The Generative AI RENAISSANCE:

Transforming Business for the Future

Dr.Arunprasad ı
Dr. Sanjay Tolani
Jai Ganesh
Marius Bgdan Pislariu
Eng. Eissa Alkamali

GUIDED SELF PUBLISHING (I)
WE CRAFT YOUR DREAMS

COPYRIGHT & DISCLAIMER:

1st Edition (August, 2025)

MRP: Rs. 999 / USD $79
ISBN: 978-93-7053-032-4
Published & Distributed by
Guided Self Publishing (I) LLP

Every effort has been made to avoid errors or omissions in this publication. In spite of this, errors may creep in. Any mistake, error or discrepancy noted may be brought to our notice which shall be taken care of in the next edition. It is notified that neither the publisher nor the author or seller will be held responsible for any damage or loss of action to any one, of any kind, in any manner, therefrom. It is suggested that, in order to avoid any doubt, the reader should cross-check all the facts, law and contents of the publication with the original Government publication or notifications.

For binding mistake, misprints or for missing pages, etc., the publisher's liability is limited to replacement within one month of purchase of the similar edition. All expenses in this connection are to be borne by the purchaser.

The information provided within this book is for general purposes only. The thoughts expressed in this book are the author's own. Therefore, any resemblance is purely coincidental. If inadvertently, we have missed announcing the due credit, future publications will give the due credit to those that are brought to the author's attention.

All disputes are subject to Delhi jurisdiction only.

CONTENTS

PREFACE

The dawn of Generative Artificial Intelligence marks one of the most profound transformations in the history of technology and business. Unlike traditional AI—largely focused on automation, prediction, and classification—Generative AI introduces creativity, adaptability, and the ability to design entirely new solutions. With the capacity to generate human-like text, create realistic images, compose music, and even write functional code, it represents not only an evolution of artificial intelligence but also a redefinition of human–machine collaboration. This book, The Generative AI Renaissance: Transforming Business for the Future, has been crafted to serve as both a comprehensive introduction and a practical guide for organizations, leaders, and innovators seeking to navigate this new frontier. Across its chapters, readers will gain an understanding of the foundations of Generative AI; the evolution of its core models such as GANs, VAEs, Transformers, and Diffusion Models; and the transformative applications emerging across industries including healthcare, finance, education, marketing, and entertainment. At the heart of this book is a dual mission: to demystify Generative AI by making its concepts accessible to a wide audience, and to equip professionals with the insights needed to harness its potential responsibly. Each chapter blends technical clarity with real-world case studies, demonstrating not only how Generative AI can increase efficiency and personalization, but also how it reshapes business models, customer experiences, and strategic decision-making.

Equally important, the book does not shy away from the challenges. It critically examines ethical dilemmas, risks of bias, and the societal implications of widespread adoption. In doing so, it calls for a culture of responsible innovation in which creativity is balanced with accountability, and disruption with sustainability. It is my hope that this work inspires readers to experiment, adapt, and embrace Generative AI as a catalyst for growth, resilience, and meaningful human progress

CHAPTER 1
INTRODUCTION TO GENERATIVE AI IN BUSINESS

The dawn of Generative Artificial Intelligence marks a transformative chapter in the evolution of technology and business. Unlike traditional AI systems designed primarily for classification, prediction, or automation, Generative AI exhibits the ability to create from generating human-like text and realistic images to composing music and writing code. This creative capacity enables machines to augment human innovation, significantly shifting the dynamics of how businesses operate, innovate, and compete in an increasingly digital and experience-driven economy. Over the past few decades, AI has evolved from rule-based automation to sophisticated machine learning and deep learning techniques. This evolution has laid the foundation for generative models like Generative Adversarial Networks (GANs), Variational Autoencoders (VAEs), and transformer-based models such as GPT and DALL·E. These technologies have unlocked new potentials across industries, enabling real-time content generation, personalized customer experiences, and novel product development cycles that were once considered futuristic. Generative AI is more than a technological upgrade; it is a strategic enabler of growth, differentiation, and resilience. Organizations embracing these tools are already seeing measurable improvements in efficiency, cost reduction, customer satisfaction, and time-to-market. By shifting from static workflows to adaptive, AI-augmented processes, businesses can harness creativity at scale turning data into insights and insights into value with unprecedented speed and precision. This chapter lays the groundwork for understanding the core principles, evolution, and business impact of Generative AI. It explores what sets generative models apart, how they developed, and why they are now at the forefront of digital transformation. As we progress through the book, these foundational insights will frame more advanced discussions on implementation strategies, industry-specific applications, ethical considerations, and future trends.

Generative AI

Generative Artificial Intelligence (Generative AI) refers to a class of AI algorithms and models that can generate new content that is similar to existing data. Unlike traditional AI systems that are primarily focused on analyzing data, making predictions, or recognizing patterns, generative AI is designed to create. It learns the underlying structure and distribution of a dataset and then uses that knowledge to produce new, original outputs whether it's text, images, music, code, or other forms of data. At the core of Generative AI are deep learning models such as Generative Adversarial Networks (GANs), Variational Autoencoders (VAEs), and Transformer-based architectures like OpenAI's GPT (Generative Pre-trained Transformer). These models are trained on vast datasets to understand and replicate the nuances of human language, visual aesthetics, and even logical reasoning. For instance, GPT-4 can generate coherent essays, conduct natural conversations, or write software code, while tools like DALL·E can create images from textual prompts.

Distinguishing Features of Generative AI

Generative AI stands apart from traditional artificial intelligence through its remarkable ability to produce new and original content. This generative capacity includes the creation of human-like text, realistic images, synthetic audio and video, 3D models, and even entire data sets. Tools such as ChatGPT, DALL·E, and other transformer-based models have demonstrated how machines can replicate, and sometimes even surpass, human creativity in specific domains. This shift from reactive, task-based automation to proactive creation signifies a groundbreaking evolution in the role of AI in business and society. One of the core enablers of this creativity is unsupervised and self-supervised learning. Unlike traditional supervised learning, where models are trained on labeled datasets with clear input-output relationships, generative AI learns from unlabeled or loosely structured data. This allows models to understand deeper patterns, semantics, and representations within data, granting them the flexibility to adapt to a wide range of tasks with minimal human intervention. It opens the door to broader applications and greater autonomy, especially in environments where labeled data is limited or expensive to obtain.

Another hallmark feature of generative AI is its context awareness and continuity, particularly evident in natural language applications. Advanced models like GPT-4 can maintain tone, coherence, and relevance over long conversations or text passages, enabling them to mimic human-like reasoning and expression. This makes generative AI well-suited for content generation, customer interaction, and any task requiring consistent messaging or communication. In addition, generative AI exhibits cross-modality versatility, allowing it to operate across text, image, audio, and video domains. Some models, like OpenAI's CLIP and DALL·E, can even bridge these modalities such as generating images from text or summarizing visual content in language creating powerful synergies in business applications. This capability unlocks new creative opportunities in advertising, education, product design, and entertainment. Lastly, generative AI thrives in interactive and collaborative settings. Unlike traditional AI that often functions behind the scenes, generative systems actively engage users responding in real time, adapting outputs based on feedback, and even participating in co-creation processes. Professionals across industries now use these tools as creative partners, enabling rapid prototyping, idea generation, and personalized content development. Far from replacing human creativity, generative AI enhances it ushering in a new era of human-AI collaboration.

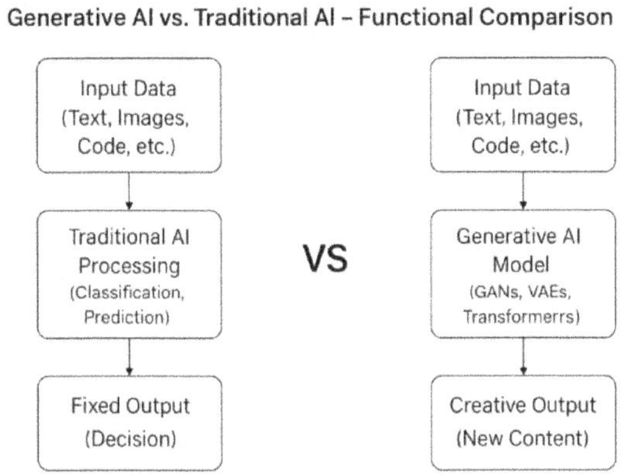

Figure 1.1: Fundamental difference between Traditional AI and Generative AI.

Figure 1.1 illustrates the fundamental difference between Traditional AI and Generative AI in terms of data processing and output. Traditional AI begins with input data such as text, images, or code, and processes it using rule-based or statistical models to perform tasks like classification or prediction. The outcome is a fixed decision—such as identifying a product category, detecting spam, or forecasting demand. These systems are optimized for automating repetitive tasks and supporting decision-making based on historical patterns. In contrast, Generative AI follows a more creative path. Starting with similar input data, it employs advanced generative models like GANs, VAEs, or transformers to learn the underlying data structures and produce entirely new content. Rather than generating a fixed response, it creates novel outputs such as a unique image, a natural language paragraph, or new software code. This shift from analytical to generative capability marks a major leap in AI's evolution—enabling businesses to move from automation to innovation, and from efficiency to creativity.

Comparison with Traditional AI

While both traditional AI and generative AI share a foundation in data-driven algorithms and machine learning principles, they differ significantly in their objectives, processes, and outputs. Traditional AI, also known as discriminative AI, is primarily focused on identifying patterns, making predictions, and automating decision-making processes. These systems excel at solving well-defined problems such as fraud detection, image recognition, demand forecasting, and customer segmentation. They use labeled datasets and produce outputs like classifications or probabilities—for instance, tagging an image as a cat or not, or predicting next month's sales. Generative AI, on the other hand, is designed not just to interpret or analyze data but to create entirely new data. It operates through models such as Generative Adversarial Networks (GANs), Variational Autoencoders (VAEs), and transformer-based architectures like GPT and DALL·E. These models learn the underlying structure of input data and use that knowledge to produce original outputs, such as generating a synthetic image that looks real, composing an email in natural language, or designing new products. The result is a system capable of creative, adaptive, and context-aware generation, going far beyond traditional classification or regression tasks. Another fundamental difference lies in their learning paradigms. Traditional AI systems often rely on supervised learning, requiring large amounts of labeled data to perform specific tasks. Generative AI systems, however, frequently utilize unsupervised or self-supervised learning, allowing them to detect patterns in unlabeled data and generalize across diverse use cases. This gives generative AI more flexibility and a broader range of applications in domains where labeled data is scarce or costly. From a business perspective, traditional AI helps optimize existing processes by automating repetitive or analytical tasks. Generative AI, however, empowers innovation by enabling the creation of new products, personalized content, and customer experiences. It shifts the role of AI from a back-office support function to a strategic driver of creativity and value, opening new horizons for businesses to differentiate and scale.

Table 1.1: Comparison of Generative AI and Traditional AI

Aspect	Traditional AI	Generative AI
Primary Function	Analyzing and interpreting existing data	Creating new and original data/content
Learning Approach	Mostly supervised learning	Mostly unsupervised or self-supervised learning
Common Models	Decision Trees, SVM, CNNs, RNNs	GANs, VAEs, Transformers (e.g., GPT, DALL·E)
Output Type	Predictive outputs (labels, scores, categories)	Creative outputs (text, image, code, audio, etc.)
Application Focus	Automation, classification, prediction	Content creation, innovation, simulation
Examples	Fraud detection, image recognition, churn prediction	Chatbots, art generation, code writing, product design
Business Impact	Improves efficiency and reduces errors	Drives innovation and enhances personalization

Table 1.1 highlights the key differences between Traditional AI and Generative AI. While Traditional AI focuses on analyzing data for tasks like prediction and

classification, Generative AI specializes in creating new, original content such as text, images, and code. It also uses more flexible learning methods and plays a more innovative and strategic role in business applications.

Types of Generative Models

Generative AI relies on a set of deep learning models designed to learn the distribution of data and generate new, similar samples. Among the most powerful and widely used are Generative Adversarial Networks (GANs), Variational Autoencoders (VAEs), and Transformer-based models like GPT and DALL·E. Each of these architectures takes a different approach to learning and generation, offering unique advantages in various applications.

1. Generative Adversarial Networks (GANs)

Generative Adversarial Networks (GANs) are one of the most innovative developments in deep learning, introduced by Ian Goodfellow in 2014. GANs consist of two neural networks a Generator and a Discriminator locked in a competitive "game." The Generator tries to create fake data that resembles the real data, while the Discriminator attempts to detect whether the input is real or generated. Over time, both networks improve, leading the Generator to produce increasingly realistic outputs. The training process of GANs is based on minimax optimization, where the Generator minimizes the chance of being caught, and the Discriminator maximizes its accuracy. This adversarial process enables GANs to generate high-fidelity images, videos, and even audio clips. Applications include deepfake generation, art creation, image enhancement, and data augmentation for training other models. However, GANs are notoriously difficult to train due to instability and issues like mode collapse, where the generator produces limited types of outputs. Despite these challenges, their realism and creative potential have made them popular in both research and industry.

2. Variational Autoencoders (VAEs)

Variational Autoencoders (VAEs) are another type of generative model built on the idea of encoding and decoding data. A VAE consists of an Encoder, which compresses input data into a smaller latent space (called a latent vector), and a Decoder, which reconstructs the original input from this compressed representation. The goal is not only to reconstruct the data accurately but to learn a probabilistic distribution over the latent space. Unlike traditional autoencoders, VAEs introduce variability into the latent space by sampling from a probability distribution (usually Gaussian). This makes it possible to generate new, diverse outputs by sampling different points in the latent space and decoding them. VAEs are widely used for image synthesis, text generation, anomaly detection, and semantic editing, where users can tweak latent features to modify outputs (e.g., turning a smiling face into a neutral one). Though their generated outputs are often less sharp than GANs, VAEs are more stable and interpretable, making them ideal for applications requiring control and structure.

3. Transformer-based Models

Transformer-based models represent the latest and most powerful architecture for generative tasks, especially in natural language processing (NLP) and multimodal generation. Introduced in 2017 by Vaswani et al., the Transformer architecture replaced sequential models like RNNs and LSTMs with attention mechanisms that can capture dependencies in data regardless of position. Models like GPT (Generative Pre-trained Transformer), BERT, and DALL·E use massive pre-training on large datasets and fine-tune on specific tasks. GPT, for example, predicts the next word in a sentence, while DALL·E generates images from textual descriptions. The strength of Transformers lies in their scalability, context understanding, and versatility across data types (text, image, code, audio). These models dominate current AI applications: GPT powers chatbots, content writing, and code generation; DALL·E and Imagen generate digital artwork; and Codex assists in programming. Due to their self-attention mechanisms, they maintain coherence and adapt outputs based on long-range context, making them highly intelligent and human-like in their generation.

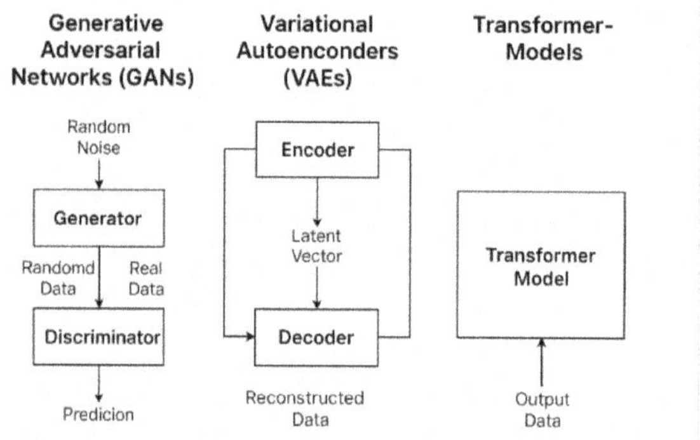

Figure 1.2: Comparing the Architectural Flow of Gans, Vaes, and Transformer-Based Models.

Figure 1.2 visually compares the architectures of three major generative models. On the left, GANs consist of a Generator that creates fake data from random noise and a Discriminator that evaluates it against real data, improving generation quality through adversarial feedback. In the center, VAEs compress input data into a latent vector using an Encoder, then reconstruct it through a Decoder, allowing structured and controllable generation. On the right, Transformer Models process input sequences to generate coherent and context-aware output data, particularly excelling in tasks like text and image generation. Each model showcases a distinct approach to generating new data from learned patterns.

1.2 Historical Evolution of Artificial Intelligence

Artificial Intelligence (AI) has undergone a profound transformation since its inception, evolving from simple rule-based systems to highly creative generative models.

This journey reflects how advances in computational power, data availability, and algorithmic design have collectively reshaped what machines can do. Today's Generative AI is built upon decades of innovation, experimentation, and foundational research.

Table 1.2: Evolution of AI Phases

AI Phase	Time Period	Key Technologies	Core Function	Examples
Rule-Based Systems	1950s – 1980s	Symbolic AI, Expert Systems	Automation	ELIZA, MYCIN
Machine Learning	1990s – 2010s	SVM, Decision Trees, Neural Networks, CNNs, RNNs	Pattern Recognition	IBM Watson, AlphaGo
Generative AI	2014–Present	GANs, VAEs, Transformers (GPT, DALL·E, BERT)	Creativity & Content Creation	ChatGPT, Midjourney, DALL·E, Bard

Table 1.2 summarizes the three major phases in the evolution of Artificial Intelligence. It outlines how AI progressed from Rule-Based Systems (1950s–1980s), which used expert-defined logic for automation, to Machine Learning (1990s–2010s), where models learned patterns from data for tasks like prediction and classification. The most recent phase, Generative AI (2014–present), introduced creativity through models like GANs, VAEs, and Transformers, enabling machines to generate new content such as text, images, and code.

The table also highlights key technologies and real-world examples that define each era.

1. The Era of Rule-Based Systems (1950s–1980s)

The earliest phase of AI was dominated by rule-based systems, also known as symbolic AI or Good Old-Fashioned AI (GOFAI). These systems relied on explicitly defined rules and logic provided by human experts. The AI did not learn or improve over time; it simply followed "if-then" statements to perform tasks such as expert decision-making or data retrieval. One of the earliest successful implementations was ELIZA, a natural language processing program developed in the 1960s that simulated a psychotherapist. Other notable systems include MYCIN, used for medical diagnosis in the 1970s. These systems worked well in narrow, clearly defined domains but failed in complex or dynamic environments where exhaustive rules were impractical. The limitations of this approach became increasingly evident as the volume and variability of data grew. Rule-based systems struggled with ambiguity, context, and scalability, leading to the need for more adaptive and data-driven approaches.

2. Rise of Machine Learning (1990s–2010s)

In response to the rigidity of symbolic systems, the field of AI shifted towards machine learning (ML) in the 1990s and early 2000s. This paradigm emphasized learning from data instead of being programmed with rules. Algorithms could now detect patterns, make predictions, and improve over time as they were exposed to more data. ML can be broadly categorized into supervised, unsupervised, and reinforcement learning. Common algorithms include decision trees, support vector machines (SVMs), k-nearest neighbors, and neural networks. The rise of deep learning, particularly convolutional neural networks (CNNs) and recurrent neural networks (RNNs), allowed machines to perform complex tasks like image recognition, speech processing, and language translation with human-like accuracy. One of the key drivers of this era was the explosion of digital data and the accessibility of computational resources such as GPUs. Landmark moments include IBM Watson's victory on Jeopardy! in 2011 and AlphaGo defeating the world champion Go player in 2016. These breakthroughs demonstrated the potential of ML to outperform humans in specific cognitive tasks.

3. Transition to Generative AI (2014–Present)

The last decade has witnessed the emergence of Generative AI, marking a shift from prediction to creation. Powered by architectures like Generative Adversarial Networks (GANs), Variational Autoencoders (VAEs), and Transformers, these models are capable of generating novel content text, images, code, audio, and more by learning the underlying structure of input data. GANs, introduced by Ian Goodfellow in 2014, allowed machines to generate hyper-realistic images. VAEs enabled semantic editing, while Transformer-based models like GPT, BERT, DALL·E, and ChatGPT revolutionized natural language and multimodal AI tasks. These models can write essays, design graphics, and even generate music or simulate voice. Unlike earlier AI systems, generative models rely on self-supervised learning, using massive datasets to pre-train on a broad range of tasks before being fine-tuned for specific applications. Their ability to understand and generate human-like content positions Generative AI as a cornerstone of the fourth industrial revolution.

4. Shifts in Capability: From Automation to Creativity

As shown in Figure 1.3, AI has evolved across three dimensions:

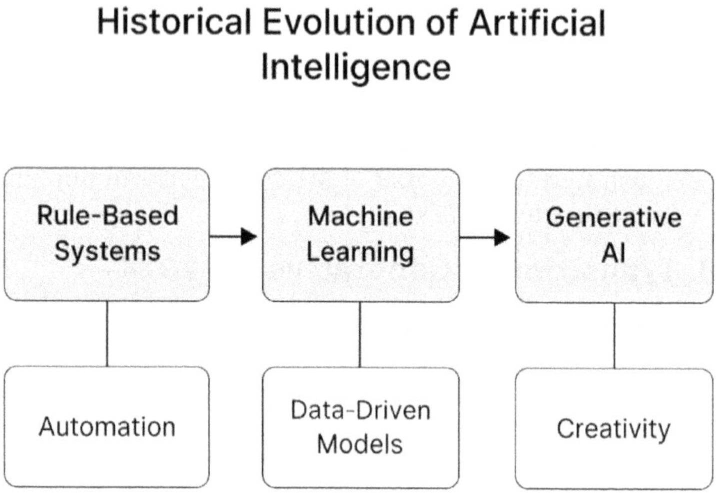

Figure 1.3: Progressive Evolution of AI Technologies.

The flowchart traces three main stages Rule-Based Systems, Machine Learning, and Generative AI each represented by a box linked in chronological order. Below each stage, the dominant capability is shown: Automation for rule-based systems, Data-Driven Models for ML, and Creativity for generative AI. This visual emphasizes how each phase added new layers of complexity, intelligence, and human-like ability to machines.

- Rule-Based Systems focused on automation through predefined logic.
- Machine Learning emphasized data-driven modeling, improving adaptability and performance.
- Generative AI introduced creativity, enabling the machine to generate unique outputs rather than follow a fixed structure.
- Each stage builds upon the previous one—leveraging greater computational power, larger datasets, and

more complex algorithms to expand the possibilities of machine intelligence.

5. Impact and Integration Across Industries

This historical evolution has significantly impacted business, healthcare, education, finance, and manufacturing. Rule-based systems automated repetitive administrative tasks. Machine learning introduced intelligent analytics, fraud detection, and recommendation systems. Generative AI now empowers industries to create marketing content, design prototypes, automate coding, and even simulate complex medical scenarios.

6. Current Trends and the Road Ahead

As AI systems become more autonomous and capable of mimicking human thought and creativity, ethical concerns have also surfaced. Transparency, accountability, and explainability remain critical areas of research, especially as Generative AI becomes more deeply embedded in society. The next decade may witness even tighter human-AI collaboration, where AI augments human creativity and decision-making.

1.3 Capabilities of Generative AI

Generative AI is revolutionizing digital capabilities by enabling machines not just to analyze or process information but to create new, original content. Among its most prominent features is text generation, as demonstrated by advanced models like ChatGPT and GPT-4. These language models are trained on vast amounts of text data, enabling them to generate human-like responses, write essays, compose poetry, draft emails, or even create entire books. They can also adapt tone and style based on context, making them powerful tools for customer service, content marketing, education, and personal productivity. Beyond language, Generative AI also excels in image, audio, and video synthesis. Tools like DALL·E, Midjourney, and Stable Diffusion generate highly detailed images from textual prompts, while AI models like Eleven-Labs and Synthesia create lifelike voice and video content. These capabilities are transforming industries such as advertising, filmmaking, virtual reality, gaming, and media, where high-quality digital assets can now be produced quickly and cost-effectively. Audio models can clone voices, generate music, or dub content into multiple languages with near-human realism.

Another key application is code generation and automated design. Tools like GitHub Copilot, powered by OpenAI's Codex, assist programmers by suggesting code snippets, generating functions, or even writing complete programs based on natural language descriptions. In the design space, generative AI tools help create user interfaces, generate architectural blueprints, and provide automated web layouts or prototypes. This not only speeds up development cycles but also empowers non-technical users to participate in software and design creation. Generative AI also plays a significant role in data augmentation and simulation. In fields like machine learning and robotics, it can generate synthetic data to train models when real data is limited, sensitive, or costly to collect. For example, it can create diverse facial images for facial recognition systems, simulate driving scenarios for autonomous vehicles, or model rare medical conditions for diagnostic tools. These synthetic datasets enhance model robustness, reduce biases, and improve generalization without compromising data privacy.

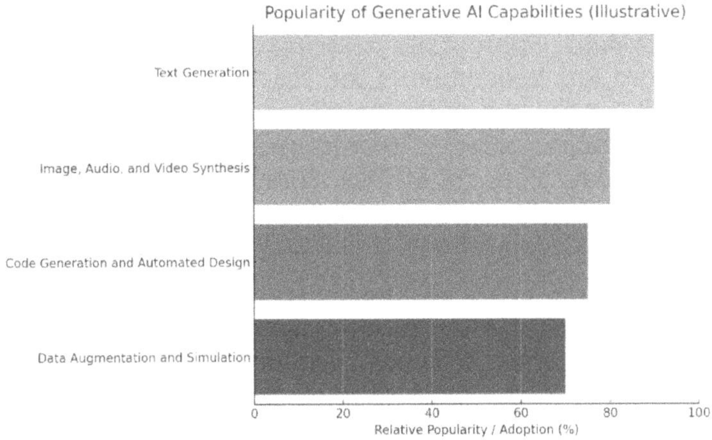

Figure 1.4: Illustrative Graph for the Four Key Capabilities of Generative AI.

The "Popularity of Generative AI Capabilities (Illustrative)" graph visually ranks four key areas of generative AI based on their relative adoption. Text generation leads in popularity due to widespread use in chatbots and content creation, followed by media synthesis, code generation, and data simulation all rapidly growing in business and research applications (Figure 1.4).

1. Text Generation (e.g., ChatGPT, GPT-4)

Text generation is one of the most mature and widely adopted applications of generative AI. Using models like OpenAI's GPT-4, Claude, and Google's Gemini, machines can now generate coherent, context-aware, and human-like text. These models are trained on massive corpora, including books, websites, articles, and dialogues, enabling them to learn grammar, semantics, tone, and even cultural nuances. One key strength of these models lies in their contextual understanding. They can maintain coherent dialogue over multiple turns, summarize long documents, translate languages, or rewrite content in different tones or styles. This has opened up new possibilities in education, journalism, marketing, customer service, and even therapy, where AI can assist in content creation, answer questions, and provide emotionally appropriate responses. The backbone of modern text generation is the Transformer architecture, which uses self-attention mechanisms to analyze relationships between words regardless of position. Unlike older RNNs or LSTMs, Transformers handle long-range dependencies efficiently, making them ideal for multi-paragraph coherence and logical structuring.

Text generators are also highly customizable. Businesses can fine-tune models on domain-specific data to create legal summaries, technical documentation, or medical advice. Some systems even allow prompt engineering or instruction tuning, where the model adjusts its response based on how questions are framed. However, despite their capabilities, these models can sometimes produce hallucinated information text that sounds accurate but is factually incorrect. As such, their deployment in high-stakes fields like healthcare or law requires human oversight and strong validation protocols. Text generation also raises ethical concerns, including misinformation, plagiarism, and impersonation. Companies must ensure transparency, consent, and content validation when integrating these tools into business processes. Still, when used responsibly, generative text models significantly reduce workload, boost productivity, and improve communication efficiency, making them indispensable in modern workflows.

2. Image, Audio, and Video Synthesis

One of the most visually and creatively impactful applications of Generative AI is its ability to synthesize images, audio, and video content from scratch or from a prompt. This capability has been popularized by tools such as DALL·E, Midjourney, Stable Diffusion, Synthesia, and Eleven-Labs, which can convert text prompts into highly detailed, photorealistic images, realistic voiceovers, and even entire AI-generated video segments. In image synthesis, AI models learn the patterns and textures of millions of images to generate entirely new visual content. Users can describe a scene in words like “a cyberpunk city at night with flying cars” and receive a corresponding high-resolution image. Artists, designers, advertisers, and content creators use this to prototype designs, illustrate ideas, and visualize concepts without needing complex software or large creative teams. Audio synthesis, especially in voice cloning and music generation, has reached new levels of realism. AI tools can mimic a person's voice from just a few seconds of audio, enabling personalized voiceovers or dubbing across multiple languages. In music, AI can generate new compositions or assist musicians by offering instrumental backing tracks or suggesting melodies based on mood and style. Video synthesis is an emerging frontier where Generative AI is capable of creating entire video clips, animating still images, or changing facial expressions and lip movements in videos to match new audio inputs (a technique known as deep-faking). Platforms like Synthesia let users create AI avatars that speak pre-written scripts, reducing the need for physical video production setups in corporate communication or online education. These technologies are highly beneficial in entertainment, marketing, education, and accessibility. Businesses use AI-generated visuals for product mockups, campaign artwork, or personalized advertising. Educational platforms produce lectures in different languages and formats. Audio tools help generate audiobook narrations or create voice interfaces for applications. However, the potential for misuse especially in deepfakes and synthetic media raises significant ethical and legal concerns, including consent, authenticity, and misinformation. Regulations and watermarking strategies are being developed to ensure that synthetic content can be distinguished from real media. When used ethically and with proper attribution, generative image, audio, and video synthesis expands creative boundaries, reduces production time, and enhances engagement across digital platforms.

3. Code Generation and Automated Design

Generative AI is increasingly revolutionizing the software development and design industries by automating the generation of code and user interfaces. Tools like GitHub Copilot, OpenAI Codex, Replit Ghostwriter, and Uizard have made it possible for AI to write functioning code snippets, full programs, or design templates based on natural language instructions. Code generation works by training models on millions of open-source repositories. When a developer types a comment or prompt like "create a login form with email and password validation," the AI responds by generating syntactically correct and context-aware code. These tools can suggest completions, fix bugs, generate test cases, and even explain what existing code is doing. This has dramatically improved developer productivity, especially in repetitive or boilerplate tasks. Beginners can learn by example, while experienced developers save time and focus on complex logic or architecture. It's also a powerful tool for non-coders—people with basic understanding can now instruct AI to generate websites, apps, or data visualizations.

In automated design, AI tools can create layouts, wireframes, dashboards, and UI components based on written input. Tools like Uizard and Diagram AI use natural language to generate visually appealing, usable designs without requiring professional design skills. This democratizes product prototyping and accelerates product development. One of the significant advantages is the ability to rapidly iterate and experiment. Designers and developers can test multiple layouts, color schemes, or coding approaches in minutes. AI also helps with accessibility, automatically checking for contrast, structure, and compliance with standards like WCAG. Despite these benefits, there are challenges—such as code quality, security, and overreliance. AI-generated code may contain vulnerabilities or inefficiencies if not reviewed. Also, some concerns exist around copyright and licensing when models are trained on open-source code without explicit permissions. Overall, generative AI empowers a new era of human-AI collaboration in technology, enhancing productivity, innovation, and access for creators at all skill levels.

4. Data Augmentation and Simulation

In fields where data is limited, expensive, or sensitive, Generative AI plays a crucial role in data augmentation and simulation. This involves generating synthetic data that mimics real-world patterns, which is especially valuable in industries like healthcare, autonomous vehicles, robotics, and finance. Data augmentation enhances existing datasets by creating new samples through modification (e.g., rotation, noise injection) or generation. For example, in computer vision, Generative AI can create additional images of the same object under different lighting or angles to improve the robustness of recognition models. In NLP, it can paraphrase sentences to increase linguistic variety during training. Synthetic data generation, powered by models like GANs or VAEs, creates entirely new data points that resemble the distribution of real data. In healthcare, for instance, synthetic patient records can be used to train diagnostic algorithms without violating patient privacy. Similarly, banks can simulate customer behavior to detect fraud patterns more effectively. Simulation environments are another application where Generative AI helps model real-world systems. Platforms like NVIDIA Omniverse or Unity ML-Agents simulate traffic scenarios, warehouse robotics, or drone navigation. These environments are used to safely train reinforcement learning models, test autonomous systems, or model edge-case scenarios without real-world risk. One major benefit of simulated or augmented data is improved generalization. By exposing models to a wider variety of conditions, they perform better on unseen real-world inputs. It also reduces the need for massive labeled datasets, which are costly and time-consuming to gather. However, synthetic data must be carefully validated. If poorly generated, it may introduce bias, noise, or unrealistic features. It's also important to ensure the data remains representative and diverse, especially in regulated domains like medicine or finance. Used thoughtfully, Generative AI becomes a powerful data multiplier, enabling safer, faster, and more inclusive development of AI systems even when real data is scarce or restricted.

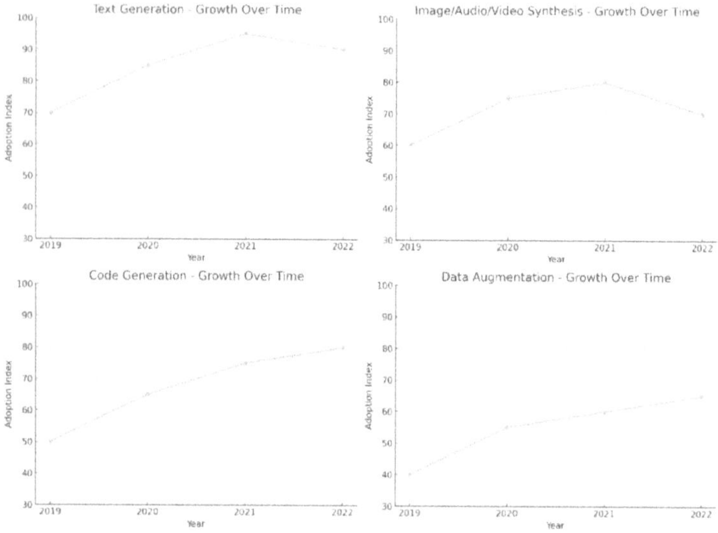

Figure 1.5: Growth Trend

Above Figure 1.5 shows four individual graphs, each showing the growth trend over time (2019–2022) for different Generative AI capabilities:

- Text Generation: Shows rapid and consistent growth, reflecting widespread adoption in tools like ChatGPT for communication, content creation, and automation.
- Image/Audio/Video Synthesis: Displays strong growth, driven by creative and media industries using AI for visuals, voice, and video production.
- Code Generation and Automated Design: Steadily rising due to increasing demand for developer assistance and low-code/no-code platforms.

- Data Augmentation and Simulation: Shows a more gradual but steady rise, especially in AI training, healthcare, and robotics simulations where data scarcity is a challenge.

1.4 Generative AI vs Traditional Automation

Traditional automation has long been associated with increasing efficiency by performing repetitive, rule-based tasks. From assembly lines to back-office operations like payroll and invoicing, traditional systems are designed to follow predefined instructions with minimal deviation. These systems typically aim to replace manual labor in predictable workflows, improving speed and accuracy while reducing costs. However, they are limited in scope, unable to adapt, learn, or innovate beyond what they are explicitly programmed to do. In contrast, Generative AI represents a paradigm shift—it moves beyond automation into the realm of creation and ideation. Rather than executing a fixed process, Generative AI systems can generate entirely new content, designs, ideas, and strategies. For example, where traditional automation might send out templated emails, Generative AI can compose personalized responses tailored to tone, intent, and past interactions. This leap from task execution to content creation is what distinguishes Generative AI from its traditional predecessors. Moreover, problem-solving approaches differ significantly. Traditional automation relies on a linear understanding of problems: identify a task, define a rule, and automate it. In contrast, Generative AI uses probabilistic models and pattern recognition to explore creative, non-obvious solutions. It can assist in brainstorming, suggest novel product designs, or provide alternate solutions in engineering challenges. This makes it a valuable tool not just for efficiency, but for enhancing innovation capacity within an organization. Generative AI also plays a transformative role in strategic planning and decision-making. It can analyze vast, unstructured datasets and generate insights or predictive scenarios that support high-level strategy development. For instance, AI can help businesses simulate market trends, generate customer personas, or visualize new business models—tasks that require both analytical depth and creative interpretation, far beyond the capabilities of traditional automation tools.

From Task Automation to Idea Generation

Traditional automation excels at performing structured, repetitive tasks with precision. It is rule-based and designed to optimize processes such as data entry, billing, scheduling, or manufacturing, where inputs and outputs are clearly defined. While effective for efficiency and consistency, it is limited to what it's programmed to do. Generative AI, however, extends automation into the realm of creativity and ideation. It doesn't just automate existing tasks—it generates new ideas, content, and solutions. For example, in marketing, it can create original ad copy or campaign ideas, while in design, it can propose entirely new visual layouts based on trends or preferences. This ability to create, not just execute, marks a significant evolution.

Creative Problem-Solving vs Repetitive Tasks

Whereas traditional systems are built for executing repeatable processes, they falter in situations requiring creativity or ambiguity. Generative AI fills this gap by supporting creative problem-solving. It can analyze complex, unstructured data and generate unique solutions, patterns, or suggestions that may not have been previously considered. For example, in product development, traditional automation might streamline testing, but Generative AI can generate innovative product concepts, simulate user interactions, or even draft marketing plans. This shift empowers teams to move from execution to innovation, with AI acting as a collaborative partner.

Impact on Strategic Planning and Innovation

Traditional automation contributes to strategy by reducing costs and improving productivity. However, it plays a limited role in innovation, offering little support in identifying market opportunities or generating future-oriented strategies. Generative AI, on the other hand, supports dynamic strategic planning. It can simulate future trends, create forecasts based on scenario modeling, and generate insightful reports. Business leaders use it to visualize new market strategies, generate alternative business models, and explore untested ideas, making it a tool for innovation-led growth.

Table 1.3: Comparison – Traditional Automation vs Generative AI

Aspect	Traditional Automation	Generative AI
Core Function	Executes predefined, rule-based tasks	Creates new ideas, content, and solutions
Nature of Output	Fixed, repetitive, and structured	Dynamic, variable, and original
Problem Solving	Limited to known problems and workflows	Capable of creative, adaptive problem-solving
Role in Innovation	Supports efficiency, not innovation	Drives innovation through simulation, ideation, and content creation
Strategic Contribution	Enhances productivity and consistency	Enables scenario planning, trend forecasting, and strategic ideation
Examples	Payroll automation,	Generating ad campaigns, product

	inventory updates, scheduling	concepts, strategic roadmaps

The Table 1.3 highlights the key differences between Traditional Automation and Generative AI, showing how traditional systems focus on fixed, rule-based efficiency, while Generative AI drives creativity, innovation, and strategic thinking through adaptive, content-generating capabilities.

1.5 Business Drivers Behind the Adoption

The rise of Generative AI in modern enterprises is not merely a technological shift—it's a strategic response to the changing demands of customers, markets, and digital ecosystems. Businesses are increasingly integrating generative models to unlock new levels of personalization, efficiency, and real-time responsiveness. These drivers are shaping how organizations invest, innovate, and deliver value.

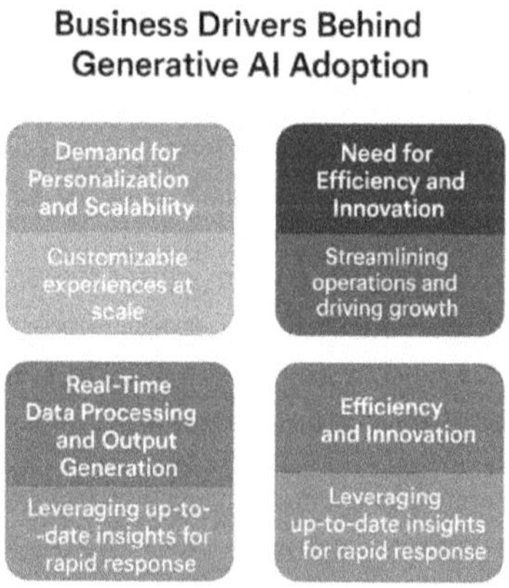

Figure 1.6: Business Drivers Behind the Adoption.

Business Drivers Behind the Adoption of Generative AI, structured around the three key drivers and aligned with the Figure 1.6 above.

1. Demand for Personalization and Scalability

In today's hyper-connected world, consumers expect brands to understand their preferences and deliver experiences that feel personal. Generic, one-size-fits-all communication no longer resonates. Generative AI responds to this by enabling hyper-personalization at scale. AI can generate customized content for emails, product recommendations, ads, and even virtual experiences based on real-time data like user behavior, browsing history, and preferences. What was once possible only through human effort for a small audience is now scalable to millions of users—thanks to tools like GPT-4, DALL·E, and AI-based content engines. Retailers use AI to generate personalized product descriptions. Financial institutions produce individualized investment reports. In e-learning, students receive tailor-made study plans and exercises based on progress. This level of customization, powered by generative models, increases engagement, satisfaction, and conversion rates—key metrics for business success. Moreover, scalability is no longer constrained by human bandwidth. Generative AI systems can operate 24/7, handling thousands of queries or generating massive volumes of content in seconds, making it a vital tool for global operations and rapid market expansion.

2. Need for Efficiency and Innovation

Organizations are under pressure to do more with less—to reduce costs while continuously innovating. Generative AI supports this dual mandate by streamlining operations and opening new creative avenues. For instance, content teams can rapidly generate marketing materials, graphics, and blog posts. Design and product teams can auto-generate concepts, wireframes, and prototypes. In software development, AI-powered code generators like Copilot assist engineers in building applications faster with fewer bugs. This boost in efficiency allows human teams to shift focus from routine tasks to higher-value, strategic work. Businesses save time, reduce dependence on outsourced labor, and cut overhead costs—all while maintaining or even enhancing output quality. On the innovation front, generative AI acts as a brainstorming partner. It generates new ideas, simulations, or visual concepts that spark human creativity. It can suggest design alternatives, marketing headlines, or even business models. By introducing creative diversity and accelerating iteration, AI becomes a catalyst for innovation-driven growth.

3. Real-Time Data Processing and Output Generation

In fast-paced industries, timing is everything. Businesses need to react quickly to customer behavior, market shifts, or internal KPIs. Generative AI excels at processing real-time data and producing actionable outputs in seconds. Consider a customer support chatbot trained on real-time CRM data—it can provide intelligent, context-aware answers instantly. In finance, generative models analyze live market data to produce real-time investment briefings. In supply chain, AI generates delivery route updates or demand forecasts on the fly. This ability to process and respond to information in real-time gives businesses a decisive edge. It improves agility, reduces downtime, and enables smarter decision-making across departments. Organizations that embed AI in their feedback loops move from being reactive to proactively adaptive. Real-time capabilities also improve user experiences. For example, AI can update content recommendations on a website instantly based on a user's click behavior. In healthcare, AI-generated triage messages or diagnosis suggestions can help frontline professionals act faster.

4. Strategic Integration and Long-Term Value

These business drivers—personalization, efficiency, and real-time responsiveness—are not siloed. When integrated strategically, they multiply one another. An AI-powered system that personalizes content (driver 1), produces it instantly (driver 3), and scales efficiently (driver 2), creates end-to-end transformation. Generative AI helps organizations redefine their value proposition, improve operational agility, and enter new markets with less risk. It is not just a cost-saving tool, but a platform for innovation and differentiation in a crowded marketplace. For businesses aiming to future-proof their strategies, investing in Generative AI is becoming a non-negotiable competitive imperative. It aligns with the growing expectation for smarter, faster, and more tailored digital experiences—pushing companies toward a more intelligent, responsive, and resilient model of operation.

1.6 Benefits for Modern Enterprises

Generative AI has emerged as one of the most impactful digital technologies, reshaping enterprise operations across sectors. As depicted in the chart, the benefits fall into three primary areas: enhanced productivity & reduced operational costs, improved customer experiences, and accelerated innovation & product development (Figure 1.7). These pillars are driving widespread adoption and investment in AI solutions across industries (Table 1.4).

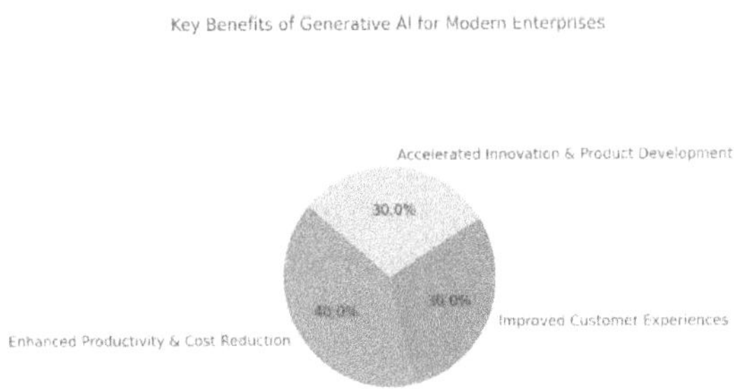

Figure 1.7: Benefits for Modern Enterprises

Table 1.4: Benefits of Generative AI for Modern Enterprises

Benefit Area	Description	Key Applications
Enhanced Productivity & Cost Reduction	Automates repetitive tasks, reduces manual effort, and optimizes workflows to lower operational costs	Automated content creation, report generation, code writing, customer service bots
Improved Customer Experiences	Delivers real-time, personalized, and multilingual interactions at scale	AI chatbots, tailored marketing messages, dynamic product recommendations
Accelerated Innovation & Product Development	Speeds up ideation, prototyping, and market testing with AI-assisted tools	AI-driven design, software development, drug discovery, campaign A/B testing
Faster Time-to-Market	Enables quicker concept-to-launch cycles by generating designs and content instantly	Prototype generation, UI/UX mockups, agile product development
Personalization at Scale	Adapts content and services based on individual preferences and behaviors	Personalized emails, custom web content, AI-curated product recommendations
Data-Driven Decision	Provides intelligent	Trend forecasting, customer

Making	insights from real-time or historical data to inform strategy	sentiment analysis, automated business reports
Operational Agility	Improves responsiveness to changes in demand, feedback, or external environments	Real-time inventory updates, dynamic content optimization, supply chain adjustments

1. Enhanced Productivity and Reduced Operational Costs

One of the most immediate and measurable benefits of Generative AI is the significant boost in productivity. Tasks that traditionally consumed hours of manual effort can now be accomplished in seconds using generative tools. Whether it's generating reports, automating email drafts, or writing software code, employees can shift from repetitive work to strategic initiatives. By offloading routine and labor-intensive processes to AI, companies reduce the time spent on low-value activities. This allows teams to refocus on decision-making, creative thinking, and long-term strategy—areas where human input remains irreplaceable. Another major advantage is the reduction in operational costs. Organizations no longer need large teams to produce content or handle customer inquiries. AI models like GPT and DALL·E can generate high-quality marketing material, visuals, and support responses at a fraction of the cost of traditional outsourcing or hiring.

The savings extend to infrastructure and resources. By optimizing supply chains with AI-generated demand forecasts or automating workflows through intelligent agents, businesses can reduce inventory waste, avoid bottlenecks, and eliminate process inefficiencies. For example, in banking, AI reduces costs by generating regulatory reports and automating KYC (Know Your

Customer) procedures. In retail, AI handles inventory planning and customer personalization without human input, freeing up staff for higher-level tasks. Overall, the compound effect of reduced time, lower costs, and better utilization of human resources contributes to leaner, more agile business operations.

2. Improved Customer Experiences

Customers today expect fast, personalized, and meaningful interactions. Generative AI enables businesses to deliver these experiences at scale. AI-powered chatbots, virtual assistants, and recommendation engines respond instantly to inquiries and adapt responses based on past behavior or sentiment. One standout capability is hyper-personalization. Generative AI can create tailored emails, suggest unique product bundles, or generate personalized homepages in real time. This fosters a deeper emotional connection between the brand and the customer. Generative AI also supports multilingual communication, expanding customer service capabilities across geographies. Tools like Synthesia and ElevenLabs allow businesses to create videos and voice content in multiple languages without requiring native-speaking staff. Customer feedback is another area enhanced by AI. Instead of manually analyzing survey results, businesses use natural language models to summarize feedback and highlight themes. This makes it easier to adapt services and correct pain points swiftly. The ability to engage customers dynamically across channels—email, web, social media, or voice—means companies are always connected, always responsive, and always evolving with customer needs. These AI-driven experiences not only improve satisfaction but also boost loyalty, retention, and lifetime customer value—core metrics for sustainable business growth.

3. Accelerated Innovation and Product Development

Innovation is no longer optional; it's a survival strategy in today's fast-moving markets. Generative AI accelerates the pace of ideation, prototyping, and deployment, helping businesses stay ahead of the curve. In product design, AI tools can generate dozens of concepts in seconds, simulate how they'll perform in real-world environments, and highlight design flaws before manufacturing begins. This reduces development cycles and shortens time-to-market. R&D teams use AI to mine patent databases, scientific articles, and market data to generate insights and identify white space opportunities. AI can also simulate chemical compounds or predict drug behavior in biotech, dramatically reducing experimentation time. Software development is also revolutionized. AI-based code assistants not only suggest code snippets but also refactor legacy systems, write test cases, and ensure compliance with security protocols—accelerating the development lifecycle.

In the creative industry, marketers use AI to A/B test visuals and messaging at scale, enabling campaigns to adapt in real time based on performance. This iterative, data-driven innovation was once impractical due to time and budget constraints. Beyond new products, AI helps develop new business models. For instance, companies now offer AI generated personalization as a premium service or create AI-curated collections in fashion and entertainment. The rapid feedback loops enabled by AI foster a culture of experimentation and learning, where ideas can be tested, refined, or replaced at speed—ensuring continuous innovation and competitive advantage.

4. Strategic Synergy of All Three Pillars

While each of these benefits—productivity, customer experience, and innovation—can deliver value individually, their combined effect is transformative. For example, a company that uses AI to reduce content production time (productivity) can also create more personalized and engaging campaigns (customer experience), and test those ideas rapidly (innovation). This synergy leads to operational excellence, brand differentiation, and market leadership. Companies that embrace all three benefits don't just survive disruption—they become disruptors.

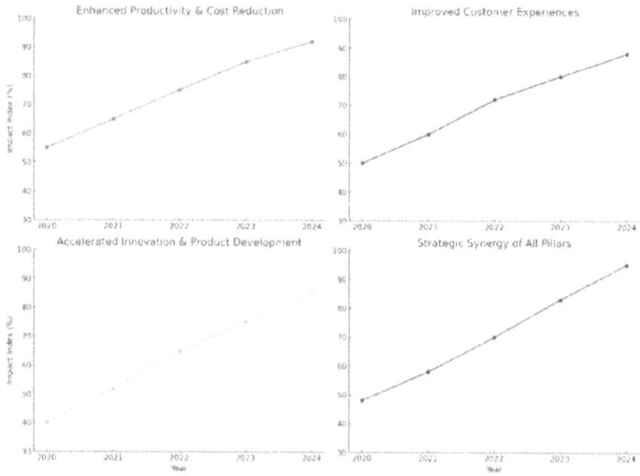

Figure 1.8: Rising Impact of Generative AI

The four graphs collectively illustrate the rising impact of Generative AI across key enterprise performance areas from 2020 to 2024. Enhanced productivity and reduced operational costs show a consistent upward trend as businesses increasingly automate workflows and eliminate manual inefficiencies (Figure 1.8). Simultaneously, customer experience metrics have improved steadily, reflecting the growing use of AI for real-time personalization, multilingual support, and instant query resolution. In the realm of innovation, the acceleration of product development and design is evident, driven by AI's ability to generate prototypes, write code, and simulate user scenarios. Most significantly, the final graph highlights the strategic synergy that emerges when all three pillars—productivity, customer experience, and innovation—are aligned. Organizations that leverage these capabilities in tandem achieve exponential improvements, positioning themselves for sustainable growth and long-term market leadership.

1.5 Generative AI as a Disruptive Force

Generative AI is not merely an enhancement to existing technologies—it is a disruptive force capable of fundamentally reshaping business models, redefining value creation, and setting new competitive benchmarks across industries. Much like the internet and smartphones, Generative AI is altering how businesses operate, engage with customers, and innovate their offerings (Figure 1.9).

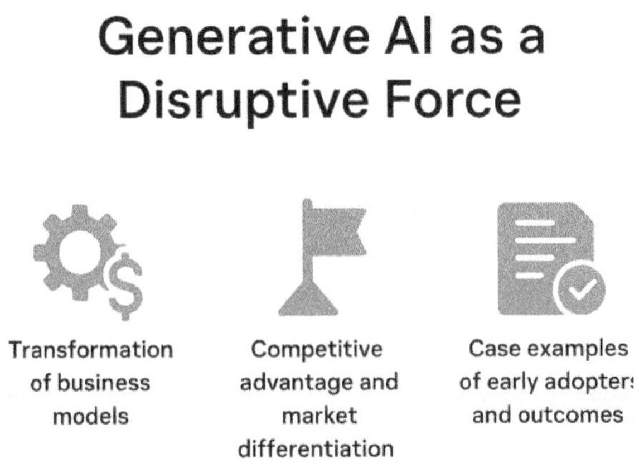

Figure 1.9: Generative AI as a Disruptive Force

Transformation of Business Models

At its core, Generative AI enables value creation through intelligent content generation, rather than just process optimization. This shift reorients business models from efficiency-centric to creativity-centric. Companies are no longer just automating tasks—they are reimagining products, services, and customer experiences with AI as a core enabler. In the media industry, for example, content production once required extensive human input—writers, designers, voice actors, editors. Today,

Generative AI tools like ChatGPT, DALL·E, and Synthesia can handle text, images, and video production at scale. This enables media companies to launch AI-driven studios that produce content rapidly and cost-effectively. In SaaS and technology, the subscription model is evolving. Companies now offer "AI as a Service" (AIaaS) where users pay for content generation, real-time analytics, or design suggestions, rather than static features. AI is becoming a revenue-generating asset rather than just a backend tool. Retailers are also leveraging AI to personalize shopping experiences. Brands use AI to create individualized storefronts, promotional content, and dynamic product recommendations—blurring the line between product and experience. These AI-driven personal commerce models redefine customer engagement. Healthcare is undergoing transformation as well. With AI generating medical summaries, risk reports, and patient education content, healthcare providers can scale consultations and enhance the patient-provider interaction—all while improving diagnostic efficiency.

Competitive Advantage and Market Differentiation

One of the biggest impacts of Generative AI is the way it enables rapid differentiation. Companies that embrace it are not just becoming faster—they're becoming smarter, more creative, and more adaptable. This leads to a sustainable competitive advantage rooted in innovation rather than scale alone. AI empowers teams to test more ideas in less time. For example, marketers can run A/B tests across thousands of variations created by AI and optimize campaigns in real time. Designers can iterate user interfaces using AI-generated layouts. This cycle of fast feedback and agile refinement gives early adopters a creative edge. Additionally, AI can help companies tap into new markets. Through multilingual content generation, localized customer interactions, and culturally adaptive messaging, businesses can expand globally without building large regional teams. This levels the playing field for startups and small businesses. Another competitive benefit is the ability to customize at scale. Where traditional mass production favored standardization, Generative AI enables individualized solutions—mass personalization that was previously cost-prohibitive. This is particularly impactful in sectors like fashion, education, and entertainment. Internally, companies using AI benefit from enhanced knowledge management. AI-generated documentation, automated training modules, and intelligent dashboards equip teams with real-time insights, improving internal efficiency and decision-making across departments.

Case Examples of Early Adopters and Outcomes

Numerous companies have already demonstrated the disruptive power of Generative AI. For instance, Coca-Cola used OpenAI's DALL·E and GPT-4 to create customized ad campaigns tailored to different demographics, reducing creative turnaround time and increasing engagement. In the legal domain, Harvey AI, built on OpenAI's GPT-4, is helping law firms automate contract review, legal research, and case summarization. This reduces billable hours spent on repetitive tasks while improving accuracy and consistency. Duolingo, the popular language learning app, integrated Generative AI to simulate real-life conversations and provide personalized grammar explanations. This significantly boosted user engagement and retention by offering adaptive learning experiences.

In the software industry, GitHub Copilot has transformed the developer workflow. By assisting with code generation, debugging, and documentation, Copilot accelerates development cycles and reduces onboarding time for new engineers. Startups are also capitalizing on Generative AI. Companies like Runway offer video editing powered entirely by AI, allowing creators to produce visual effects, scene transitions, and animations with simple text commands—democratizing professional video production. In education, platforms like Sana Labs use Generative AI to create personalized learning paths, quizzes, and content in real-time, revolutionizing e-learning for corporate training and academic institutions.

Generative AI is more than a tool—it is a catalyst for organizational reinvention. It not only optimizes how businesses function but redefines what businesses can become. By transforming business models, creating new revenue streams, and enabling continuous innovation, it positions early adopters as leaders in their domains. The companies that succeed in this new era will not be those that simply adopt AI, but those that embed it strategically into their core operations, culture, and vision. As AI continues to evolve, the next wave of industry leaders will be those who treat it not as a disruptor to react to—but as a foundation to build upon.

Conclusion

Generative AI is rapidly emerging as a transformative force across industries, redefining how businesses operate, innovate, and engage with customers. Unlike traditional automation that focuses on repetitive tasks, Generative AI brings creativity, adaptability, and intelligence into workflows—enabling content generation, real-time personalization, automated design, and enhanced decision-making. Its capabilities span across text, image, audio, video, and code generation, making it a versatile tool for improving productivity, reducing operational costs, and scaling customer experiences. As organizations increasingly adopt this technology, they unlock the potential for hyper-personalized services, agile product development, and data-driven strategies. Beyond operational efficiency, Generative AI is reshaping business models and delivering competitive advantage through faster innovation, scalable solutions, and customized offerings. Early adopters across sectors such as media, healthcare, education, and finance have demonstrated measurable improvements in output quality, customer engagement, and market differentiation. By integrating Generative AI strategically, modern enterprises are not only staying ahead of digital disruption—they are setting new standards in speed, creativity, and intelligence. This chapter lays the foundation for understanding these powerful capabilities and their strategic significance in the future of business.

Exercise Question:

- Define Generative AI. How does it differ from traditional artificial intelligence systems?
- Explain the historical evolution of AI from rule-based systems to machine learning and then to Generative AI.
- List and describe three major types of generative models. Provide examples of each.
- How does Generative AI support business model transformation? Provide examples from any two industries.
- Compare Generative AI with Traditional Automation based on functionality, output, and strategic impact.
- What are the key capabilities of Generative AI in content creation? Explain each with practical applications.
- How does Generative AI enhance customer experiences? Illustrate with real-world tools or use cases.
- What are the business drivers behind the adoption of Generative AI in modern enterprises?
- Describe how Generative AI contributes to operational cost reduction and productivity improvement.
- Discuss the role of Generative AI in accelerating product development and innovation cycles.
- How can organizations achieve strategic synergy by integrating personalization, efficiency, and innovation through Generative AI?

- Provide two case examples of companies that have successfully implemented Generative AI. What were the outcomes?
- What are the potential challenges or ethical concerns associated with using Generative AI in business?
- Create a comparison table highlighting at least five differences between Machine Learning and Generative AI in terms of business impact.
- Imagine you are a consultant for a retail company. Propose three ways they could implement Generative AI to improve operations and customer engagement.

CHAPTER 2
THE CORE CONCEPTS OF GENERATIVE AI

As Generative AI continues to redefine digital innovation, it becomes essential to understand the foundational concepts that power these intelligent systems. This chapter delves into the underlying technologies, models, and methodologies that form the backbone of generative intelligence. From machine learning paradigms to deep learning architectures, it explores how neural networks have evolved to support the creative capacities of modern AI applications. We begin with an overview of machine learning and deep learning, laying the groundwork for understanding how systems learn from data. The chapter then transitions into key generative models, including GANs, VAEs, and Transformer-based architectures like GPT and DALL·E—each with unique mechanisms and applications. A dedicated section discusses the critical role of data, from quality and preprocessing to ethical concerns like bias and fairness. Finally, we examine model training, evaluation techniques, and the pressing importance of developing responsible and reliable AI systems. Together, these concepts provide a comprehensive technical framework to grasp how Generative AI works and why it matters in today's rapidly evolving digital landscape.

2.1 Foundations of Machine Learning and Deep Learning

The foundation of Generative AI rests on the broader fields of Machine Learning (ML) and Deep Learning (DL). These subdomains of artificial intelligence focus on enabling machines to learn from data and make intelligent decisions or predictions without being explicitly programmed for every task. Machine learning involves creating algorithms that can detect patterns, classify data, and improve performance over time based on experience. It is categorized into three main paradigms: Supervised Learning, Unsupervised Learning, and Reinforcement Learning. Each of these serves a different purpose and is applied based on the problem type and the structure of the available data. Supervised learning uses labeled data to teach models to map input to output—for instance, spam detection in email systems. Unsupervised learning finds hidden patterns in data without pre-labeled outcomes, as seen in customer segmentation or anomaly detection. Reinforcement learning is centered on agents that learn optimal strategies through trial and error in dynamic environments, making it effective in robotics and gaming applications. These paradigms form the basis of how machine intelligence is taught and evaluated in real-world applications.

At the heart of deep learning lies the artificial neural network, inspired by the human brain's structure. Deep learning involves multiple layers of neurons where each layer processes a set of features and passes the results to the next. Two widely used architectures in deep learning are Convolutional Neural Networks (CNNs) and Recurrent Neural Networks (RNNs). CNNs are highly effective in image and visual processing, using filters to detect edges, shapes, and features, while RNNs are designed for sequential data such as time series and natural language, maintaining memory of previous inputs for context. Deep learning architecture involves three key layers: an input layer, which receives the raw data; hidden layers, where transformation and abstraction of data occur; and an output layer, which produces the final prediction or classification. Each neuron applies a mathematical operation to incoming data and uses activation functions to introduce non-linearity, allowing the model to capture complex relationships in data.

The model development process follows three stages: training, testing, and evaluation. During training, the model learns by adjusting its weights based on loss functions and backpropagation. Testing involves applying the trained model to unseen data to check its performance, while evaluation quantifies this performance using metrics such as accuracy, precision, recall, or F1 score. These stages ensure that the model generalizes well and is not overfitting or underfitting the data. Together, machine learning and deep learning form the essential groundwork that makes Generative AI possible. The ability of these systems to learn data distributions, extract features, and produce new outputs has enabled a wide array of generative applications—from AI-written content to realistic image synthesis and beyond.

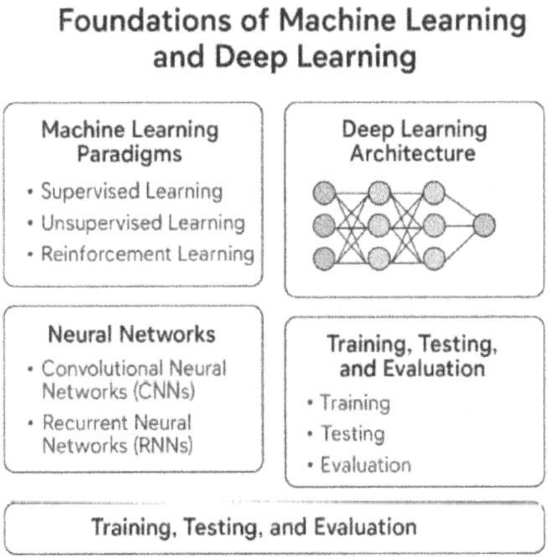

Figure 2.1: Training, Testing and Evaluation

Machine learning and deep learning form the core of Generative AI by enabling systems to learn patterns from data and make intelligent decisions. While machine learning includes paradigms like supervised, unsupervised, and reinforcement learning, deep learning uses neural networks (e.g., CNNs and RNNs) to handle complex tasks such as image recognition and language processing (Figure 2.1). These models are trained, tested, and evaluated to ensure accurate and scalable AI performance.

1. Supervised, Unsupervised, and Reinforcement Learning

Supervised Learning

Supervised learning is a foundational approach in machine learning where the algorithm learns from labeled data. This means each training example includes both the input and the correct output. The model analyzes these inputs to learn a function that maps inputs to outputs. Once trained, the model can predict the output for new, unseen inputs. Common use cases include classification (e.g., detecting spam emails, diagnosing diseases) and regression (e.g., predicting housing prices). Algorithms such as Linear Regression, Support Vector Machines (SVM), and Neural Networks are popular in this category. A critical advantage of supervised learning is its predictive accuracy, especially when provided with a large, well-labeled dataset. However, it is limited by the availability and cost of labeled data, which is often resource-intensive to collect. Training involves minimizing a loss function that measures the difference between predicted and actual outputs. Through techniques like gradient descent and backpropagation, the model iteratively improves until it achieves satisfactory performance. Model performance is assessed using metrics like accuracy, precision, recall, and F1-score for classification, and mean squared error (MSE) for regression. Cross-validation is often used to prevent overfitting. Supervised learning is widely applied in industries such as finance (fraud detection), healthcare (disease prediction), and e-commerce (recommendation systems), making it a versatile and powerful tool in the machine learning toolkit.

Unsupervised Learning

Unsupervised learning deals with unlabeled data, meaning the model must discover hidden patterns or structures without predefined outcomes. The main goal is data exploration, pattern discovery, and dimensionality reduction. The most common tasks in unsupervised learning include clustering and association rule mining. For instance, in marketing, customer segmentation based on purchasing behavior is a classic example of clustering. Algorithms like K-Means, DBSCAN, and Hierarchical Clustering are widely used. Another key technique is Principal Component Analysis (PCA), which reduces the number of variables in a dataset while preserving most of the variance. This is useful in visualizing high-dimensional data or speeding up other algorithms. Unsupervised learning is inherently more challenging to evaluate because there are no "correct" answers. Validation often relies on domain knowledge, visualization, or metrics like Silhouette Score for clustering coherence. A significant strength of unsupervised learning is its ability to uncover unknown insights, making it suitable for exploratory data analysis. It's especially valuable when labeled data is unavailable or too expensive to obtain. This paradigm is used in fraud detection (finding outliers), genomics (gene clustering), and social network analysis (community detection), offering a powerful way to make sense of raw data.

Reinforcement Learning

Reinforcement learning (RL) is a paradigm where an agent learns to make decisions by interacting with an environment. It learns by trial and error, receiving rewards or penalties based on its actions, and its goal is to maximize cumulative rewards over time. Key components in RL include the agent, environment, state, action, and reward. The agent observes a state, takes an action, receives a reward, and transitions to a new state. This loop continues until the task is complete or a termination condition is met. Unlike supervised learning, reinforcement learning does not require labeled input/output pairs. Instead, the agent explores the environment and learns from consequences, making it highly effective in dynamic and uncertain domains.

Algorithms such as Q-learning, SARSA, and Deep Q Networks (DQNs) are commonly used. These methods allow agents to build policies—a mapping from states to optimal actions—based on learned experience.

RL has been successfully applied in high-stakes environments like robotics, autonomous driving, finance, and games (e.g., AlphaGo and Dota 2). It supports complex decision-making where outcomes are influenced by sequential actions. A challenge in reinforcement learning is the exploration-exploitation trade-off—the agent must explore to discover new strategies while exploiting known good strategies for rewards. Effective balance is key to successful learning. Due to its focus on learning from interaction, reinforcement learning is ideal for applications where systems need to adapt over time and respond intelligently to changing conditions.

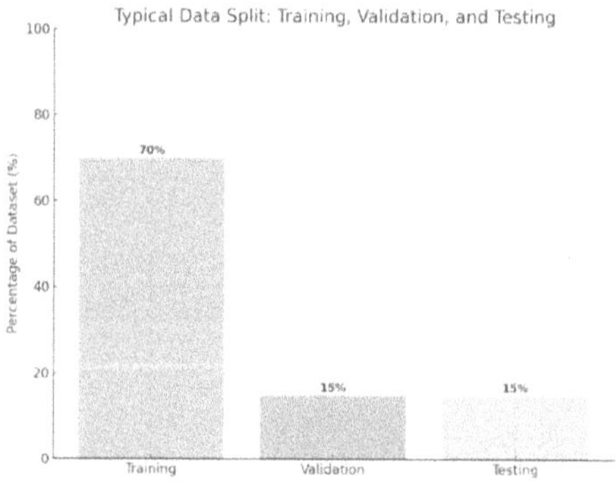

Figure 2.2: Illustrates a Typical Dataset Split Used in Machine Learning.

Figure 2.2 illustrates a typical dataset split used in machine learning: 70% for training, 15% for validation, and 15% for testing. This ensures the model learns effectively from the training data, tunes its performance during validation, and is finally evaluated on unseen testing data for generalization.

2. The Architecture of Deep Learning: Neural Networks, CNNs, and RNNs

Neural Networks

At the heart of deep learning lies the artificial neural network (ANN), inspired by the structure of the human brain. A neural network consists of layers of interconnected nodes (neurons), each performing simple computations. These layers include an input layer, hidden layers, and an output layer. Each neuron receives inputs, processes them using a weighted sum and activation function, and passes the result to the next layer. The activation function introduces non-linearity, allowing the network to model complex relationships. Common functions include ReLU, sigmoid, and tanh. The network learns by adjusting weights through backpropagation and gradient descent, minimizing a loss function that quantifies the error between predicted and actual outputs. Neural networks can model virtually any function and are particularly effective in pattern recognition tasks, such as handwriting recognition or stock price forecasting. However, they require large datasets and significant computational power. The depth and complexity of a neural network determine its capacity to learn intricate data patterns. This leads to more advanced forms like deep neural networks, which consist of multiple hidden layers. Despite their power, neural networks can suffer from overfitting, where the model performs well on training data but poorly on unseen data. Techniques like dropout, batch normalization, and early stopping are used to counteract this.

Convolutional Neural Networks (CNNs)

CNNs are a specialized form of neural networks designed for image and spatial data processing. Unlike traditional neural networks, CNNs use convolutional layers that apply filters to detect features like edges, textures, and shapes in images. The key components of CNNs include convolutional layers, pooling layers, and fully connected layers. Convolution layers perform the filtering operation, pooling layers reduce dimensionality, and fully connected layers make the final classification. CNNs are extremely effective in computer vision tasks, including object detection, face recognition, and medical image analysis. They can learn spatial hierarchies—meaning they understand both local features and their global arrangement. Because of parameter sharing and local connectivity, CNNs are more efficient than traditional deep networks when working with images. They reduce the number of parameters significantly, which helps with faster training and better generalization. Popular architectures like AlexNet, VGGNet, ResNet, and EfficientNet have achieved remarkable performance on image classification benchmarks like ImageNet. CNNs are also being used beyond vision—such as in speech recognition, where spectrograms (visual representations of sound) are analyzed. Their robustness and accuracy have made CNNs the go-to architecture in AI applications that rely on visual or grid-like data.

Recurrent Neural Networks (RNNs)

RNNs are neural networks designed to process sequential data, such as time series, audio, or natural language. Unlike feedforward networks, RNNs have loops in their architecture, allowing information to persist and influence future outputs. Each neuron in an RNN not only receives input from the current time step but also from the previous step's output, creating a form of memory. This makes RNNs ideal for modeling temporal dependencies. However, standard RNNs face problems like vanishing gradients, which make it hard to learn long-term dependencies. To solve this, advanced architectures like Long Short-Term Memory (LSTM) and Gated Recurrent Units (GRU) were developed. LSTMs and GRUs use gating mechanisms to control information flow, allowing them to retain relevant context over longer sequences. This is essential in tasks like language translation, sentiment analysis, and speech recognition.

RNNs are used in chatbots, voice assistants, real-time stock prediction, and music generation—anywhere the order of inputs affects the output. Despite their power, RNNs are gradually being replaced by Transformer models for many NLP tasks, due to the latter's superior efficiency and parallelization capabilities. Still, RNNs remain foundational in understanding how neural networks process sequence-based information.

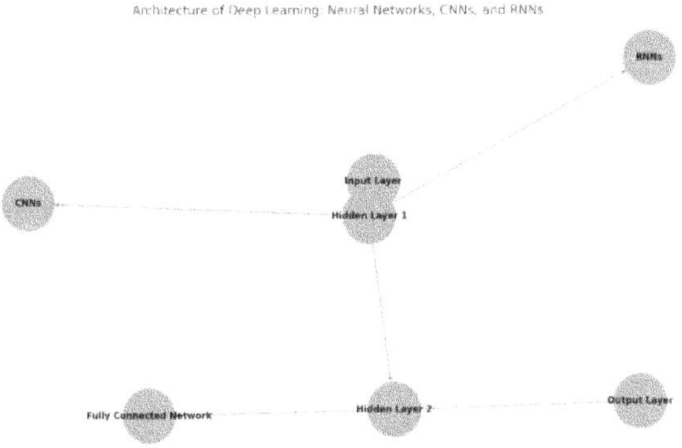

Figure 2.3: Deep Learning Architecture

Figure 2.3 of Deep Learning Architecture, showing how neural networks consist of input, hidden, and output layers, and how specialized architectures like CNNs and RNNs branch from the hidden layers to address specific data types and tasks.

3. The Significance of Training, Testing, and Evaluation

In any machine learning or deep learning project, the process of training, testing, and evaluation is fundamental to building reliable, accurate, and generalizable models. These phases ensure that the model not only learns from the data but also performs well when applied to new, unseen scenarios. Understanding each step is crucial for avoiding common pitfalls like overfitting, underfitting, or misleading performance metrics.

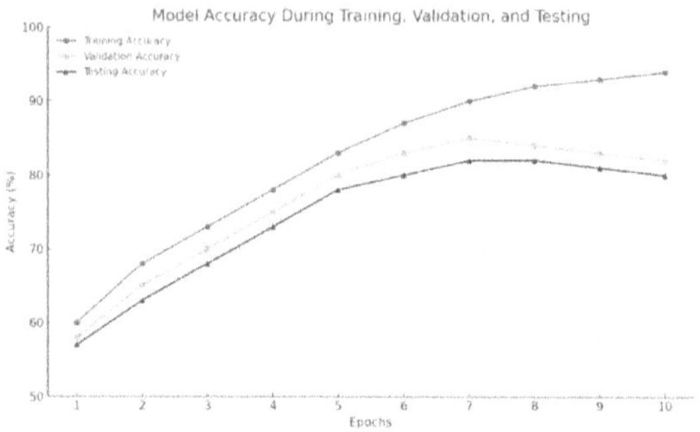

Figure 2.4: Machine Learning Model's Accuracy

Figure 2.4 illustrates how a machine learning model's accuracy evolves across training, validation, and testing over 10 epochs. Training accuracy consistently increases, while validation and testing accuracy peak and then plateau—highlighting the importance of early stopping to prevent overfitting and ensure generalization.

1. Training Phase

The training phase is where the model learns patterns from a labeled dataset. This dataset contains known inputs and corresponding outputs (in supervised learning), which the model uses to adjust internal parameters (weights and biases) via optimization algorithms such as gradient descent. The goal during training is to minimize a loss function, which measures how far the model's predictions are from the actual results. Through multiple iterations, the model becomes increasingly better at predicting outputs for the data it has seen. However, if the model is trained excessively on this data, it may memorize the dataset instead of learning general patterns—a problem known as overfitting.

2. Validation

Often, a validation set is used as a checkpoint during training. This set is not used to update the model's weights but helps in tuning hyperparameters, selecting architectures, and implementing early stopping. The validation set acts as a simulated test set to monitor the model's performance during training. If validation accuracy starts to decrease while training accuracy continues to improve, it's a signal that overfitting may be occurring. Hyperparameters such as learning rate, number of layers, and regularization strength are fine-tuned using validation performance, not training accuracy.

3. Testing Phase

The testing phase evaluates the final model's performance on a completely separate set of data that the model has never seen before. This step measures the model's ability to generalize to new scenarios and provides an unbiased assessment of real-world performance. Testing should only be done once after training and validation are complete to avoid tuning the model based on test results, which would compromise the integrity of the evaluation. Metrics such as accuracy, precision, recall, F1-score (for classification tasks), and mean squared error or R^2 (for regression tasks) are commonly used for this purpose.

4. Evaluation Metrics and Interpretability

Evaluating a model is not just about getting a high score—it's about understanding where and why the model succeeds or fails. For instance, a high accuracy may hide poor performance in minority classes in an imbalanced dataset. Confusion matrices, ROC curves, AUC scores, and classification reports provide deeper insights. For generative models, metrics like BLEU score (for text), FID score (for images), or Inception Score are used to assess the quality of generated content. Moreover, evaluation helps identify bias, data leakage, or distributional shifts between training and deployment environments, which could harm model reliability in production.

5. Importance in Real-World Deployment

In production, a well-evaluated model helps ensure robustness, reliability, and fairness. Businesses rely on these metrics to make high-stakes decisions—be it approving loans, diagnosing diseases, or recommending legal actions. Without proper testing and evaluation, a model might perform well in the lab but fail catastrophically in real-world applications, leading to financial loss, ethical violations, or damaged user trust. Thus, the training-testing-evaluation cycle is not just a technical routine—it's a critical quality control mechanism for ensuring AI solutions deliver consistent and responsible outcomes.

2.2 Understanding Generative Models

2.1. Difference Between Discriminative and Generative Models

Generative and discriminative models represent two fundamentally different approaches in machine learning. While both aim to support prediction, classification, or decision-making tasks, they do so by modeling different aspects of data. Understanding their distinctions is essential to grasp the foundation of modern AI systems, particularly those used in generative applications. Discriminative models focus on modeling the boundary between different classes. In technical terms, they aim to learn the conditional probability $P(Y|X)$, which predicts the label (Y) given the input features (X). They are designed to excel in classification or regression tasks by distinguishing one category from another. Examples of discriminative models include Logistic Regression, Support Vector Machines (SVMs), Decision Trees, and Neural Networks used for classification.

On the other hand, generative models learn the joint probability $P(X, Y)$ and often model the full distribution of the input data. These models can generate new data points similar to those in the training set. They are capable not only of classification but also of creating new content, such as generating realistic text, images, or audio. Examples include Naive Bayes, Generative Adversarial Networks (GANs), Variational Autoencoders

(VAEs), and GPT models. A significant practical difference is in use case flexibility. Discriminative models are best suited for tasks like spam filtering, sentiment analysis, and disease prediction, where accuracy and efficiency in classification are key. Generative models, by contrast, are used in applications requiring creativity and synthesis, such as data augmentation, content generation, and image-to-image translation.

Another point of distinction is complexity. Generative models are computationally more intensive and often require larger datasets and more training time. However, they offer greater potential for learning deeper representations of data and are often more versatile. As shown in the visual diagram, discriminative models take in input data and output a class label. Generative models, in contrast, can simulate both the features and the class, and can generate new data samples that resemble the training data distribution. Understanding when to use each model depends on the goal of the task: if you aim to predict a label, a discriminative model suffices; but if your task involves understanding, modeling, or generating data itself, then a generative model is more appropriate (Table 2.1).

Table 2.1: Discriminative and Generative Models

Aspect	Discriminative Models	Generative Models
Model Type	Models that learn boundary between classes	Models that learn joint probability distribution
Learning Goal	Predict label Y given input X (P(Y|X))	Model how data is generated (P(X,Y))
Data Distribution	Do not model distribution of input data	Model full input data distribution
Examples	Logistic Regression, SVM, Decision Trees	Naive Bayes, GANs, VAEs, GPT

Output	Class probabilities or labels	New data samples, reconstructions
Use Cases	Spam detection, Sentiment analysis	Text/image generation, Data augmentation
Training Complexity	Generally simpler and faster	More complex, requires more data

2.2. Overview of common generative models

Generative models are designed to learn the underlying structure of data so they can generate new, realistic samples. These models have broad applications in AI, ranging from creative content generation to simulations. Among the most popular are Generative Adversarial Networks (GANs), Variational Autoencoders (VAEs), Autoregressive Models, Transformer-based architectures, and Diffusion Models. GANs use a Generator-Discriminator structure to create high-quality images, with the Generator crafting fake data and the Discriminator distinguishing real from fake. This competition leads to outputs that closely resemble real data, making GANs a go-to choice for image synthesis and deepfake generation. In contrast, VAEs use probabilistic encoding and decoding to model data distributions, offering stability and interpretability. They're well-suited for tasks like image reconstruction and smooth data interpolation, though the outputs tend to be slightly blurrier than GANs.

Autoregressive models generate sequences by predicting each value conditioned on previous values, excelling in applications like audio generation (WaveNet) and image modeling (PixelRNN). However, their sequential nature makes them slower to train and less scalable. Enter Transformers, which revolutionized generative modeling by using self-attention to capture long-range dependencies across sequences. Models like GPT-4 and

DALL·E are built on transformer foundations and are highly effective across text, image, and code generation. Diffusion models, a more recent breakthrough, work by gradually denoising random noise to form meaningful data. These models are slower than GANs or Transformers but often produce the most photorealistic results. Tools like Stable Diffusion and Imagen are examples of diffusion-based models that generate stunning visuals with high consistency. While each model has strengths and trade-offs, their selection depends on the specific task: GANs for realism, VAEs for structured data, Transformers for versatile sequence generation, and Diffusion Models for image quality (Figure 2.5). The chart above visually compares these models based on general performance and generation quality.

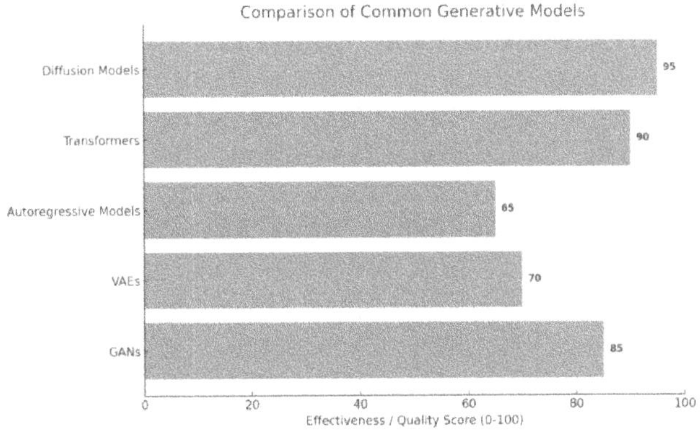

Figure 2.5: Overview of Common Generative Models

2.3. Use cases of generative models in real-world applications

1. Content Creation and Marketing

Generative models are revolutionizing how businesses create and deliver content. In marketing, tools like GPT-4 are used to generate ad copy, blog articles, email newsletters, and SEO-friendly website text. These models can quickly produce high volumes of content while maintaining relevance and contextual coherence. What makes this impactful is personalization? AI can tailor content to different audiences by changing tone, language, or formatting based on user data or demographics. For example, a product description for the same shoe can be written differently for tech-savvy customers versus style-conscious shoppers. Image generation tools like DALL·E and Midjourney complement this by producing custom graphics, promotional posters, and visual elements without needing graphic design skills. This allows small businesses to scale creative output without large in-house teams.

2. Media and Entertainment

In the entertainment industry, generative models are enabling unprecedented levels of creative automation. GANs and Diffusion models are used to produce high-resolution textures, landscapes, and animated characters for movies, games, and virtual environments. Platforms like Runway ML allow video editors and VFX artists to apply effects, modify frames, or even generate entire scenes using simple text prompts. This reduces both the cost and time of post-production workflows, making professional tools more accessible. Voice synthesis tools such as ElevenLabs let content creators generate realistic voiceovers for dubbing, animation, or narration. These tools can mimic specific voices, adjust tone or emotion, and produce multilingual outputs—enabling global content delivery at scale.

3. Healthcare and Biomedical Research

Generative models play a critical role in medical imaging and data simulation. Tools built on VAEs or GANs can create synthetic CT scans, ECG readings, or pathology slides that closely mimic real patient data. This is essential for training AI models while preserving patient privacy. In medical research, AI is accelerating drug discovery by generating possible molecular structures that could bind to disease targets. Instead of testing thousands of physical compounds, generative models simulate chemical interactions and prioritize the most promising candidates. Companies like Insilico Medicine and Atomwise use such models to reduce drug development timelines from several years to just a few months. This has the potential to speed up cures for diseases and drastically lower R&D costs in pharmaceuticals.

4. Finance and Fraud Detection

In the financial sector, generative models are used for both data generation and predictive analytics. Synthetic transaction data helps train fraud detection systems, especially in regions or markets where real data is scarce or restricted. Generative AI can also simulate economic scenarios for stress testing and risk analysis. By modeling hypothetical market behaviors or consumer trends, banks and investment firms gain insights without relying solely on historical data. Institutions like JPMorgan Chase use large language models to summarize financial documents, analyze trends, and assist analysts in making investment decisions. This significantly reduces manual effort while increasing decision accuracy and responsiveness.

5. Personalized Education and Learning Platforms

Education platforms now use generative models to deliver adaptive learning experiences. AI systems can create individualized quizzes, study plans, and explanations tailored to a learner's strengths and weaknesses. Tools like Khanmigo and Sana Labs simulate one-on-one tutoring by understanding a student's context and generating real-time responses. This is particularly helpful in remote or self-paced learning environments where live teacher interaction may be limited. Language learning apps such as Duolingo use AI to generate natural conversations and contextual practice scenarios, making the learning experience more immersive, engaging, and effective for users around the world.

6. Design and Architecture

Generative AI is transforming how design and architectural concepts are developed. Tools like Uizard and Diagram help product teams convert rough sketches or verbal descriptions into fully designed UI mockups and application screens. In architecture, GANs and diffusion-based models are being used to generate conceptual building layouts, façade designs, and interior visuals based on specific constraints such as size, function, or local climate. This accelerates the iteration phase, allowing teams to explore multiple design ideas quickly, receive client feedback earlier, and make better-informed decisions without redrawing plans manually.

7. Legal and Business Document Automation

Generative AI models are now capable of drafting contracts, legal memos, and business reports with impressive fluency and consistency. They can follow legal templates, include jurisdiction-specific clauses, and adjust for tone or audience. Firms using tools like Harvey AI benefit from reduced document review time, fewer human errors, and faster contract turnaround. These tools also assist with document summarization and compliance reporting. In corporate settings, generative models are used to create meeting notes, strategy briefs, and performance dashboards from raw input like transcripts, KPIs, or databases—saving teams hours of routine work.

Table 2.2: Real-World Use Cases of Generative Models by Industry

Industry	Use Case	Generative Model(s) Used	Example Tools / Platforms
Marketing & Content	Automated ad copy, blogs, social media graphics	Transformers, DALL·E, GPT	ChatGPT, Jasper AI, DALL·E, Midjourney

Media & Entertainment	Synthetic image/video/audio generation & editing	GANs, Diffusion Models, Voice Cloning Models	Runway ML, ElevenLabs, Synthesia
Healthcare & Biotech	Synthetic medical imaging, drug discovery simulation	VAEs, GANs, Graph-based Generative Models	Insilico Medicine, DeepMind AlphaFold
Finance	Fraud detection, synthetic transaction data, trend reports	Autoregressive Models, GPT	JPMorgan AI Labs, Kinetix AI
Education	Adaptive learning, personalized tutoring	Transformers, GPT	Duolingo, Khanmigo, Sana Labs
Design & Architecture	UI/UX mockup generation, concept building design	GANs, Diffusion, NLP-based Layout Generators	Uizard, Diagram, Autodesk AI
Legal & Enterprise	Drafting contracts, summarizing legal documents	GPT, Legal-specific Language Models	Harvey AI, Spellbook AI

Table 2.2 highlights how generative models are applied across diverse industries—from marketing and media to healthcare, finance, and education. It shows the specific use cases, the types of generative models involved (e.g., GANs, Transformers), and real-world tools that

implement these applications, demonstrating the versatility and impact of generative AI in practical scenarios.

2.3 Generative Adversarial Networks (GANs)

Generative Adversarial Networks (GANs) are a class of machine learning frameworks introduced by Ian Goodfellow in 2014. They are designed to generate new, realistic data by pitting two neural networks against each other in a competitive setting: a Generator and a Discriminator. This dynamic forms the core of what is known as adversarial learning, where the Generator tries to create fake data that looks real, and the Discriminator tries to identify whether input data is real or generated. As shown in the figure, the Generator receives input as a random noise vector (Z) and transforms it into a synthetic output (e.g., an image). The Discriminator, meanwhile, receives both real data and the Generator's output, and it tries to correctly classify each as real or fake. Over time, the Generator improves its output to better fool the Discriminator, while the Discriminator sharpens its classification skills. This adversarial feedback loop pushes the Generator to produce outputs that closely resemble real data distributions. GANs are especially powerful in image synthesis and enhancement, having been used to generate human faces (StyleGAN), perform image-to-image translation (CycleGAN), and upscale low-resolution images (SRGAN). They are also used in generating artwork, synthetic medical data, deepfakes, and even new molecular structures for drug discovery. However, GANs are not without challenges. Training can be unstable, often requiring careful tuning of hyperparameters. One common issue is mode collapse, where the Generator produces limited variations of outputs. Despite these challenges, continued innovations—such as improved loss functions and architecture tweaks—have made GANs more robust and practical over time.

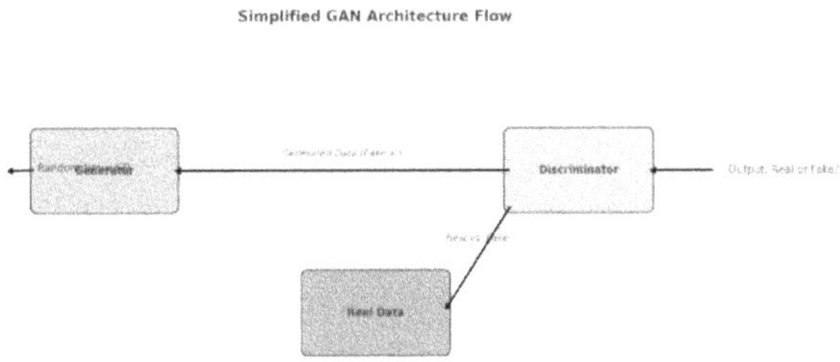

Figure 2.6: The GAN Architecture

Structured diagram of the GAN architecture, visually separating the Generator, Discriminator, and Real Data inputs (Figure 2.6). It clearly shows how random noise is converted into fake data by the Generator and then evaluated alongside real data by the Discriminator to determine authenticity.

Concept of adversarial learning

Adversarial learning is the foundational concept behind Generative Adversarial Networks (GANs). It is a training methodology where two neural networks commonly referred to as the **Generator (G)** and the **Discriminator (D)** engage in a strategic game. The Generator attempts to produce data that is indistinguishable from real data, while the Discriminator's job is to identify whether a given input is real (from the training data) or fake (produced by the Generator). This **game-theoretic setup** forms a dynamic loop that improves the capabilities of both networks over time.

At the heart of adversarial learning is the idea of **competition driving improvement**. The Generator's objective is to “fool” the Discriminator by generating increasingly realistic data samples. Conversely, the Discriminator strives to become more accurate in detecting which data samples are real and which are generated. This adversarial dynamic ensures that both models are constantly learning from each other, much like a forger and a detective continually refining their techniques. The Generator starts with **random noise input (z)**, typically sampled from a uniform or normal distribution. It uses this noise to generate synthetic data samples that resemble the training distribution (e.g., faces, texts, or sounds). The Discriminator receives both real and fake samples and predicts a probability score indicating the likelihood of a sample being real. Initially, both networks perform poorly, but as training progresses, they evolve together. The training of GANs is guided by a **minimax loss function**. The Generator tries to minimize the Discriminator's ability to detect fakes (i.e., minimize the Discriminator's success), while the Discriminator tries to maximize the probability of correctly identifying real and fake inputs. Mathematically, this is described as a two-player zero-sum game:

$$\min_G \max_D V(D, G) = \mathbb{E}_{x \sim p_{data}(x)}[\log D(x)] + \mathbb{E}_{z \sim p_z(z)}[\log(1 - D(G(z)))]$$

This adversarial framework provides a powerful way to train unsupervised models without requiring labeled data, as the Generator is implicitly learning the data distribution by attempting to mimic it. Despite its power, adversarial learning is notoriously **unstable**. Since the Generator and Discriminator are improving simultaneously, finding equilibrium is complex. If one becomes too dominant, the other fails to learn resulting in **mode collapse** (where the Generator outputs limited diversity) or failure to converge. To mitigate instability, researchers have proposed improvements such as **feature matching**, **mini-batch discrimination**, **label smoothing**, and **Wasserstein loss** (used in WGANs), which stabilize training by adjusting the objectives or the training regime. Another fascinating aspect of adversarial learning is its **generalizability**.

Beyond GANs, the adversarial paradigm has been applied in **domain adaptation**, **adversarial training for robustness**, and **privacy-preserving learning**, where an adversary attempts to reverse-engineer private data.

Adversarial learning also mimics **human learning in adversarial settings**, such as a student learning from a critical teacher or a game player improving against a more skilled opponent. This natural analog has helped popularize GANs as biologically inspired systems. Furthermore, adversarial learning fosters **creativity in AI**. Unlike conventional classification models, GANs generate entirely new samples, opening doors for applications in art, music, fashion, and storytelling. The adversarial loss allows the Generator to refine outputs in ways that resemble creative exploration. Importantly, adversarial learning models are also being used in **AI safety and security**, including detecting deepfakes and generating adversarial examples to test model robustness. Thus, the framework is not just about generation but also about preparing models for complex real-world adversaries.

Architecture: Generator vs. Discriminator

The architecture of a Generative Adversarial Network (GAN) revolves around two main components the Generator (G) and the Discriminator (D) that work in tandem under an adversarial framework. These two networks are trained simultaneously but have opposing goals: while the Generator aims to create data that looks real, the Discriminator tries to distinguish between real and generated (fake) data. The Generator is responsible for producing synthetic data by transforming a random input (usually a noise vector zzz) into a sample that resembles the real data distribution. The idea is to "fool" the Discriminator into believing that the generated sample is genuine. Structurally, the Generator is a neural network, often composed of fully connected layers or transposed convolution layers (in image-related tasks), which upscale the input noise vector into a high-dimensional output like an image, audio waveform, or text embedding.

The Discriminator, on the other hand, functions like a traditional binary classifier. It receives as input either real data (from the training dataset) or fake data (from the Generator), and outputs a probability value between 0 and 1 indicating whether it believes the sample is real. The Discriminator is typically built with convolutional layers (for images), fully connected layers (for tabular or embedded data), or RNNs/Transformers (for sequences). During training, both models update their parameters through backpropagation. The Discriminator minimizes a binary cross-entropy loss by trying to accurately classify real and fake data. The Generator tries to maximize the probability that the Discriminator misclassifies its outputs as real—effectively minimizing the Discriminator's ability to identify fakes. This setup forms a minimax game, with the two networks locked in competition. As the Generator gets better, the Discriminator's job becomes harder, and vice versa. Ideally, the training reaches a Nash equilibrium, where the Generator produces perfectly realistic samples and the Discriminator cannot do better than random guessing (i.e., 50% accuracy).

In practice, achieving balance between G and D is challenging. If the Discriminator becomes too strong early in training, it quickly overpowers the Generator, which then struggles to learn. Conversely, if the Generator becomes too efficient, the Discriminator may stop learning. To manage this, techniques like alternating updates, gradient penalty, label smoothing, and batch normalization are often applied. GAN architectures differ based on application. For example, DCGAN uses convolutional and transposed convolutional layers to handle image data. StyleGAN introduces style vectors and progressive growing to generate high-quality, controllable images. Text-based GANs may replace CNNs with recurrent layers or Transformers, depending on sequence length and structure. The latent space (input noise vector) plays a crucial role in Generator design. It allows for interpolation and manipulation of generated outputs. For example, tweaking the vector can morph a generated face from smiling to neutral, showing how semantic features are encoded within the network.

One powerful concept in GAN architecture is the feedback loop. The Discriminator's feedback (i.e., how convincingly it spots fake samples) helps the Generator improve. This loop is what allows GANs to generate sharper and more natural-looking outputs than older generative models like VAEs. Visualization of the data flow—from noise to fake sample to Discriminator decision—helps grasp the interaction. The Generator pushes data forward, while the Discriminator acts as a gatekeeper evaluating both real and generated data (Table 2.3). Over time, many enhancements to GAN architecture have emerged. These include conditional GANs (cGANs), where both G and D receive additional labels or context, and Wasserstein GANs (WGANs), which replace the traditional loss with a Wasserstein distance to improve training stability. The modularity of GANs means they can be adapted for diverse applications. The Generator and Discriminator can be tailored independently to handle text, speech, music, time-series, or tabular data, making GANs a versatile tool in modern AI.

Table 2.3: Comparison Generator vs. Discriminator in GANs

Aspect	Generator (G)	Discriminator (D)
Purpose	Generate fake data that mimics real data	Distinguish real from fake data
Input	Random noise vector zzz	Real or fake data sample
Output	Synthetic data sample (e.g., image, text,	Probability that input is real (0 to 1)

	audio)	
Type of Network	Transposed CNN, FC, RNN, Transformer	CNN, FC, or sequence models (depending on data type)
Loss Function	Minimize log(1 - D(G(z))) or maximize log(D(G(z)))	Maximize log D(x) and minimize log D(G(z))
Training Goal	Fool the Discriminator	Accurately classify real vs fake
Backpropagation	Uses Discriminator's gradient to improve	Updates directly based on prediction accuracy
Common Layers	Deconvolution, BatchNorm, ReLU, Tanh	Convolution, LeakyReLU, Sigmoid
Challenges	Mode collapse, blurry outputs, unstable gradients	Overconfidence, overfitting on early fake patterns
Key Variants	DCGAN, StyleGAN, BigGAN, cGAN	Part of all GAN variants, tailored to application

Variants of GANs (e.g., DCGAN, StyleGAN, CycleGAN)

As Generative Adversarial Networks (GANs) gained popularity, researchers began developing specialized variants to improve stability, quality, control, and application scope. While the original GAN laid the theoretical foundation, these variants—DCGAN, StyleGAN, CycleGAN, and others—introduced architectural innovations and domain-specific adaptations that made GANs far more practical and powerful across fields like image synthesis, domain translation, and design.

1. Deep Convolutional GAN (DCGAN)

DCGAN is one of the earliest and most influential GAN architectures tailored for image generation. Introduced in 2015, DCGAN replaces fully connected layers with convolutional and transposed convolutional layers, making it ideal for learning spatial hierarchies in image data. It also uses techniques like batch normalization, LeakyReLU in the Discriminator, and ReLU in the Generator to stabilize training. DCGAN demonstrated that GANs could learn meaningful representations, such as object shapes, textures, and background layouts. For example, a DCGAN trained on face datasets like CelebA could produce realistic-looking human faces with proper alignment and lighting. The simplicity of DCGAN's architecture makes it a common starting point for new GAN-based projects and an educational model for understanding the fundamentals of convolutional GANs.

2. StyleGAN

Developed by NVIDIA, StyleGAN introduced a significant leap in the control and quality of generated images. Unlike traditional GANs where the latent vector *z* directly drives the Generator, StyleGAN first maps *z* into an intermediate latent space (W) and applies style modulation at each convolutional layer. This separation of content and style allows fine-grained control over features such as facial expression, hairstyle, age, or background. For example, users can adjust one latent dimension to make a face smile, while keeping the other features intact. StyleGAN also introduced progressive growing, where training starts with low-resolution images and gradually adds layers to increase resolution. This technique improves stability and output quality, enabling the generation of photorealistic faces at resolutions like 1024x1024. Its most famous application is ThisPersonDoesNotExist.com, where each page refresh generates a brand-new, hyperrealistic human face.

3. CycleGAN

CycleGAN focuses on image-to-image translation without requiring paired training data. Traditional supervised models need aligned pairs (e.g., a horse image and its zebra equivalent), but CycleGAN uses cycle consistency loss to learn mappings between domains. It works using two Generators (G and F) and two Discriminators (D_X and D_Y). One Generator translates images from domain X to Y (e.g., horse to zebra), and the other translates them back from Y to X (zebra to horse). The cycle consistency ensures that an image translated back and forth remains unchanged, even in the absence of paired examples. CycleGAN has been widely used for artistic style transfer, converting photos into paintings (e.g., Monet to Van Gogh), seasonal changes in landscapes, or even transforming facial expressions.

4. BigGAN

BigGAN, also developed by DeepMind and Google, is a large-scale GAN trained on massive computational resources and datasets (like ImageNet). It leverages class-conditional training, which allows the model to generate specific categories (e.g., dogs, birds, cars) by feeding in a class label alongside the noise vector. BigGAN achieves high diversity and realism, setting benchmarks for high-resolution image synthesis. It introduced advanced training techniques like orthogonal regularization, shared embeddings, and truncation trick to control diversity vs. fidelity trade-offs. The outputs from BigGAN models often appear indistinguishable from real photos, and it remains one of the most powerful public image generators to date.

5. Conditional GAN (cGAN)

Conditional GANs (cGANs) extend the GAN architecture by feeding additional label or context information into both the Generator and Discriminator. This allows for more control over the generated output. For example, in a digit-generation task, feeding the label “7” into the

Generator allows it to create handwritten "7" images. In image generation tasks, cGANs can generate images based on text descriptions or segmentation masks. This added supervision improves model consistency and usability in controlled synthesis applications such as data augmentation, image-to-image translation, and medical image simulation.

6. Pix2Pix

Pix2Pix is a supervised image-to-image translation framework based on cGANs. Unlike CycleGAN, it requires paired data. It is used in applications where precise image transformation is needed, such as sketch-to-photo translation, satellite-to-map generation, or black-and-white to color image restoration. Pix2Pix uses a U-Net architecture for the Generator, which preserves spatial information via skip connections, and a PatchGAN Discriminator, which evaluates image realism at the patch level for sharper results.

7. StarGAN

StarGAN enables multi-domain translation using a single Generator and Discriminator, unlike CycleGAN which requires separate models for each domain pair. It can translate facial attributes (like age, gender, expression) across multiple categories in a unified architecture. StarGAN feeds domain labels along with input images to control the translation target, making it ideal for multifaceted image manipulation tasks in face editing, fashion, and entertainment applications.

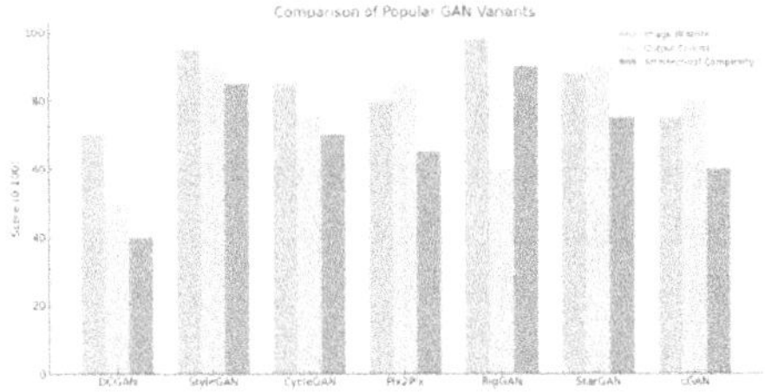

Figure 2.7: Popular GAN variants

The comparison Figure 2.7 for popular GAN variants, showing how they score across three key dimensions:

- Image Realism: Quality and photorealism of generated content
- Output Control: User control over style, content, or domain
- Architectural Complexity: Depth, layers, and resource needs

This helps visualize how different GANs are suited for various applications based on trade-offs between quality, usability, and implementation effort

Strengths, limitations, and use cases

Strengths of GANs

Generative Adversarial Networks (GANs) are widely celebrated for their ability to produce highly realistic synthetic data, especially in visual domains. Unlike older generative models, GANs don't rely on reconstruction losses, which allows them to generate sharper and more visually appealing outputs. Their ability to learn complex, high-dimensional data distributions without requiring explicit labels makes them ideal for unsupervised learning scenarios. GANs are also flexible; with slight architectural modifications, they can be tailored to a wide range of data types, including images, audio, video, and text.

Limitations of GANs

Despite their capabilities, GANs come with notable challenges. The training process is notoriously unstable, often suffering from non-convergence, vanishing gradients, and mode collapse, where the Generator produces limited varieties of outputs. Tuning GANs requires careful balancing between the Generator and Discriminator to avoid overpowering one over the other. Moreover, GANs can be resource-intensive, especially when generating high-resolution images, making them less practical for low-resource environments. Finally, evaluating the quality of GAN outputs is still a challenge, as existing metrics like Inception Score or FID don't fully capture subjective visual quality or diversity.

Use Cases Across Industries

GANs have found applications in various sectors. In entertainment and media, they're used to generate hyper-realistic human faces, deepfakes, and visual effects. In healthcare, GANs generate synthetic medical images for training diagnostic models while preserving patient privacy. Retail and e-commerce leverage GANs for product design and virtual try-ons. In autonomous systems, GANs simulate environments for training reinforcement learning agents. Their ability to generate unseen yet plausible samples also makes them valuable in data augmentation, improving the performance of classifiers when real data is limited or imbalanced.

Ethical and Practical Considerations

With great power comes responsibility—GANs raise important ethical concerns. Deepfakes and synthetic media can be misused for disinformation, identity theft, or content manipulation. As such, businesses and researchers must ensure responsible deployment, incorporate watermarking, and follow fairness guidelines when using GAN-generated content (Table 2.4). On the practical side, combining GANs with techniques like transfer learning, conditional generation, and semi-supervised learning can significantly enhance both utility and control over the outputs.

Table 2.4: Overview of GANs Strengths, Limitations, and Use Cases

Category	Description	Examples / Notes
Strengths	- Generates highly realistic data - Works with unlabeled data	Used for image, video, audio, and text generation

	- Flexible across data types	
	- Learns complex distributions - Adaptable to different domains	From faces to molecular structures
Limitations	- Training instability - Mode collapse (limited output diversity) - Requires large resources	Needs careful tuning of Generator and Discriminator
	- Evaluation is challenging - Sensitive to hyperparameters	Inception Score and FID are common but not perfect metrics
Use Cases	- Image synthesis and deepfakes - Data augmentation - Domain translation	StyleGAN (faces), CycleGAN (image-to-image), BigGAN (high-res objects)
	- Medical imaging simulation - Fashion design & virtual try-on - Simulation for RL agents	Useful in privacy-preserving training and low-data scenarios
Ethical Concerns	- Deepfake misuse - Disinformation - Synthetic identity	Must apply safeguards like watermarking and authenticity

	fraud	verification

2.4 Other Generative Models

Variational Autoencoders (VAEs): structure and applications

Variational Autoencoders (VAEs) are a class of probabilistic generative models that merge deep learning and Bayesian inference to generate new data samples. First introduced by Kingma and Welling in 2013, VAEs stand out for their structured and interpretable latent space, stable training behavior, and capability to model complex data distributions. Unlike traditional autoencoders, which deterministically compress and reconstruct input data, VAEs encode inputs into a probabilistic latent space, allowing them to generate diverse outputs from learned distributions.

A standard VAE consists of two neural networks—an Encoder and a Decoder. The Encoder maps input data into a latent space characterized by a mean and variance, essentially learning parameters of a Gaussian distribution. Rather than using fixed outputs, the model samples from this distribution using the reparameterization trick ((i.e., $z=\mu+\sigma\cdot\epsilon$) to ensure gradients can flow during training. The Decoder then reconstructs data from this sampled latent vector, attempting to recreate the original input as closely as possible. The VAE training objective includes two components: the reconstruction loss, which penalizes differences between original and reconstructed data, and the Kullback–Leibler (KL) divergence, which regularizes the latent space by ensuring it follows a standard normal distribution. This dual objective helps prevent overfitting while promoting generalization and smooth interpolation in the latent space. The stochastic nature of sampling further allows the model to explore various plausible representations for a given input. One of the major strengths of VAEs is the interpretability of their latent space. Latent dimensions often capture distinct and semantically meaningful features, such as object orientation, color, or size. This makes VAEs especially useful for tasks that require representation learning or semantic manipulation. For instance, by modifying individual latent variables, one can alter specific attributes of generated images, like making a face smile or adding glasses.

Although VAEs tend to produce blurrier images compared to GANs—mainly due to the reliance on mean squared error for reconstruction—they offer higher mode coverage and fewer training difficulties. Their stability makes them suitable for applications where diversity and robustness are more critical than ultra-sharp realism. VAEs have been effectively used in image generation, text generation, and audio synthesis. In healthcare, they're deployed for synthetic data generation, anomaly detection in ECG/EEG, and privacy-preserving diagnostics by simulating medical images without compromising patient identities. In natural language processing, VAEs, when combined with RNNs or Transformers, are applied for paraphrasing, sentence generation, and unsupervised translation. They are also useful in semi-supervised learning tasks, where they enhance generalization by modeling both labeled and unlabeled data. The Conditional VAE (CVAE) extends the base model by feeding label information into both Encoder and Decoder, enabling conditional sample generation based on user-specified features. Beyond NLP and vision, VAEs are used in music generation—such as in Google's NSynth project—where they interpolate sounds between instruments in latent space. They're also critical in anomaly detection, as unusual data points tend to have high reconstruction errors. Moreover, β-VAE and other variants promote disentangled representation learning, where individual latent variables capture independent factors of variation, making models more explainable and controllable.

VAEs also have applications in data compression, where only the latent vector needs to be stored or transmitted. Their robust structure allows them to denoise corrupted inputs, making them effective for signal restoration. In hybrid models like VAE-GAN or VQ-VAE, researchers have combined the expressiveness of GANs with the structured learning of VAEs to improve both output quality and controllability. VQ-VAE in particular has been used in OpenAI's DALL·E and Jukebox for text-to-image and music generation. Despite their strengths, VAEs are not ideal when ultra-realistic image quality is paramount. However, they offer invaluable benefits when interpretability, latent structure, and diversity matter. Their probabilistic framework allows for principled likelihood estimation and better control over data generation. Supported in popular frameworks like PyTorch and TensorFlow, VAEs continue to be a foundational tool for researchers and practitioners alike.

Autoregressive models: PixelRNN, WaveNet

Autoregressive models are a class of generative models that predict data one step at a time, using previously generated values as input for the next prediction. The core idea is based on the chain rule of probability, which expresses the joint distribution of a sequence as a product of conditional distributions. This approach is foundational in sequence modeling and has been widely applied in domains such as language, audio, and image generation.

Formally, for a sequence $x = (x_1, x_2, ..., x_n)$, the model estimates the probability as:

$$P(x) = \prod_{t=1}^{n} P(x_t | x_1, x_2, ..., x_{t-1})$$

This formulation is the basis for powerful autoregressive models like PixelRNN for images and WaveNet for audio.

PixelRNN

PixelRNN is an autoregressive model designed to generate images pixel by pixel, introduced by DeepMind. It models the joint distribution of pixel values in an image by conditioning each pixel on all previously generated pixels. This is done in a row-wise or diagonal fashion to respect spatial dependencies. The architecture includes recurrent neural networks—typically LSTM layers—that operate across the pixels of an image. These LSTMs process the image one row at a time, maintaining a memory of all prior pixels. The prediction of each pixel takes into account not only its neighbors in the same row but also in previous rows. To preserve the 2D spatial structure of images, PixelRNN uses two key variants: Row LSTM and Diagonal BiLSTM. Row LSTM processes each row sequentially, while Diagonal BiLSTM captures dependencies in both dimensions, though at higher computational cost.

PixelRNN handles images as matrices, and each pixel (especially in color images) has multiple channels (RGB), which are generated sequentially as well. This ensures high fidelity and coherence, even though it introduces significant time complexity during inference. Despite its effectiveness, PixelRNN suffers from slow generation speed due to its strictly sequential nature. To address this, PixelCNN was introduced as a faster alternative, using convolutional layers instead of RNNs to model pixel dependencies. PixelCNN retains many of PixelRNN's benefits while allowing for more parallelizable training. PixelRNN and PixelCNN have inspired many modern image completion and super-resolution tasks, as they can infer missing parts of an image by conditioning on known pixels.

WaveNet

WaveNet, also developed by DeepMind, applies the autoregressive principle to audio generation. Unlike traditional methods that use predefined vocoders or spectral models, WaveNet generates raw audio waveforms sample by sample, achieving unprecedented naturalness and detail in synthetic speech and music. WaveNet models the conditional distribution of the next audio sample given all previous samples. Since audio signals can have tens of thousands of samples per second (e.g., 16,000 or 24,000 Hz), the model must make a vast number of predictions even for short audio clips. The key architectural innovation in WaveNet is the use of dilated causal convolutions, which allow the model to maintain a large receptive field without requiring excessive depth or sequential computation. Causal convolutions ensure that the prediction at time t only depends on samples before t, maintaining temporal coherence. Dilated convolutions introduce gaps between filter elements, enabling exponential growth of the receptive field with depth. This allows WaveNet to model long-range dependencies efficiently, capturing both short-term details (like phonemes) and long-term structure (like intonation and rhythm).

WaveNet also incorporates residual and skip connections, improving training dynamics and convergence speed. The output is typically a softmax over quantized waveform values, though later versions used continuous distributions for better audio fidelity.

Initially, WaveNet was very slow during inference, requiring one sample generation per forward pass. Optimized implementations and student-teacher models like Parallel WaveNet were later introduced to enable real-time generation. WaveNet revolutionized text-to-speech (TTS) systems, surpassing classical approaches in naturalness. It has since been integrated into commercial systems like Google Assistant and Amazon Alexa, powering high-quality voice responses. Beyond speech, WaveNet has been adapted for music generation, acoustic modeling, and seismic waveform synthesis. Its success inspired architectures in non-audio domains as well, such as time-series forecasting and sensor signal processing.

Comparison and Relevance

Both PixelRNN and WaveNet showcase the strength of autoregressive models in capturing complex local dependencies in structured data—images and waveforms, respectively. Their ability to model fine-grained details makes them powerful in tasks where realism and continuity are essential. However, their main limitation is generation speed. Because each step depends on the previous one, these models cannot fully parallelize generation. This has prompted the development of hybrid or alternative models such as Transformers (which use masked attention) and diffusion models (which reverse noise gradually).

Despite this, autoregressive models remain important. They form the conceptual backbone of many sequence-based models, including language models like GPT, which can be viewed as autoregressive Transformers. The autoregressive principle ensures that generated outputs remain consistent and temporally coherent. In summary, autoregressive models like PixelRNN and WaveNet demonstrate the ability of deep networks to model sequential dependencies with high fidelity. They laid the foundation for modern generative models and continue to influence developments in audio, image, and sequential data modeling.

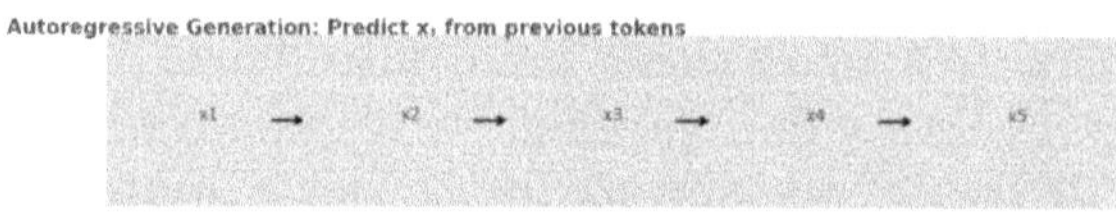

Figure 2.8: Autoregressive Generation

Figure 2.8 illustrating Autoregressive Generation, where each output x_t is predicted sequentially based on the previous values. This principle forms the core of autoregressive models like PixelRNN and WaveNet.

Transformer-based models (GPT, DALL·E, BERT): capabilities and innovations

The Transformer architecture, introduced by Vaswani et al. in the 2017 paper "Attention Is All You Need", revolutionized how machines process sequential data. Unlike RNNs and LSTMs, which process sequences step-by-step, Transformers use self-attention mechanisms to process all tokens in parallel, enabling greater scalability and performance. Transformers consist of Encoder and Decoder stacks. While BERT uses only the encoder (for understanding tasks), GPT uses only the decoder (for generative tasks), and DALL·E combines both with vision modules for multimodal generation. The core innovation is the attention mechanism, particularly multi-head self-attention, which allows models to dynamically weigh the relevance of different input tokens when encoding information.

1. GPT (Generative Pretrained Transformer)

GPT, developed by OpenAI, is a unidirectional decoder-based Transformer. It generates text one token at a time, conditioned on previous tokens. GPT's architecture enables powerful language modeling, where it learns to predict the next word in a sentence. Trained on massive datasets from books, websites, and articles, GPT models (GPT-2, GPT-3, and GPT-4) generate coherent paragraphs, answer questions, summarize texts, write code, and more. A key strength of GPT is its pretraining-finetuning paradigm. First, it's trained unsupervised on a large corpus; then it is fine-tuned for specific downstream tasks (e.g., translation, summarization). Later versions like GPT-3 and GPT-4 use few-shot and zero-shot learning, where they perform tasks based on example prompts without needing task-specific training. GPT's decoder-only setup uses masked self-attention, meaning each token can only attend to previous tokens—preserving causality for generative tasks. This architecture is ideal for tasks like text generation, code completion, and dialogue systems.

2. BERT (Bidirectional Encoder Representations from Transformers)

BERT, developed by Google, is based on the encoder side of the Transformer. Unlike GPT, it is bidirectional, meaning it attends to both left and right contexts of a word simultaneously. This makes BERT ideal for language understanding tasks, such as question answering, sentiment analysis, and named entity recognition. BERT uses two novel pretraining tasks: Masked Language Modeling (MLM) and Next Sentence Prediction (NSP). In MLM, random words are masked and the model learns to predict them using context. In NSP, the model learns relationships between sentence pairs. This two-pronged pretraining gives BERT a deep understanding of syntax and semantics. Variants of BERT include RoBERTa, DistilBERT, and ALBERT, each improving efficiency or performance. BERT has set new benchmarks on several NLP tasks and is widely used in enterprise search, chatbots, and information retrieval systems.

3. DALL·E Text-to-Image Generation

DALL·E extends Transformer architecture to the multimodal domain, generating images from textual descriptions. Developed by OpenAI, it fuses the Transformer with image modeling by treating pixels or image tokens as a language. DALL·E 1 uses a discrete VAE to tokenize images into learnable codebook entries, then trains a Transformer to generate these tokens based on input text. DALL·E 2 improves over its predecessor by separating image generation into two stages: generating a CLIP-guided image embedding from text, then using diffusion models to generate high-resolution images. This two-step process enhances realism, style control, and alignment with user prompts. One of DALL·E's biggest innovations is zero-shot image synthesis, where it generates complex, creative, or surreal images without task-specific training. Use cases include graphic design, storytelling, concept art, advertising, and even fashion prototyping.

Capabilities of Transformer Models

The success of Transformer models lies in their ability to scale with data and parameters. Unlike older architectures, Transformers improve in performance when scaled to billions of parameters and trillions of training tokens. This scaling law, validated through GPT and BERT variants, enables unprecedented generalization across diverse tasks. Transformers also support transfer learning. A pretrained Transformer can be fine-tuned or prompted to perform well on new tasks with minimal additional data, saving computational resources. In domains like healthcare or legal AI, this adaptability allows models to be applied to domain-specific text with minimal retraining. The use of attention maps provides some interpretability. Attention weights can show which words a model is focusing on, useful in explaining why a model made a certain prediction. Although not perfect, it's a step toward explainable AI.

Innovations in Architecture and Training

Modern innovations like sparse attention, efficient Transformers, and long-context models address the quadratic time complexity of attention. Models like Longformer, BigBird, and FlashAttention process long documents efficiently without sacrificing performance. The integration of Reinforcement Learning from Human Feedback (RLHF) in models like ChatGPT fine-tunes responses based on human preferences, improving alignment, safety, and engagement. Similarly, instruction tuning helps models better follow commands and behave predictably. Transformers also enable multimodal models, combining text, images, audio, and video. For instance, CLIP aligns image and text embeddings in the same latent space, allowing flexible tasks like text-guided image retrieval or classification.

Challenges and Ethical Considerations

Despite their power, Transformer models come with challenges. Their size and energy consumption make training environmentally costly. They are also prone to hallucination, generating confident but incorrect information. In real-world applications, this can lead to misinformation or biased outputs. To mitigate this, researchers are working on model compression, knowledge distillation, and safety alignment techniques. OpenAI, Google, and others have emphasized ethical deployment, transparency, and bias detection frame.

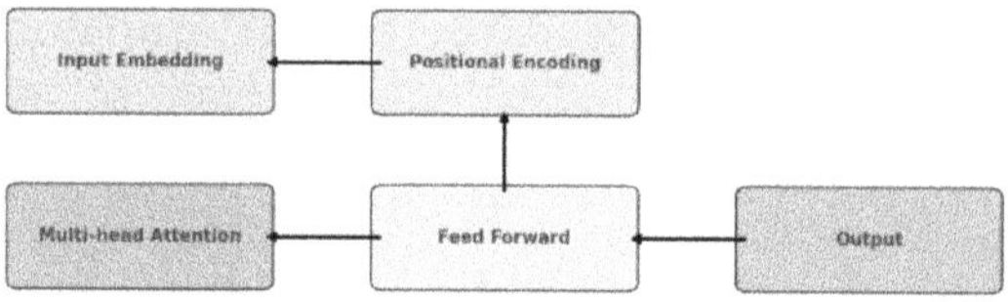

Figure 2.9: Transformer Architecture Diagram

Transformer architecture diagram, showcasing core components like input embeddings, positional encoding, multi-head attention, and feed-forward layers—used in models such as GPT, BERT, and DALL·E (Figure 2.9).

2.5 The Role of Data in Generative AI

In Generative AI, data is the foundation upon which intelligent systems learn to mimic, synthesize, and innovate. Unlike traditional models that rely on labeled inputs and outputs, generative models learn to understand the underlying distribution of data to generate new samples that resemble the original inputs. This makes the quality, diversity, and quantity of data pivotal to the model's success. If the data used to train a generative model is biased, incomplete, or noisy, the generated outputs will inherit these flaws, leading to poor generalization or even harmful consequences like reinforcing stereotypes or misinformation. The quality of data directly influences the fidelity and realism of generative outputs. High-resolution images, grammatically correct text, and accurately transcribed audio are essential for models like GANs, VAEs, and Transformers to learn meaningful patterns. Preprocessing steps such as normalization, noise removal, and augmentation enhance data quality and make it more suitable for robust training. Moreover, well-curated and balanced datasets help prevent overfitting to specific patterns or over-representation of certain categories, ensuring that the model learns a fair and comprehensive view of the data distribution. Diversity of data is equally crucial. A model trained only on Western faces, for instance, would struggle to generate or understand faces of other ethnicities, demonstrating a lack of generalization. In applications like image synthesis, language modeling, and video generation, exposure to diverse datasets ensures that the AI can generate outputs that are more inclusive, creative, and context-aware. Diversity in linguistic patterns, visual content, and cultural references enables generative AI systems to respond effectively in global, real-world scenarios. Another vital aspect is the size of the dataset. Generative models—especially large-scale ones like GPT or DALL·E—require vast amounts of data to capture complex relationships and contextual nuances. However, more data is not always better; it must be relevant and representative of the task or domain. Recent approaches also emphasize data efficiency, leveraging transfer learning, synthetic data, and semi-supervised learning to minimize reliance on massive datasets while still achieving state-of-the-art performance.

Importance of data quality, quantity, and diversity

In the realm of Generative AI, the entire capacity of a model to create realistic, coherent, and meaningful outputs hinges on the quality, amount, and diversity of the training data. These three elements form the core foundation of how well a model can learn, generalize, and perform across varied tasks—whether generating text, synthesizing images, composing music, or simulating speech. Without a solid data foundation, even the most advanced architectures like GANs, VAEs, or Transformers can produce flawed or biased outputs. Data quality refers to how accurate, clean, and well-structured the training inputs are. High-quality data allows a model to extract meaningful patterns and avoid learning from noise, inconsistencies, or errors. For instance, grammatically sound and contextually rich text trains language models like GPT to write coherent paragraphs. Conversely, poor-quality data—like mislabeled images or noisy recordings—leads to distorted outputs and confusion during learning. In sensitive domains such as medical imaging or financial data generation, compromised data quality can severely impact the reliability and safety of AI outputs.

Beyond quality, the quantity of data plays a crucial role in how deeply a model can learn and how well it generalizes to new scenarios. Large datasets expose generative models to a broader spectrum of patterns, increasing their capacity to create complex and contextually rich outputs. Language models like GPT-4 and image models like DALL·E 2 are trained on vast corpora comprising hundreds of billions of words and images. This sheer volume allows them to recognize and mimic subtle details like sarcasm, idioms, shadows, or artistic brush strokes. However, having lots of data is not enough—it must be relevant and not just repetitive or noisy, which can lead to overfitting or model bloat without actual performance gains. Equally important is data diversity, which ensures that the AI learns from a broad array of inputs encompassing multiple languages, cultures, age groups, genders, styles, and formats. A model trained only on English news articles might perform poorly on informal conversation, regional dialects, or creative writing. Similarly, an image generator trained only on Western faces may lack the ability to represent global demographics, leading to unintentional exclusion or bias. Data diversity not only improves generalization and fairness but also enhances a model's creative scope—allowing it to blend ideas from different sources, mimic varied aesthetics, and produce outputs relevant to wider audiences.

These three elements—quality, quantity, and diversity—must be balanced. A large dataset with poor quality can still mislead the model, just as a diverse but tiny dataset may fail to teach robust patterns. High-quality, diverse data in inadequate volumes can also limit the model's ability to generalize. Thus, a holistic approach to data curation is essential, where all three factors are considered in tandem. This includes steps such as de-duplication, deducing biases, augmenting minority classes, and normalizing inconsistencies. As AI development advances, the focus is shifting toward better—not just bigger—data. Techniques like synthetic data generation, data filtering, active learning, and human-in-the-loop validation are helping refine datasets to enhance learning outcomes. Simultaneously, ethical considerations such as data provenance, consent, transparency, and auditability are becoming central to dataset management. In the end, the integrity and breadth of data used in training generative models not only shape the capability of AI, but also its responsibility, inclusivity, and trustworthiness in real-world applications (Table 2.5).

Table 2.5: Importance of Data Attributes in Generative AI

Attribute	Definition	Importance	Examples
Quality	Accuracy, cleanliness, and correctness of data	Prevents hallucinations, improves realism and structure	Well-labeled images, grammatically correct text
Quantity	Volume of training data	Enables learning of deep patterns and long-range dependencies	GPT trained on billions of tokens
Diversity	Range of	Reduces bias,	Multi-

	variation in content and context	enhances generalization and cultural/contextual inclusivity	lingual corpora, global face datasets
Combined Impact	Interaction between all three attributes	Balancing them leads to high-performing, ethical, and robust AI	CLIP, DALL·E, and GPT benefit from massive, diverse data

Dataset curation and preprocessing

In the context of Generative AI, the process of dataset curation and preprocessing is foundational—it ensures that the models are built upon structured, reliable, and ethically sourced information. Generative models are only as good as the data they are trained on. Therefore, careful attention must be paid to collecting, organizing, refining, and validating the data before it ever reaches the model training phase. This comprehensive process enhances the quality of generative outputs and ensures the fairness, accuracy, and efficiency of the system. The first stage in the pipeline is raw data collection, which involves sourcing unstructured data such as text, images, audio, or video from various domains. Whether the data is collected from public repositories, web scraping, APIs, or internal enterprise databases, the goal is to amass a broad and representative dataset. However, this raw input is often messy, containing duplicates, irrelevant items, or even harmful content. Therefore, cleaning and filtering becomes the second vital step. This involves removing noise, resolving inconsistencies, de-duplicating entries, and filtering out sensitive or unethical material that might lead to problematic AI behavior.

Next, many datasets require annotation and labeling, especially for semi-supervised or conditional generative tasks. This could involve tagging image classes, labeling emotions in audio, or assigning part-of-speech tags in text. Proper annotation enhances the semantic understanding of the model, allowing it to generate contextually accurate and tailored outputs. Once labeled, the data undergoes normalization and scaling—a step where numerical values are standardized, images are resized, or text is tokenized. This consistency ensures that all data points are processed uniformly by the model without introducing scale-related biases. To further strengthen model generalization and robustness, data augmentation techniques are applied. In vision tasks, this might involve rotating, flipping, or adding noise to images. In text, paraphrasing or back-translation is used, while audio data can be pitch-shifted or compressed. Augmentation synthetically increases dataset volume while preserving core semantics, making the model less sensitive to noise and outliers. After augmentation, data is typically split into training, validation, and testing subsets. Care must be taken to maintain balance across these subsets—ensuring equal representation of classes, styles, and domains—so that models generalize well without overfitting or underperforming on rare cases.

Integrity checks are essential throughout the process. Before finalizing the dataset, teams must perform audits to verify consistency in labels, test for class imbalance, and validate the distribution of different features across the dataset. This process is especially critical in regulated sectors like healthcare or finance, where erroneous predictions can have serious consequences. Additionally, ethical and legal considerations must be observed throughout dataset curation. Datasets should comply with data protection regulations such as GDPR or HIPAA, avoid encoding bias or stereotypes, and respect user privacy and consent when using human-generated content. The modern data pipeline often leverages tools and frameworks such as TensorFlow Datasets, Hugging Face Datasets, and PyTorch's torchvision. These platforms streamline the curation process by offering utilities for transformation, loading, and documentation. Domain-specific preprocessing is also essential. For instance, in healthcare, anonymization and quality are prioritized; in NLP, multilingual and syntactic preprocessing is emphasized; and in vision tasks, pixel normalization and spatial cropping are common. In scenarios where real-world data is scarce, sensitive, or unavailable, synthetic data—often generated by earlier models—can be used to supplement training datasets. For example, in self-driving car simulation or rare disease diagnosis, synthetic examples are generated to train models on low-frequency edge cases. Along with synthetic enhancement, maintaining version control over datasets using tools like DVC ensures reproducibility and traceability over time.

Continual improvement is part of responsible dataset curation. As the AI model learns, it might expose gaps or biases in the data. Active learning, feedback loops, and iterative retraining enable teams to patch these weaknesses and improve future model iterations. In many workflows, human-in-the-loop validation plays a key role—subject matter experts validate difficult or sensitive examples, offering judgment where statistical preprocessing may fall short. Dataset curation and preprocessing is not a one-off technical chore, but an ongoing, strategic activity that defines the limits and capabilities of generative models. It affects not only the technical performance of AI but also its fairness, interpretability, and social responsibility. A well-curated dataset ensures the development of high-performing, ethical, and scalable generative AI systems—making it a cornerstone of modern AI development (Figure 2.10).

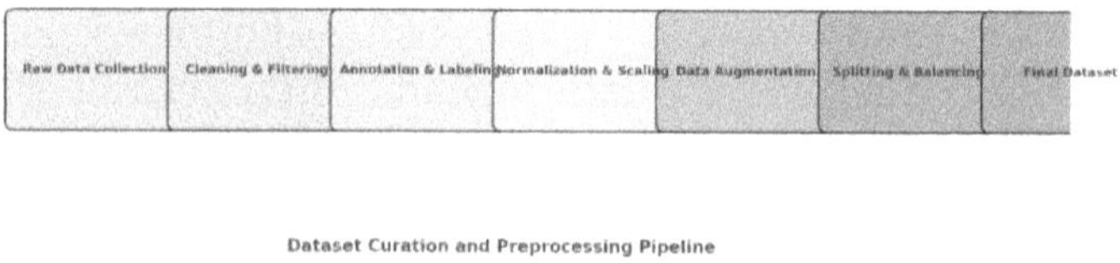

Figure 2.10: Visual representation of the Dataset Curation and Preprocessing Pipeline.

Bias and fairness considerations

Bias in Generative AI is one of the most critical challenges faced in ensuring ethical and equitable deployment of intelligent systems. Because generative models are trained on vast datasets, they inevitably learn and replicate the patterns, prejudices, and imbalances present in those datasets. If these biases go unaddressed, they can lead to discriminatory outputs, exclusion of underrepresented groups, and reinforcement of harmful stereotypes. The most prevalent form is data bias, which originates from the underlying training data. If a text model is trained predominantly on content from one language, demographic, or political perspective, it will mirror that bias in its outputs. Similarly, image generators trained on non-diverse datasets might produce results that exclude people of color, non-Western cultures, or non-binary gender identities. This is particularly problematic when generative AI is used in domains like education, healthcare, law, or recruitment, where fairness is essential.

Another type is representation bias, where certain classes, traits, or groups are either overrepresented or underrepresented. This causes the model to favor the dominant features it has seen most often, potentially marginalizing minority viewpoints or features. For instance, if a face-generation model is mostly trained on young adults, it may generate unrealistic or less frequent representations of elderly individuals. Historical bias arises even when datasets accurately reflect real-world data, but that data itself is historically skewed. An example includes employment data that reflects systemic inequality—if a generative model is trained on such data, it may inadvertently suggest biased hiring patterns or replicate outdated gender roles in generated content.

To counteract these issues, developers use fairness-aware preprocessing techniques. These involve cleaning datasets to balance classes, removing or masking sensitive attributes, and reweighting samples to promote equity. Fairness metrics like demographic parity or equal opportunity are applied to assess whether the outputs align with fair distribution goals. Bias mitigation techniques also include in-training interventions, such as adversarial debiasing, which penalizes the model when it relies on protected attributes like race or gender for predictions. Post-processing steps can also filter or adjust outputs to ensure they meet fairness criteria without needing to retrain the entire model.

A critical part of the solution lies in ethical dataset design—carefully curating training data with explicit attention to inclusivity, transparency, and consent. This includes sourcing content from diverse communities, avoiding copyrighted or harmful content, and documenting data provenance and structure. The final goal is to ensure equitable model output—where the generative model performs equally well across all groups, creates content that is culturally and socially inclusive, and avoids perpetuating harmful ideologies. Achieving this often requires continuous feedback loops, monitoring deployed outputs, and involving diverse stakeholders in evaluation.

Transparency and explainability also contribute to fairness. If users and developers can understand why a model generated a particular output, they are more equipped to identify and correct biases. Tools like attention visualization, saliency mapping, and prompt engineering analysis are helpful in this regard. Organizations increasingly apply ethical AI principles, with frameworks like Google's AI Principles or OECD's AI Guidelines promoting fairness, inclusivity, and non-discrimination. Compliance with regulations such as the EU AI Act or the U.S. Algorithmic Accountability Act is also pushing AI developers to design systems that proactively mitigate bias. The field is also moving toward participatory AI, where underrepresented communities help define what fairness means and how it should be achieved. This helps counteract the top-down design bias that often comes from homogeneous development teams. In conclusion, bias and fairness considerations in

Generative AI are not only technical issues but also societal imperatives. By addressing bias in data, training, and deployment, developers can build systems that are not only powerful and creative—but also just, inclusive, and worthy of public trust (Figure 2.11).

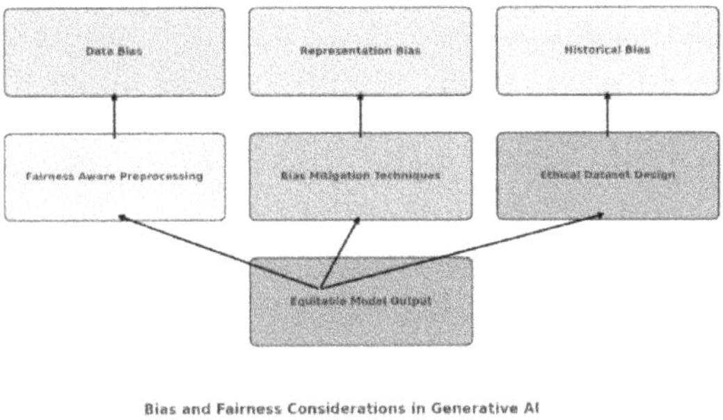

Figure 2.11: Illustrating the key stages and concepts in addressing Bias and Fairness in Generative AI

Synthetic Data Generation and Augmentation

Synthetic data generation refers to the process of artificially creating data using algorithms rather than collecting it from real-world events. In the context of Generative AI, this is typically done using models such as GANs, VAEs, and diffusion models that learn the distribution of a dataset and generate new, realistic samples. This synthetic data can serve as a replacement or supplement to real data, offering several advantages in terms of scalability, cost, privacy, and balance. The most compelling use case for synthetic data is in privacy-sensitive environments. For example, in healthcare or finance, sharing real data for training AI systems can violate patient or client confidentiality. Synthetic data, which statistically mirrors real data but contains no identifiable personal information, provides a viable and legally safe alternative. This enables wider collaboration, research, and model training without compromising ethical boundaries.

Another major application is data augmentation, which involves expanding an existing dataset by transforming or generating new variants of the original data. In image tasks, this might include rotating, flipping, or adding noise to images. In text generation, augmentations may include paraphrasing, synonym replacement, or back translation. These transformations help improve model generalization and reduce overfitting. Generative models like GANs and VAEs are at the forefront of synthetic data creation. For instance, GANs can generate new human faces, simulate rare diseases, or create synthetic traffic scenes for autonomous vehicle training. VAEs, while less visually sharp than GANs, are more stable and useful in generating variations with semantic consistency. Diffusion models, like those behind DALL·E 2 and Imagen, offer high-resolution and photorealistic outputs suitable for complex creative tasks.

Synthetic data is especially useful in class imbalance scenarios. In many real-world datasets, certain categories are underrepresented—such as fraud cases in banking, or rare tumors in medical imaging. Generative models can synthesize minority class examples to balance the dataset and improve classifier accuracy. Techniques like SMOTE (Synthetic Minority Oversampling Technique) are widely used in such settings. Beyond class balance, synthetic data also enables domain transfer and adaptation. For example, a model trained on European traffic signs can be fine-tuned using synthetic images of Indian road scenes, created using a GAN or simulation engine. This reduces the need for costly manual data collection in every new deployment context.

Another benefit is the ability to simulate edge cases or hazardous conditions that are difficult to capture in reality. In autonomous driving, synthetic data can simulate night driving, snowstorms, or accident scenarios. Similarly, synthetic malware or attack data can train cybersecurity models more robustly without exposing actual systems to risk. Despite these advantages, synthetic data is not without challenges. One major concern is distribution drift, where the synthetic data diverges too much from the real-world domain, leading to poor model performance. Moreover, over-reliance on synthetic data can lead to lack of generalization if the generated samples do not sufficiently capture real-world variability.

To ensure quality, synthetic data must undergo rigorous evaluation. Techniques like visual inspection, diversity metrics, and performance benchmarks (e.g., training classifiers on synthetic vs real data) are used to assess the utility of synthetic datasets. Human-in-the-loop validation is often used in domains like healthcare and law to validate synthetic outputs.

The legal and ethical landscape of synthetic data is evolving. While synthetic data solves many privacy issues, it can also introduce new risks—such as deepfakes or synthetic misinformation. Therefore, regulatory guidelines and watermarking technologies are being developed to distinguish synthetic from real and ensure ethical usage. In terms of tooling, open-source libraries like SDV (Synthetic Data Vault), DataSynthesizer, and CTGAN (Conditional GAN for tabular data) enable organizations to generate synthetic datasets for research, production, and compliance. Major platforms like AWS and Google Cloud now offer synthetic data generation services as part of their AI stacks (Table 2.6).

Table 2.6: Synthetic Data Generation vs Augmentation

Aspect	Synthetic Data Generation	Data Augmentation
Definition	Creating entirely new data samples using generative models	Modifying existing data to create new variants

Techniques Used	GANs, VAEs, Diffusion Models, CTGAN, SMOTE	Rotation, flipping, noise injection, paraphrasing, etc.
Use Case	When real data is scarce, private, or imbalanced	When more variety is needed to prevent overfitting
Application Domains	Healthcare, cybersecurity, finance, autonomous driving	Image classification, NLP, speech recognition
Risk Factors	Domain shift, synthetic bias, deepfake misuse	Loss of semantic meaning, redundancy
Evaluation Methods	Statistical similarity, classifier performance, human review	Accuracy and generalization metrics on downstream models
Benefits	Scalability, privacy-preservation, edge case simulation	Better model robustness, reduced overfitting

2.6 Model Training and Evaluation

Training Workflows and Hyperparameters

Training a generative model involves guiding it to learn the underlying data distribution so that it can produce new, high-quality, and realistic data samples. The typical training workflow includes several key stages: data loading, model initialization, forward pass, loss computation, backward pass (gradient computation), weight updates, and performance tracking on validation data. The training process starts with initializing model parameters—random values assigned to the weights and biases of the neural network layers. Data is then fed into the model in batches, where it produces an output (e.g., a generated image, sentence, or audio signal). This output is compared to the ground truth using a loss function to determine the error. This error is then used in backpropagation, where gradients are calculated and propagated backward through the network to update the weights. This step is repeated for multiple epochs, during which the model learns to improve its predictions.

The choice of hyperparameters is crucial in determining the effectiveness and efficiency of model training. Key hyperparameters include the learning rate, which determines the step size during gradient descent; batch size, which affects memory use and convergence speed; and number of epochs, which defines how many times the entire dataset is passed through the model. Other important hyperparameters in generative models include the latent dimension size (for VAEs and GANs), number of layers and hidden units, and architecture-specific settings like dropout rate, activation functions, and normalization techniques. Tuning these parameters is often done through grid search, random search, or increasingly through automated methods like Bayesian optimization or Hyperband. In GANs, both the Generator and Discriminator must be trained in a coordinated manner. If one improves too quickly, the other may fail to learn. This adversarial balance adds complexity to the training workflow and necessitates practices like gradient clipping, learning rate scheduling, and alternating training updates.

Evaluation Metrics for Generative Models

Evaluating generative models is significantly more challenging than evaluating discriminative ones. Unlike classification tasks where accuracy is a clear-cut metric, generative tasks often require subjective or domain-specific evaluations to measure realism, diversity, and semantic accuracy. One of the most widely used metrics in image generation is the Fréchet Inception Distance (FID). FID measures the distance between feature distributions of real and generated images using the Inception-v3 network. Lower FID scores indicate higher similarity to real images. FID is preferred over earlier metrics like Inception Score (IS) because it penalizes lack of diversity and accounts for distributional differences.

In text generation tasks, metrics like BLEU (Bilingual Evaluation Understudy) are used. BLEU calculates the degree of overlap between the generated text and reference text, typically in terms of n-gram matches. While useful, BLEU doesn't capture semantic quality and is sensitive to variations in word choice, making it less reliable for open-ended generation. ROUGE and METEOR are also used in NLP to assess recall and synonymic matches, respectively. However, these metrics struggle to evaluate the creativity and contextual appropriateness of text—a limitation that has led to the development of newer metrics like BERTScore, which uses contextual embeddings for comparison. In audio and speech generation, metrics like PESQ (Perceptual Evaluation of Speech Quality) and MOS (Mean Opinion Score) are commonly used, often in conjunction with human evaluation. Perceptual similarity, style transfer consistency, and rhythmic accuracy are also relevant depending on the application. Some evaluations rely on domain-specific metrics. For example, in drug discovery, the novelty and binding affinity of a generated molecule are key indicators. In data-to-text generation, factual consistency is often assessed using entailment models or rule-based checks. Finally, human evaluation remains a gold standard in many cases. Crowd-sourced ratings or expert judgments can provide insights into fluency, realism, and appropriateness that are difficult to quantify otherwise.

Overfitting, Underfitting, and Generalization

A fundamental challenge in model training is managing the balance between underfitting and overfitting. Underfitting occurs when the model fails to learn the data patterns due to insufficient capacity or inadequate training. Symptoms include high training and validation loss and poor generation quality. Overfitting, on the other hand, occurs when the model learns the training data too well—including noise and specific patterns that don't generalize to new inputs. In generative models, overfitting manifests as reduced diversity, repeated outputs, or memorization of training samples. This trade-off is best understood through training vs validation loss graphs. In the early stages of training, both losses decrease. As overfitting begins, training loss continues to decline while validation loss starts increasing, indicating a drop in generalization.

To mitigate overfitting, several techniques are used. Early stopping halts training when validation performance worsens. Dropout randomly deactivates neurons during training to encourage redundancy and robustness. Regularization methods like L1 or L2 penalties constrain model complexity. Data augmentation can also help prevent overfitting by introducing variation in training examples. In generative models, techniques like noise injection or latent space perturbation help the model generalize better by exploring broader data representations. Achieving generalization is the ultimate goal—where the model performs well on unseen inputs while maintaining diversity and realism. In generative AI, generalization doesn't just mean accuracy—it also means the ability to produce creative, diverse, and contextually appropriate outputs in response to novel prompts. Robust generalization often comes from proper validation strategies, including k-fold cross-validation, testing on out-of-distribution data, and evaluating on adversarial inputs. Additionally, transfer learning and fine-tuning pre-trained models on domain-specific datasets improve performance with less data and training time.

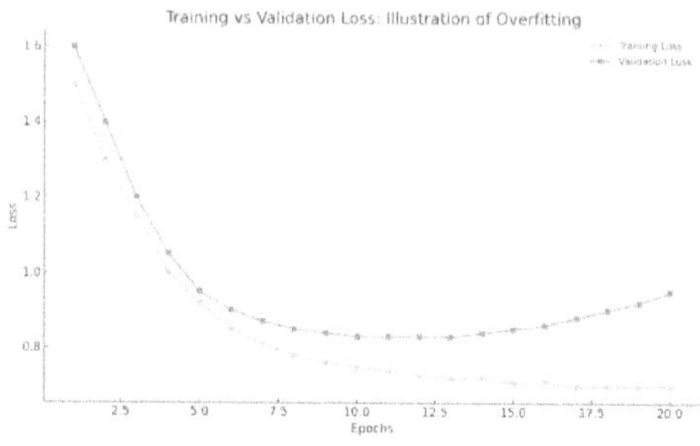

Figure 2.12: Training vs Validation Loss

Figure 2.12 showing Training vs Validation Loss across 20 epochs, which illustrates the concept of overfitting—where training loss continues to decrease while validation loss begins to rise after a certain point, indicating the model is memorizing training data rather than generalizing.

Example: Training a GAN to Generate Fashion Apparel Designs

You're building a GAN model to generate new fashion apparel designs (e.g., shirts, dresses, shoes) for an e-commerce brand. You start with a dataset of 100,000 product images, each labeled by category.

Training Workflow & Hyperparameters

- You design a DCGAN architecture with a Generator (transposed CNN layers) and a Discriminator (convolutional layers).
- You set a latent dimension of 100, learning rate of 0.0002, and use Adam optimizer.
- You train the GAN for 150 epochs with a batch size of 64 using binary cross-entropy loss.
- You alternate between training the Discriminator and Generator every batch to maintain balance.

Evaluation Metrics

- After every 10 epochs, you evaluate the quality of generated images using FID (Fréchet Inception Distance).
- The FID drops from 45 → 28 → 15, indicating improved realism.
- You also conduct a blind test with designers, who rate realism on a scale of 1 to 5. Average score improves from 2.8 to 4.2 by the 100th epoch.

Overfitting

- By epoch 120, FID begins to increase slightly (from 15 to 18) and human ratings plateau.
- You notice some generated samples start resembling real training images—a classic sign of overfitting.

To resolve this, you enable early stopping at epoch 110 and apply dropout (0.3) in the Discriminator.

Underfitting

Initially, with only 30 epochs, outputs looked noisy and unrecognizable. Training and validation loss were high—clear signs of underfitting. You addressed it by training for more epochs and tuning the learning rate, which helped the model learn stable features.

Generalization

Once trained properly, you input noise vectors and receive creative yet plausible new apparel designs some combining styles (e.g., "sneaker-boot hybrids") that weren't in the original dataset. The model generalizes well, imagining new fashion concepts by combining and remixing learned patterns creatively.

This single example showcases how the entire lifecycle of model training and evaluation plays out in a real-world Generative AI project.

2.7 Ethics and Reliability in Generative Modeling

Generative AI has made remarkable strides in creating text, images, video, audio, and synthetic data. However, as its capabilities grow, so do the ethical implications and societal risks associated with it. From misinformation and bias to consent and surveillance, ethical considerations must guide the development, deployment, and governance of these powerful systems.

Data Privacy in Generative AI

At the core of any AI system lies data—and generative models often require vast amounts of it. Data privacy becomes a critical concern when personal or sensitive data is used for training. For instance, models trained on patient medical records or user communications may inadvertently memorize and reproduce sensitive information. This not only violates ethical standards but can breach legal frameworks like GDPR, HIPAA, or India's DPDP Act. Developers must implement privacy-preserving techniques such as differential privacy, which ensures that the presence or absence of a single individual in the training dataset does not significantly affect the model's output. Techniques like federated learning, where data remains on-device and only model updates are shared, also support decentralized privacy protection.

Transparency and Explainability

Generative models, particularly deep learning-based ones, often function as black boxes, making it difficult to understand how they arrive at specific outputs. This lack of transparency raises questions of accountability—especially when these systems are used in high-stakes scenarios like education, healthcare, or public policy. Explainability refers to the ability to interpret a model's decisions and outputs in human-understandable terms. Tools like attention heatmaps (in NLP), activation visualizations (in vision), and latent space interpolation (in VAEs and GANs) provide insights into how a model is learning and generating content. However, improving explainability without compromising performance remains a central challenge. Transparency also involves being open about model limitations, data sources, and biases. Public documentation such as model cards and datasheets for datasets helps foster trust and responsibility, providing stakeholders with necessary information about how models were trained and should be used.

Risks of Misuse: Deepfakes and Misinformation

Perhaps the most discussed ethical issue in generative AI is the potential for misuse. Deepfake technologies, which can swap faces in videos or mimic voices with stunning realism, pose serious threats to public trust, personal security, and democracy. Fake political speeches, manipulated evidence, and identity theft are all real possibilities enabled by misused generative tools. Text generators can produce convincing fake news articles, phishing emails, or hate speech, especially if fine-tuned on biased or malicious content. With minimal effort, bad actors can automate misinformation campaigns that are hard to trace and combat. To mitigate this, platforms and researchers have developed deepfake detectors, digital watermarking, and traceable fingerprints in AI-generated content. Companies like OpenAI have strict API usage policies that restrict malicious deployment, and governments are now exploring legislation to mandate disclosure labels on synthetic media.

Bias, Fairness, and Representation

Bias in generative models is an ethical issue with far-reaching consequences. If a text generator associates specific jobs with certain genders, or an image generator fails to represent diverse skin tones, the AI system amplifies existing stereotypes and exclusion. Fairness requires curating diverse, inclusive datasets, using bias mitigation techniques, and regularly auditing model behavior across different demographics. Intersectional fairness—ensuring equity across combinations of identities (e.g., race and gender)—is particularly important to prevent compounded biases. Open, inclusive development teams, participatory AI practices, and feedback mechanisms from affected communities can all help make AI fairer and more inclusive.

Environmental and Resource Ethics

Training massive generative models like GPT-4 or DALL·E involves enormous computational resources, raising environmental concerns. High carbon footprints, excessive water use in cooling data centers, and energy consumption all contribute to AI's environmental cost. Ethical development involves efficiency-aware training, using smaller fine-tuned models, and deploying only when necessary. Green AI initiatives advocate for performance metrics that include energy usage and environmental impact, not just accuracy or realism.

Consent and Intellectual Property

Generative AI often scrapes data from the web, including copyrighted materials, social media posts, and public databases. This raises questions about data consent and intellectual property (IP). Artists, writers, and developers argue that their work is being repurposed without permission. Regulators and developers must strike a balance between innovation and ownership. Some platforms now allow creators to opt out of dataset inclusion, and copyright laws are beginning to adapt to address ownership of AI-generated content.

Accountability and Governance

As AI becomes integrated into daily life, accountability for generative models becomes more important. Who is responsible when a chatbot generates harmful advice, or an AI-generated image causes reputational damage?

Developers must follow ethical guidelines, maintain detailed audit trails, and ensure that systems include failsafes, such as human review loops or content moderation tools. AI governance frameworks like OECD's AI Principles or UNESCO's Ethics of AI Recommendation provide policy guidelines for responsible use.

Trust and Reliability

To be adopted at scale, generative models must earn public trust. This requires not only technical reliability—models producing consistent, error-free outputs—but also social reliability. Users must feel confident that the system will act ethically and transparently. Trustworthy AI involves adhering to principles of beneficence, non-maleficence, autonomy, and justice. It also includes investing in robust testing, human-centered design, and accessible interfaces that empower rather than confuse end users.

Future Directions in Responsible Generative AI

The future of ethical generative AI lies in hybrid systems—where automation is complemented by human oversight, and models are co-developed with diverse users in mind. Innovations like federated GANs, explainable diffusion models, and open-sourced audit tools are paving the way. Education is also key. As generative models become democratized, users need AI literacy—the skills to identify, question, and responsibly use AI-generated content. Public awareness campaigns, ethics training for developers, and interdisciplinary collaboration can help close the gap.

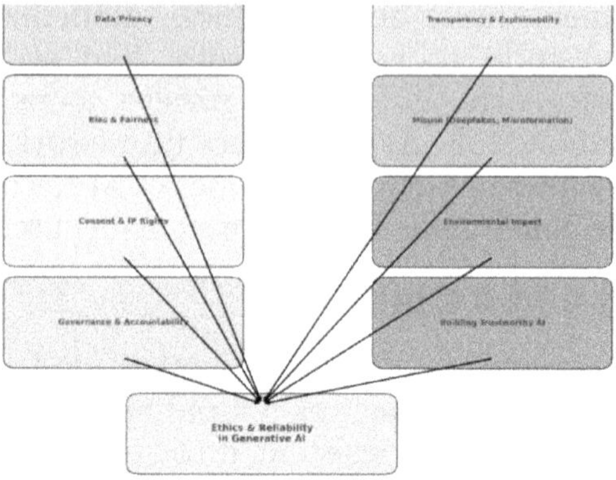

Figure 2.13: Dimensions of Ethics and Reliability in Generative AI

Figure 2.13 illustrating the key dimensions of Ethics and Reliability in Generative AI. It highlights interconnected elements such as Data Privacy, Transparency, Bias & Fairness, Misuse Prevention, Consent & IP, Environmental Impact, Governance, and Trust-building—all feeding into the central goal of ethical and reliable AI development.

CONCLUSION

As generative AI continues to evolve, mastering its training, evaluation, and ethical implications becomes essential for building robust, impactful, and responsible systems. From designing effective training workflows and tuning hyperparameters to selecting the right evaluation metrics, every step must be optimized to ensure quality, creativity, and generalization. Equally important is embedding ethical practices—from safeguarding data privacy and mitigating bias to ensuring transparency, fairness, and accountability. By aligning technological advancements with human values, we can develop generative models that not only perform well but also act in ways that are just, trustworthy, and socially beneficial. This chapter emphasizes that the future of generative AI lies not only in innovation, but also in reliable, inclusive, and ethical deployment across domains.

Exercise Questions

- Define and explain the core components of a typical training workflow in generative AI.
- What are hyperparameters? List and describe five important hyperparameters in training GANs or VAEs.
- Explain the difference between training loss and validation loss. How can they be used to detect overfitting?
- Describe how FID (Fréchet Inception Distance) is calculated and interpreted. Why is it preferred over the Inception Score?
- What are BLEU and BERTScore? Compare their strengths and weaknesses in evaluating text generation.
- Explain with examples the concepts of underfitting and overfitting. How can each be mitigated?
- What is generalization in the context of generative models? Why is it important for model performance?
- List and describe three bias mitigation techniques applicable in generative model training.
- How can transparency and explainability be improved in deep generative models? Give practical tools or methods.
- What are the ethical risks associated with deepfakes and synthetic media generation? How can they be controlled?
- Discuss the role of differential privacy and federated learning in protecting data privacy in generative AI.
- Explain the environmental concerns related to training large-scale generative models. How can they be mitigated?

- What is the importance of human-in-the-loop systems in building trustworthy generative AI? Provide examples.
- Why is it important to document training data sources and model limitations? What tools can help in this process?
- Design a mini-project to train a VAE on a small image dataset. Describe the dataset, architecture, evaluation plan, and ethical safeguards.

CHAPTER 3
GENERATIVE AI ACROSS INDUSTRIES

Generative Artificial Intelligence (Generative AI or GenAI) represents a transformative branch of AI capable of creating new, original content across multiple modalities—text, images, audio, video, code, and even 3D designs—by learning from vast datasets. Unlike traditional AI models that primarily classify, detect, or predict based on input data, generative models synthesize novel outputs by identifying patterns, structures, and relationships within training data. At the heart of GenAI are deep learning architectures such as Generative Adversarial Networks (GANs), Variational Autoencoders (VAEs), and Transformer-based models like GPT and DALL·E. This paradigm shift from analytical to creative AI marks a new era where machines are not only tools for decision-making but also collaborators in ideation, design, and problem-solving. The rapid advancements in computational power, availability of large-scale datasets, and breakthroughs in neural network architectures have accelerated GenAI's adoption across industries. What began as experimental research in AI labs has now matured into commercially viable solutions that are reshaping workflows in healthcare, education, finance, manufacturing, and entertainment. Cloud-based AI platforms and APIs have democratized access to powerful generative models, enabling startups, enterprises, and even individual creators to integrate GenAI into their operations. This widespread adoption is driven not only by efficiency gains but also by the strategic advantage of producing unique, personalized, and high-quality outputs at scale. Across industries, GenAI is augmenting human capabilities, automating complex creative processes, and unlocking new business models. In healthcare, it is used to design novel drug molecules, generate synthetic medical data for research, and assist in medical imaging analysis. In the creative arts, GenAI supports scriptwriting, music composition, and concept art generation. In engineering and manufacturing, AI-powered generative design optimizes product structures for performance and sustainability. These capabilities are not limited to replacing repetitive tasks but extend to enhancing human creativity, enabling professionals to explore more possibilities in less time while reducing costs. Generative AI's potential extends beyond productivity improvements; it also reshapes competitive landscapes. Companies leveraging GenAI can rapidly prototype, personalize customer experiences, and innovate at speeds previously unattainable. In marketing, personalized ad copy and visuals can be generated for micro-targeted campaigns. In finance, AI-generated scenarios aid in risk assessment and forecasting. In supply chain management, GenAI assists in simulating disruptions and testing adaptive strategies. This competitive advantage is amplified by the scalability of AI-generated outputs, which allows organizations to respond quickly to market changes while maintaining consistency and quality. Despite its transformative potential, GenAI raises critical challenges and ethical questions. Issues such as deepfake creation, copyright infringement, misinformation, and algorithmic bias demand rigorous governance frameworks. The authenticity and trustworthiness of AI-generated content are under increasing scrutiny, especially in journalism, politics, and scientific research. Moreover, the environmental cost of training large-scale generative models—measured in energy consumption and carbon footprint—cannot be overlooked. Industries adopting GenAI must balance innovation with responsible deployment, ensuring that societal, legal, and cultural norms are respected. The trajectory of Generative AI points toward deeper integration with industry-specific systems, blending creativity with domain expertise. As models become more multimodal, context-aware, and capable of reasoning, their role will evolve from being mere assistants to becoming co-creators and strategic partners. Future developments may see GenAI embedded into immersive environments like augmented and virtual reality, enabling real-time collaborative content creation. For industries, the challenge will be to harness this power ethically, transparently, and inclusively, ensuring that the benefits of GenAI are equitably distributed while mitigating potential risks. In essence, the coming decade may well be defined by the industries that successfully align human ingenuity with generative intelligence.

Revolutionizing content creation and marketing

Generative AI

Machine learning, a subfield of artificial intelligence, includes generative AI. Generative AI is used to create or "generate" a wide variety of written, visual, audio, and video content, whereas earlier forms of AI were primarily used to analyze data. In addition, the technology can be used to write computer code, create new medications, answer queries, analyze data and make inferences, and resolve challenging real-world issues. Although the technology of generative AI is not new, recent developments have made some models the technical term for an AI tool user-friendly despite their fundamental complexity. By employing "deep learning," a technique modeled after the way the human brain creates associations, these models are able to replicate human speech, writing, drawing, planning, and strategy.

Generative AI for marketing

Generative AI is already widely used among marketers and is here to stay: According to a 2022 MIT Technology Review study, only 20% of marketing firms were using generative AI extensively across various use cases, and only 5% of them regarded it as "critical" to their operations. However, 20% of marketing executives anticipate that generative AI will play a significant role in their department's operations by 2025, and 44%

anticipate using it in a variety of applications. 41% of marketing, sales, and customer service organizations had implemented generative AI in limited or at-scale settings, ranking second only to IT and cybersecurity departments, according to a 2023 Deloitte study. According to a 2023 Salesforce survey of 1,000 marketers, 22% of them intend to use generative AI in the upcoming year, and more than half are already using it. 73% of 1,000 B2B and B2C marketing professionals surveyed by Statista in 2023 said they currently use generative artificial intelligence in some capacity. 67% of marketing executives are investigating generative AI for personalization, 49% for content creation, and 41% for market segmentation, according to a 2023 Boston Consulting Group cross-industry survey. According to the same survey, between 40% and 50% of people who are currently utilizing generative AI do so for chatbot marketing, social listening, predictive analysis, and creating unique product descriptions.

Generative AI use cases in marketing

Numerous applications of generative AI are being discovered by marketing firms. Here are a few of the most typical in Figure 3.1.

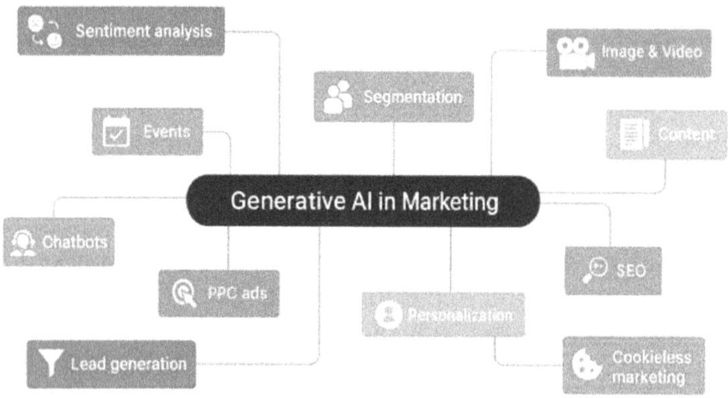

Figure 3.1: Generative AI use cases in marketing. (delve.ai)

Content creation

Generative AI models are useful for short-form content such as blog posts, emails, social media posts, and digital advertising because they can write copy based on an outline or prompt. However, their capacity to produce content extends beyond simple text generation and comprises:

1. Making pictures out of a description in text
2. Researching data-driven reports and locating citations
3. Converting information into various languages
4. Using data sets or descriptions to create charts and graphs
5. The process of creating audio from written text, or text-to-voice
6. Creating short-form video
7. Music composition without royalties
8. Condensing lengthy content, improving messaging, or rewriting it in a different voice or tone
9. Using technical data to create prospect-facing product descriptions
10. Investigating longtails, topic clusters, and SEO keywords
11. Enhancing current content for search engines

Content Personalization

Generative AI transforms marketing by delivering hyper-personalized content at scale. Using customer data such as browsing history, purchase patterns, and demographic details, AI can create unique messaging that resonates with individual preferences. It enables real-time adjustments in tone, offers, or formats based on user behavior, geolocation, or trending hashtags. This not only enhances engagement but also improves conversion rates by ensuring content relevance. Generative AI also helps build dynamic customer personas, updating them as preferences evolve. Moreover, AI-driven journey mapping allows businesses to visualize customer touchpoints, ensuring personalized interactions throughout the customer lifecycle for higher satisfaction and loyalty.

Content Ideation

Marketers often face creative blocks while generating campaign ideas, and this is where generative AI provides immense value. By analyzing industry trends, competitor strategies, and consumer preferences, AI tools can propose innovative campaign concepts aligned with brand goals. Marketers can prompt AI to explore different tones, styles, and messaging angles to match specific personas or objectives. This accelerates brainstorming sessions and sparks creativity by offering fresh perspectives. Beyond text, AI can also suggest visual themes, headlines, or taglines that resonate with target audiences. Ultimately, AI acts as a collaborative partner, making ideation more efficient, diverse, and strategically focused.

Automated Customer Service and Support

Generative AI has elevated customer support by powering chatbots and virtual assistants with natural, human-like communication abilities. Unlike traditional scripted bots, AI-driven systems can interpret intent, context, and even emotional tone using sentiment analysis. They provide accurate and empathetic responses across multiple languages, catering to global audiences. Generative AI can also handle complex technical queries by drawing insights from vast knowledge bases, reducing the load on human agents. In addition, these chatbots can proactively engage with users on websites or social media, resolving issues instantly. This leads to improved customer satisfaction, reduced wait times, and stronger brand-customer relationships.

Market Research and Data Analysis

Generative AI revolutionizes market research by analyzing vast volumes of structured and unstructured data to uncover actionable insights. Businesses can leverage these insights for segmenting markets, identifying trends, and optimizing campaigns. Predictive forecasting is one key application, enabling organizations to anticipate churn, demand cycles, and campaign performance. AI tools can process customer reviews, surveys, and social media data to understand shifting consumer preferences. Unlike traditional methods, AI works at real-time speed and adapts continuously, allowing dynamic decision-making. This reduces guesswork and provides a data-driven foundation for strategic planning, product development, and competitive positioning in fast-changing markets.

Demand and lead generation

Generative AI is revolutionizing demand and lead generation by automating the identification of potential customers and nurturing them with personalized content. By analyzing customer behavior, online interactions, and historical purchase data, AI systems generate tailored campaigns that resonate with each audience segment. These intelligent tools create compelling product descriptions, targeted emails, and engaging ad copy designed to capture interest. Furthermore, generative AI predicts lead quality by assigning scores, enabling marketers to prioritize high-value prospects. The result is a seamless pipeline where businesses attract more qualified leads, reduce manual intervention, and accelerate conversions, ultimately driving sustainable growth and efficiency. Marketers rely on strategic generative AI tools for numerous strategic marketing applications:

Automating Campaign Execution, Cross-Channel Coordination, and Lead Scoring

AI-powered automation tools are transforming campaign execution by ensuring consistent and timely delivery of marketing messages across multiple channels, including social media, email, and paid advertising platforms. Generative AI automates repetitive tasks such as scheduling posts, sending emails, and personalizing messages, saving marketers time and effort. It also provides cross-channel coordination, ensuring campaigns remain consistent in tone and messaging regardless of the medium. Additionally, AI enhances lead scoring by evaluating customer interactions, purchase intent, and engagement data, assigning each prospect a predictive score. This prioritization helps sales teams focus on the most promising opportunities, boosting efficiency and maximizing ROI.

Adjusting Advertising Strategies in Real Time

Generative AI enables marketers to adjust advertising strategies dynamically in real time, responding instantly to market shifts, customer behavior, and competitor actions. Through continuous monitoring of ad performance metrics such as click-through rates, conversions, and engagement, AI systems fine-tune campaigns without manual intervention. For example, if a campaign underperforms, AI can modify the message, reallocate the budget, or change targeting parameters instantly. This adaptability ensures businesses make the most of advertising spend while reducing waste. Real-time optimization not only boosts campaign effectiveness but also improves customer experience by delivering relevant ads at the right time and through the right channels.

Optimizing Customer and Market Segmentation

Generative AI brings precision to customer and market segmentation by analyzing vast amounts of structured and unstructured data. Instead of relying on broad demographic categories, AI identifies nuanced behavioral and psychographic patterns, creating micro-segments for highly personalized marketing. For instance, AI tools can cluster customers based on purchase history, browsing behavior, or sentiment analysis from social media. This level of segmentation enables businesses to craft tailored campaigns, ensuring messages resonate deeply with target audiences. Moreover, generative AI continually updates these segments as customer preferences evolve, allowing marketers to stay aligned with changing needs and trends, thereby enhancing engagement and loyalty.

Orchestrating SEO Strategies

Search engine optimization (SEO) has become more data-driven and creative with the integration of generative AI. These tools analyze search trends, competitor strategies, and user intent to recommend keyword-rich content structures that drive higher visibility. AI can generate blog outlines, metadata, and optimized headlines aligned with search algorithms, ensuring improved rankings. It also predicts future keyword shifts by studying user queries, allowing marketers to adapt strategies proactively. Furthermore, generative AI assists in creating high-quality content at scale without compromising originality or relevance. By orchestrating SEO strategies with precision, businesses achieve stronger online presence, improved organic traffic, and better conversion rates.

Generative AI in marketing: Examples

Marketers in a variety of industries can benefit greatly from generative AI. Here are some instances of how businesses across various sectors are using generative AI in their marketing campaigns:

1. Finding trends in past data and applying them to forecast the effectiveness of upcoming digital advertisements will help determine the optimal bid range for Google AdWords.

2. By creating customized loyalty programs with incentives based on each customer's unique purchasing habits, churn can be decreased.
3. By avoiding a generic approach and only sending product offers that are pertinent to each individual customer, spam can be decreased and customer affinity can be increased.
4. Identifying the touchpoints that have the greatest direct impact on sales in order to build advertising budgets around them.
5. Customizing an interactive customer journey with data will probably turn a lead into a prospect in real time.
6. Automating the reporting of several digital ad programs' ad performance at once.
7. Creating content and images for an email nurture campaign automatically and using micro market segmentation to tailor messaging based on several customer data points.

The risks of using generative AI for marketing

Any application of generative AI comes with risks. For marketers, the most serious risks involve problems with content generation and include:

Plagiarism and Data Piracy

One of the most significant risks of using generative AI in marketing is plagiarism and data piracy. Since AI models are trained on massive datasets scraped from various sources, they may unintentionally replicate sentences, ideas, or even entire passages verbatim. This can lead to legal consequences, as using someone else's work without permission violates intellectual property laws. For marketers, this not only risks lawsuits but also damages brand credibility and trust. Furthermore, companies may face reputational harm if accused of stealing intellectual content, even if the replication was unintentional, making careful oversight essential.

Proliferating Intentionally False or Misleading Information

Generative AI models often rely on large datasets that may contain inaccurate, outdated, or intentionally misleading information. When these models generate content for marketing, they can unintentionally spread propaganda, fake news, or harmful misinformation. For marketers, this is particularly risky because publishing false claims can damage consumer trust, attract regulatory penalties, and cause long-term brand harm. In industries like healthcare or finance, misleading content could have even more serious consequences. To prevent this, marketers must implement strict fact-checking and human review processes, ensuring that AI-generated materials do not inadvertently mislead audiences.

Bias

Bias is another critical risk inherent in generative AI. Since models are trained on vast datasets collected from human-created content, they may inherit biases related to race, gender, culture, or ideology. When used in marketing, this bias could manifest in discriminatory language, unfair stereotypes, or content that alienates specific customer groups. Such incidents not only lead to public backlash but also regulatory scrutiny. For businesses, biased marketing content can significantly damage brand reputation and limit inclusivity. Marketers must therefore actively audit AI-generated outputs, diversify training data where possible, and apply fairness checks to mitigate bias.

Copyright Violation

Generative AI models are often trained on copyrighted material without explicit permissions from creators. This means the content they generate may inadvertently incorporate or mimic copyrighted elements. For marketers, this poses a serious legal risk because publishing AI-generated text, images, or videos that infringe on someone else's copyright can result in lawsuits, financial penalties, and brand damage. Even if the violation is accidental, businesses are still accountable. To reduce this risk, marketers should use AI tools that are transparent about their data sources and always apply human review before distributing generated content publicly.

Violation of Users' Data Privacy

Generative AI tools often collect user prompts, queries, and other inputs to improve model performance. However, if this data is stored or shared without explicit consent, it can lead to serious privacy violations. For marketers, mishandling customer data damages trust and may violate data protection regulations such as GDPR or CCPA. In marketing campaigns, sensitive customer information could even be unintentionally revealed or misused by the AI system. This creates ethical, reputational, and legal challenges. Marketers must therefore prioritize transparency, use privacy-compliant tools, and ensure that sensitive customer data is never exposed or exploited.

Unpredictable Behavior Beyond Planned Functionality

Generative AI is a complex and evolving technology, and it does not always behave as intended. In marketing, this unpredictability can result in inappropriate, irrelevant, or even offensive content being generated. Such outputs may not align with a brand's values or campaign goals, causing reputational harm. For instance, an AI tool might create insensitive slogans, hallucinate facts, or misunderstand cultural nuances. Since marketers cannot fully control these outcomes, reliance on AI without oversight is risky. The only safeguard is to implement strong human-in-the-loop systems, ensuring AI-generated content undergoes rigorous review before public release.

Types of Regulation

Advocacy groups are pushing for the regulation of generative AI usage, and some governments, as well as public and private companies, have responded.

The European Union

Applications like content creation are deemed "low risk" and are subject to less strict regulations, but the EU has banned the use of AI that presents "unacceptable risks." These rules consist of:

1. Identifying content generated by AI
2. Designing models to prevent it from generating illegal content
3. Publishing summaries of copyrighted data used to train generative AI models
4. Disclosing the source for content generated by AI

Since non-EU nations that conduct business in or with the EU are typically subject to EU regulations, American and British businesses are also subject to them.

The United States

In the United States, regulatory oversight of artificial intelligence, particularly generative AI, is shaped by existing frameworks designed to protect consumers from deceptive practices. The Federal Trade Commission (FTC), already responsible for monitoring false and misleading advertising, is positioned to extend its authority into AI-generated content such as deepfakes. While the U.S. government has not enacted sweeping AI-specific legislation, policymakers are exploring measures that emphasize accountability in the development of AI models rather than restricting their use outright. This means developers may need to follow stricter transparency, safety, and ethical compliance rules, influencing how algorithms are trained and deployed.

Private Industry

Private industry plays a critical role in shaping AI regulation and governance. Leading technology companies including Microsoft, Google, Amazon, OpenAI, Apple, Nvidia, and IBM are at the forefront of both innovation and scrutiny. These corporations recognize that proactive measures can reduce regulatory risks, so they are implementing self-regulation frameworks, internal safeguards, and ethical guidelines for AI use. At the same time, they invest heavily in lobbying to ensure regulations do not stifle innovation or impose unrealistic burdens. Their dual approach compliance with evolving rules and advocacy for flexible policies demonstrates a balancing act between corporate interests, public trust, and government oversight.

Risks for Brands

For now, the primary legal risks in generative AI fall on the companies that design and train the technology rather than on brands that use AI-generated tools. Lawsuits have emerged around issues such as copyright infringement, licensing disputes, and misuse of private data in training datasets. This legal landscape creates uncertainty for technology providers, who must address intellectual property concerns and privacy safeguards. Brands using AI for marketing, design, or communication currently face less direct scrutiny, but this may change as regulations evolve. In the future, liability could extend to end-users, requiring more cautious and transparent adoption strategies.

Although there haven't been any lawsuits against AI-using brands yet, the possibility exists. Additionally, brands might no longer have access to generative AI tools that are now essential to their operations. Additionally, public complaints regarding their unauthorized use of copyrighted content or their use of plagiarized text and images could damage their brand image.

Implementing Generative AI in marketing

Risk mitigation for using generative AI

The most crucial defense against any of the dangers posed by generative AI is human oversight. AI tools should only be used with a well-defined plan and objectives. Marketing executives should put in place and enforce guidelines and workable methods that control the use of generative AI and require human evaluations of content produced by AI.

Such procedures should include:

1. Investigating generative AI models thoroughly to make sure they were constructed using correct and lawfully obtained data
2. Putting in place an AI roadmap that restricts applications of generative AI to appropriate use cases
3. Before implementing use cases across the entire organization, test them.
4. Examining material for prejudice and other moral issues
5. Adding a disclaimer for content produced by AI
6. Putting in place a thorough data strategy, a data infrastructure for gathering data, and an activation process that verifies data to manage risk.

Generative AI tools for marketers

Tools for content generation

These three content-related generative AI tools below are popular among marketers and becoming integral to their mar tech stack:

OpenAI's ChatGPT

ChatGPT has quickly become one of the most indispensable tools for marketers due to its versatility and user-friendly design. It can handle multiple content-related tasks such as brainstorming creative ideas, conducting quick research, drafting outlines, generating long-form articles, or even summarizing complex information into digestible formats. Marketers value it because of its ability to understand natural language prompts and provide contextually relevant responses in seconds. This speed and efficiency enable professionals to streamline their workflows, save time, and reduce creative fatigue. Its popularity made it the fastest-growing consumer application ever, signaling its vital role in modern digital marketing strategies.

Google's Gemini (formerly Bard)

Google's Gemini, previously known as Bard, stands out as a strong competitor to ChatGPT. Its primary advantage lies in the variety of responses it generates, giving users multiple content options from a single prompt. This flexibility allows marketers to compare tones, structures, and messaging styles before finalizing content. Gemini integrates seamlessly with Google's ecosystem, making it especially useful for those who rely heavily on search and related tools. It can also search the internet for images based on natural language queries, helping marketers enrich their campaigns with relevant visuals. Its adaptability makes it increasingly valuable in digital marketing contexts.

OpenAI's DALL·E

DALL·E revolutionizes visual content creation by allowing marketers to generate images in countless artistic styles from just a written prompt. Unlike traditional stock imagery, it produces unique, tailored visuals that align perfectly with specific campaign themes. Beyond creation, it also enables image editing, retouching, and generating alternative variations of existing visuals. This is particularly powerful for marketing teams seeking to personalize graphics without investing heavily in design resources. Its creative flexibility fuels advertising, social media, and website design efforts, ensuring brands stand out in competitive digital spaces. DALL·E empowers marketers with imaginative control previously restricted to professional designers.

Other content-generation tools include:

Stable Diffusion

Stable Diffusion is an open-source image generation technology that has gained massive popularity for its accessibility and customization options. Unlike proprietary tools, marketers can fine-tune and deploy Stable Diffusion models to generate visuals aligned precisely with their branding guidelines. This flexibility is crucial for organizations seeking complete creative ownership and cost control. It enables production of social media graphics, ads, and product visuals at scale without relying on external design services. Its open-source nature also fosters continuous innovation by developers worldwide, ensuring rapid improvements. Marketers benefit from cutting-edge capabilities while avoiding licensing limitations typically tied to closed AI platforms.

Progen

Progen is designed to streamline professional communications by generating high-quality written content quickly. It is especially effective for producing emails, reports, blogs, and other communication assets marketers need daily. The platform integrates social sharing features, allowing content to be distributed seamlessly across multiple digital channels. One of its standout attributes is its built-in plagiarism safeguards, ensuring originality and maintaining brand credibility. By reducing the risk of duplicated content, Progen supports marketers in achieving SEO compliance and audience trust. Its automation capabilities save time and effort, allowing marketing teams to focus on strategy and creativity while ensuring polished, professional outputs.

GAN.ai

GAN.ai addresses a critical marketing challenge: personalization at scale. It enables brands to create customized video content tailored to different audience segments without manually editing each version. This means marketers can deliver personalized product recommendations, greetings, or offers via video to thousands of customers simultaneously. Video personalization enhances engagement, as audiences feel directly addressed and valued by the brand. By leveraging generative AI, GAN.ai reduces production costs and turnaround times significantly. The platform's scalability makes it particularly effective for large campaigns, where personalized video messaging can dramatically improve conversion rates. It bridges efficiency and human-like connection in digital marketing.

Anthropic's Claude

Claude, developed by Anthropic, is a generative AI tool that specializes in summarization, search, and creative writing. For marketers, it provides support in synthesizing large volumes of information into concise and actionable insights. This is particularly useful when analyzing customer feedback, market reports, or competitive data. Claude also enhances content creation by collaborating on campaign ideas, slogans, and narratives, offering a more conversational approach to creative writing. Its safety-focused design emphasizes trustworthy outputs, minimizing risks of generating misleading or harmful content. Marketers rely on Claude to maintain credibility while boosting efficiency, making it a valuable ally in content-heavy workflows.

Omneky

Omneky focuses on optimizing advertising creative across multiple digital platforms, using generative AI to customize ad visuals and copy for diverse audiences. Instead of producing one-size-fits-all advertisements, Omneky analyzes performance metrics and generates variations designed to resonate with specific demographics. Its integration with platforms like Facebook, Instagram, and Google Ads ensures seamless deployment. By personalizing ads, Omneky helps marketers maximize engagement, reduce wasted spend, and achieve higher ROI. The platform's adaptive approach ensures campaigns stay fresh and relevant in fast-changing markets. For digital advertisers, Omneky combines creativity with data-driven insights to deliver highly targeted, effective marketing campaigns at scale.

Hypotenuse

Hypotenuse AI automates the creation of product descriptions, advertising captions, and other promotional text that typically consumes significant time for marketing teams. Using natural language processing, it generates consistent, engaging, and SEO-friendly content that aligns with brand voice. This is especially beneficial for e-commerce businesses managing large product catalogs, where manual description writing is impractical. Hypotenuse's automation reduces workload, speeds up go-to-market timelines, and ensures product pages are optimized for search visibility. By combining creativity with accuracy, it helps marketers attract customers while maintaining professionalism. It has become a preferred solution for businesses aiming to scale product-related content efficiently.

Flick

Flick is a social media-focused generative AI tool that streamlines the process of creating engaging posts. It not only generates captions and content ideas but also suggests targeted hashtags tailored to audience behavior and industry trends. Beyond creation, Flick optimizes scheduling by identifying the best posting times to maximize visibility and engagement. This holistic approach enables marketers to maintain a consistent online presence without spending hours manually managing accounts. By combining creativity, data insights, and automation, Flick empowers brands to build stronger digital identities. It is particularly popular among small businesses and influencers seeking professional-grade marketing with limited resources.

Strategic generative AI tools

There are dozens of generative AI tools to help with all aspects of marketing strategy, some of which may overlap with platforms already part of a company's martech stack. Because generative AI tools can be more intuitive and easier to use, they provide access to information and functionality previously reserved for specialists and data scientists.

Among the most commonly used are:

Alteryx

Alteryx is a powerful platform designed to automate data engineering, analytics, and reporting, making it a vital tool in strategic marketing powered by generative AI. Traditionally, data preparation and advanced analytics required technical expertise in coding or statistical software. Alteryx democratizes this by offering drag-and-drop workflows, automated data blending, and intuitive AI-driven insights. For marketers, this means faster access to clean, structured data and actionable insights without dependency on data scientists. It streamlines reporting, highlights hidden trends, and helps organizations make evidence-based decisions. By automating repetitive data tasks, Alteryx frees professionals to focus on strategy, innovation, and creative marketing execution.

Data-Robot

DataRobot is an open AI platform that empowers organizations to develop growth strategies by leveraging automated machine learning (AutoML). It simplifies building, training, and deploying predictive models at scale, providing marketers with deep foresight into customer behavior, demand forecasting, and campaign outcomes. Instead of relying on guesswork or delayed analytics, DataRobot enables real-time strategy optimization. Its generative AI capabilities transform raw data into strategic insights for market entry, pricing strategies, and segmentation. Businesses can predict churn, identify growth opportunities, and simulate scenarios. With its accessible interface, even non-technical users can generate predictive models, ensuring informed, data-backed decision-making at every level.

Skai

Skai is an omnichannel marketing intelligence platform that applies generative AI to automate ad spend optimization across search, social, retail, and programmatic channels. Marketers often struggle with fragmented data and complex campaign management. Skai solves this by unifying performance data and using AI algorithms to continuously optimize investments in real time. It enables smarter budget allocation, audience targeting, and performance forecasting across channels, ensuring higher ROI. By integrating generative insights, Skai allows teams to simulate outcomes, test scenarios, and refine messaging. This strategic automation reduces inefficiencies, enhances cross-channel collaboration, and empowers marketers to focus on creativity and customer experiences instead.

Braze

Braze is a customer engagement platform that orchestrates personalized, cross-channel marketing journeys with the help of generative AI. Its strength lies in dynamic segmentation, behavioral triggers, and real-time data integration. Using Braze, organizations can create customized campaigns across email, in-app messaging, SMS, and push notifications. Generative AI enhances Braze by generating adaptive customer journeys and tailoring content to individual user preferences. For marketers, this means higher engagement, loyalty, and retention through hyper-personalized interactions. Braze also provides advanced analytics to measure campaign effectiveness and refine strategies. By combining automation with personalization, it bridges the gap between data-driven insights and meaningful customer connections

Custom generative AI tools for marketing

1. Marketing companies can also use task-specific or proprietary datasets to create their own AI models. This enables them to increase the analysis's relevance and narrow its scope, even though it can be a big undertaking. Using brand guidelines or data from past campaigns, a custom dataset can also help more precisely create campaigns or content tailored to a particular industry.

2. The risk associated with using third-party tools, whose data might not have been sufficiently checked for bias, errors, misinformation, or copyright concerns, can also be managed by controlling the data that an AI model is trained on.

3. With the help of proprietary data sources, developers can create, train, and implement customized machine learning models with Amazon SageMaker.

4. Most companies, however, are unable to develop proprietary generative AI models. Usually, most organizations start with publicly accessible models such as Gemini and GPT-4. After that, the companies

use prompt engineering, reinforcement learning based on user feedback, and other methods to improve the models and update them frequently.

Applications in Healthcare: Drug discovery and patient care

Drug Discovery

Accelerated Molecular Design

Generative AI is transforming molecular design by rapidly generating drug-like compounds with desired pharmacological traits. Instead of relying on slow, costly laboratory experiments, models such as GANs, VAEs, and diffusion networks can explore vast chemical spaces in silico. These AI systems learn from extensive chemical databases and propose molecules with optimized binding affinity, solubility, and toxicity profiles. This drastically reduces the burden of trial-and-error experimentation in drug discovery. As a result, pharmaceutical research timelines are compressed, allowing researchers to identify potential candidates in hours rather than years. This paradigm shift reduces drug development cycles from 10–15 years to 3–5 years, saving billions.

Protein Structure Prediction

AI-powered protein structure prediction goes beyond AlphaFold's achievement of accurate folding predictions. Generative models are now being applied to design entirely new proteins, opening possibilities for vaccines, biologics, and antibodies. By analyzing folding patterns and molecular interactions, AI can engineer enzymes that degrade pollutants, proteins that resist mutation, or antibodies tailored for rare diseases. This is particularly vital for precision medicine, where customized biologics can address patient-specific needs. Such capabilities accelerate research in immunology, oncology, and infectious disease control. Ultimately, AI-driven protein design has the potential to revolutionize how therapies are conceived, making treatments more effective and highly personalized.

Virtual Clinical Trials

Generative AI introduces the concept of virtual clinical trials by simulating diverse patient populations using synthetic data. These digital twins replicate human physiology, demographics, and medical histories, allowing drug candidates to be tested for efficacy and safety before human trials. This approach enhances trial diversity by including underrepresented groups, reduces ethical risks by minimizing unnecessary exposure, and provides early insights into adverse reactions. Virtual trials can also optimize dosage, predict side effects, and identify biomarkers of response. By reducing reliance on large-scale real-world trials, pharmaceutical companies can accelerate approvals, cut costs, and improve patient safety in the long run.

Patient Care

Generative AI is transforming patient care by enabling precision, efficiency, and timely interventions. By analyzing multimodal data sources such as electronic health records, lab reports, and imaging studies, AI can identify risk factors and highlight early warning signs of disease. This proactive approach supports preventive care, reducing the likelihood of complications. AI also assists in continuous monitoring through wearable devices, generating insights from real-time health data streams. Healthcare providers can therefore anticipate deteriorations and adjust care accordingly. This intelligent augmentation of clinical practice not only enhances accuracy but also saves time, allowing doctors to focus on empathetic, human-centered care.

Personalized Treatment Plans

Generative AI enables highly personalized treatment strategies by integrating medical history, genetic information, imaging scans, and lifestyle patterns. Unlike traditional one-size-fits-all methods, AI models generate care pathways tailored to an individual's unique profile and predicted response. This ensures better outcomes while minimizing risks. For instance, in oncology, AI can propose optimized chemotherapy schedules that balance therapeutic effectiveness with side-effect management, improving patient comfort and adherence. Similarly, in chronic disease management, generative models simulate different medication regimens or lifestyle interventions to find the most effective plan. This customization enhances precision medicine, driving a paradigm shift toward truly individualized healthcare.

Medical Imaging Enhancement

Medical imaging has been significantly improved by generative AI, which creates clearer, more accurate diagnostic visuals. Techniques like GANs (Generative Adversarial Networks) reconstruct high-quality images from low-dose or noisy scans, reducing risks associated with repeated exposure to radiation. AI also fills in missing or corrupted scan data, enabling earlier detection of subtle abnormalities that might otherwise go unnoticed. For example, low-dose CT scans for lung cancer screening can be enhanced with generative AI to achieve the clarity of standard-dose scans without compromising patient safety. This advancement empowers radiologists to make faster, more reliable diagnoses, leading to timely interventions.

Clinical Decision Support

Generative AI strengthens clinical decision-making by simulating disease progression under different treatment scenarios. It helps physicians evaluate the potential outcomes of various interventions before applying them in practice. In critical care settings such as ICUs, AI models can predict how patients might respond to ventilation strategies, medication adjustments, or surgical procedures. This forward-looking capability reduces trial-and-error approaches and supports evidence-based medicine. Moreover, AI-generated predictions assist in risk stratification, identifying patients who may require more intensive monitoring or early intervention. By combining predictive accuracy with clinical expertise, generative AI enhances safety, optimizes care delivery, and fosters better patient outcomes.

Patient Engagement and Virtual Care

Generative AI also enhances patient engagement through interactive tools like chatbots and virtual assistants. These systems provide personalized health reminders, explain complex medical concepts in simple terms, and even simulate empathetic conversations to reduce patient anxiety. This improves adherence to treatment regimens and strengthens the patient–doctor relationship. In mental health, AI-driven virtual companions can deliver supportive dialogues, monitor emotional states, and encourage self-care practices. Furthermore, patients in remote or underserved areas gain access to reliable, AI-powered virtual consultations. By bridging communication gaps and empowering patients with knowledge, generative AI significantly improves the overall healthcare experience and long-term wellness.

Broader Implications Across Industries

Healthcare + Pharma

Generative AI is transforming healthcare and pharmaceutical industries by streamlining research, development, and patient care. In drug discovery, AI models can rapidly analyze molecular structures and generate potential compounds, reducing timelines from years to months. This efficiency lowers R&D costs while increasing the probability of finding effective treatments. In clinical trials, synthetic data generated by AI helps in simulating diverse patient populations, minimizing recruitment challenges. Personalized medicine also benefits as AI-driven models tailor therapies based on genetic and clinical data. Overall, the integration of generative AI accelerates innovation, reduces expenditure, and enhances patient outcomes in healthcare and pharmaceuticals.

Regulatory Challenges

Despite its potential, generative AI faces significant regulatory hurdles in healthcare and pharmaceuticals. Agencies like the U.S. Food and Drug Administration (FDA) and European Medicines Agency (EMA) require stringent validation before approving AI-driven innovations. Synthetic data used to augment clinical trials must demonstrate reliability, accuracy, and representativeness to gain acceptance. AI-generated drug designs, while promising, must undergo rigorous safety and efficacy testing before approval. Regulators also demand transparent documentation of how AI models are trained and validated. Balancing innovation with compliance remains a challenge, requiring collaboration between technology developers, pharmaceutical firms, and regulators to ensure safe, ethical adoption.

Ethical Considerations

The ethical use of generative AI in healthcare is as critical as its technical capabilities. Transparency is essential so that clinicians and patients can trust AI-generated insights in decision-making processes. Explainability ensures that medical professionals understand how an AI model arrives at recommendations, avoiding "black-box" risks. Bias reduction is equally crucial because skewed data can lead to unfair treatment outcomes across demographic groups. When patient health is at stake, even minor errors or hidden biases may have life-threatening consequences. Therefore, embedding fairness, accountability, and clear communication into generative AI systems is vital to uphold ethical medical practices.

Transforming Finance: Automated Reporting and Risk Modeling

A central European bank discovered an elaborate fraud scheme in 2023 that had eluded conventional detection systems for months. By analyzing enormous amounts of transaction data and generating fraud scenarios that were predictive, generative AI was able to identify anomalies that human analysts had missed. Potential losses of millions of dollars were halted in a matter of days. This is just one example of how finance is being transformed by generative AI. Financial institutions use AI-driven compliance audits, automated risk modeling, and customized investment strategies to increase efficiency, security, and decision-making.

Large language models (LLMs) and deep learning networks trained on enormous datasets are two examples of the highly sophisticated machine learning models that generative AI in financial services depends on to produce new insights, automate difficult procedures, and improve decision-making. In contrast to conventional AI systems, which frequently adhere to preset guidelines or concentrate on specific predictive tasks, generative AI is able to produce innovative financial models, replicate authentic market scenarios, and even automate customer interactions with responses that resemble those of a human. It allows financial forecasting, fraud detection, and portfolio management—tasks that previously required a great deal of human labor—to be automated by banks, insurance companies, and investment firms.

Traditional AI vs. Generative AI in Finance: Key Differences

The following differences on Traditional AI vs. Generative AI in Finance in Table 3.1.

Table 3.1: Key Differences between the Traditional AI vs. Generative AI in Finance.

Feature	Traditional AI in Finance	Generative AI in Finance
Functionality	Follows rule-based algorithms	Generates new data, insights, and scenarios
Application	Predictive modeling, automation	Market simulation, personalized financial advice

Decision-making	Data-driven but limited by pre-defined inputs	Can synthesize new insights based on multiple data points
Examples	Credit scoring models, automated trading	AI-generated financial reports, synthetic market data

Generative AI in finance work

Several elements are needed to integrate generative AI into financial processes in order to facilitate data analysis, produce insights, and aid in decision-making. By combining an organization's unique knowledge base with potent LLMs, it improves conventional financial operations. Because of the insightful information this architecture produces, people and financial institutions can make well-informed decisions in real time.

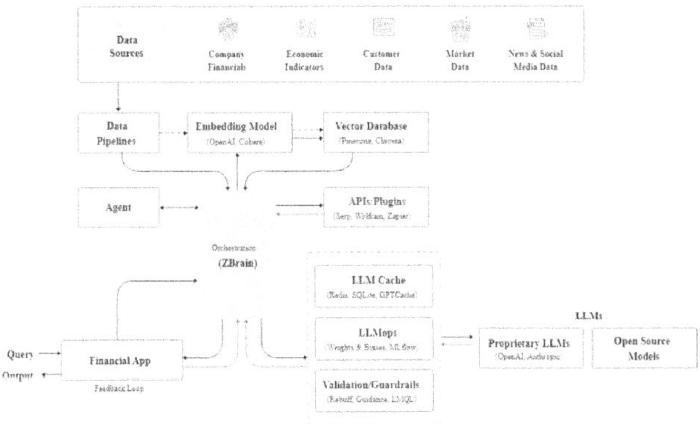

Figure 3.2: Generative AI in finance work. (leewayHertz)

Here's a detailed breakdown of how generative AI works in finance:

- Data sources: The process starts with gathering data from various relevant sources, including:
- Market data: Information on stock prices, indices, commodities, and market trends from financial markets and stock exchanges.

- Company financials: Financial statements, earnings reports, and forecasts from public companies.
- Customer data: Information about customer transactions, account balances, credit histories, and spending patterns from banks and financial institutions.
- News and social media: Real-time news, social media trends, and sentiment analysis from platforms like Bloomberg, Reuters, and Twitter.
- Data pipelines: The gathered data is routed through data pipelines responsible for ingestion, cleaning, and structuring the data, making it ready for further analysis.

Embedding model: The prepared data is then processed by an embedding model, which transforms textual data into numerical representations (vectors) that AI models can understand. Popular models include those from OpenAI, Google, and Cohere.

Vector database: The generated vectors are stored in a vector database, allowing for efficient querying and retrieval. Examples of vector databases include Pinecone, Weaviate, and PGvector.

APIs and plugins: APIs and plugins like Serp, Zapier, and Wolfram connect different components and enable additional functionalities, such as accessing extra data or performing specific tasks with ease.

Orchestration layer: The orchestration layer manages the workflow. Tools like ZBrain are examples of this layer, which simplifies prompt chaining, manages interactions with external APIs, retrieves contextual data from vector databases, and maintains memory across multiple LLM calls. This layer generates prompts or a series of prompts for processing by a language model. It ensures seamless coordination across all components within the architecture.

Query execution: The data retrieval and generation process is triggered when the user submits a query to the financial app. This query can be about anything relevant to finance and banking, such as stock price fluctuations or evaluating investment options.

LLM processing: The app transmits the query to the orchestration layer, which retrieves relevant data from the vector database and LLM Cache and sends it to the appropriate LLM. The choice of LLM depends on the nature of the query.

Output: The LLM generates an output based on the query and the received data. This output can take various forms, such as a summary of stock price fluctuations, investment recommendations, or financial insights.

Financial app: The validated output is then presented to the user through the financial app. This core application consolidates all the data, analysis, and insights, presenting them in a user-friendly format for financial professionals and individual investors.

Feedback loop: User feedback on the LLM's output helps improve the accuracy and relevance of future outputs, forming a crucial part of the architecture.

AI agents: AI agents handle complex problems, interact with the external environment, and enhance learning through post-deployment experiences. They achieve this purpose by using advanced reasoning/planning, strategic tool utilization and leveraging memory, recursion, and self-reflection.

LLM cache: Tools like Redis, SQLite, or GPTCache are employed to cache frequently accessed information, speeding up the AI system's response time.

Logging/LLMOps: LLMOps tools like Weights & Biases, MLflow, Helicone, and Prompt Layer log actions and monitor performance, ensuring LLMs function optimally and improve performance through feedback loops.

Validation: A validation layer is incorporated to ensure the LLM's output is accurate and reliable, using tools like Guardrails, Rebuff, Guidance, and LMQL.

LLM APIs and hosting: LLM APIs and hosting platforms execute financial tasks and host applications. Depending on requirements, developers can select from LLM APIs offered by companies like OpenAI and Anthropic or use open-source models. Hosting platforms include AWS, GCP, Azure, and Core weave, or opinionated clouds like Databricks, Mosaic, and Anyscale.

This structured flow demonstrates how generative AI in finance leverages various data sources and technological tools to generate accurate and actionable insights, automate financial tasks, and provide a personalized and optimized financial experience.

Key Components of Generative AI in Financial Services

Generative AI is reshaping financial services by introducing advanced tools that drive innovation and efficiency. As financial institutions strive for smarter decision-making and enhanced customer experiences, a few core components stand out:

Natural Language Processing (NLP)

Natural Language Processing (NLP) is a cornerstone of generative AI in financial services, enabling systems to interpret, process, and generate human-like language. In finance, NLP plays a vital role in automating report writing, analyzing large volumes of documents, and providing precise financial summaries. It helps institutions decode unstructured data such as customer emails, contracts, regulatory texts, and research reports. NLP-powered chat interfaces facilitate seamless customer communication, reducing human workload. Sentiment analysis of market news and social media further empowers investment decisions. By bridging human language with financial intelligence, NLP enhances accessibility, efficiency, and decision-making in complex financial ecosystems.

Deep Learning Models

Deep learning models empower financial services by uncovering intricate relationships hidden in massive datasets. Through layered neural architectures, these models detect subtle anomalies, predict market fluctuations, and optimize credit risk assessment. They continuously evolve by learning from new data, making them highly adaptive against fraud and cyber threats. In trading, deep learning enhances algorithmic strategies by forecasting price movements and asset correlations. Their predictive power supports more accurate loan approvals and insurance claims processing. Financial institutions leverage these models to refine strategies, improve compliance, and minimize risks. Ultimately, deep learning drives resilience and innovation in the rapidly shifting financial landscape.

Synthetic Data Generation

Synthetic data generation has become a game-changer in financial innovation, addressing challenges related to privacy, data scarcity, and bias. By creating artificial yet realistic datasets, institutions can simulate diverse market conditions, customer behaviors, and risk scenarios without exposing sensitive information. This technique enables robust testing of fraud detection systems, credit scoring models, and trading algorithms. It allows banks to anticipate risks under rare but high-impact events such as economic recessions or market crashes. Moreover, synthetic datasets enhance fairness by balancing underrepresented financial cases. As a result, financial services achieve stronger compliance, improved resilience, and more reliable data-driven decision-making.

Conversational AI

Conversational AI redefines customer engagement in financial services by powering intelligent chatbots, voice assistants, and digital advisors. These systems handle routine inquiries such as balance checks, transaction tracking, and loan eligibility with speed and accuracy, reducing call-center burden. Beyond simple queries, advanced conversational AI offers personalized investment advice, real-time portfolio updates, and proactive alerts on spending patterns. Its 24/7 availability ensures customers receive instant support, enhancing trust and satisfaction. By integrating emotional intelligence and contextual understanding, conversational AI delivers human-like financial guidance. Institutions benefit from cost efficiency, while customers enjoy seamless, tailored interactions that strengthen long-term financial relationships.

Importance of Generative AI in Financial Services

The financial services industry, driven by billions of daily transactions and stringent regulatory requirements, is rapidly evolving. Generative AI is emerging as a transformative force, empowering institutions to automate complex processes, derive actionable insights, and elevate customer experiences.

Enhancing Risk Assessment and Fraud Detection

Generative AI significantly enhances fraud detection by analyzing massive volumes of historical and real-time transaction data to uncover subtle anomalies. Unlike rule-based systems that rely on predefined conditions, AI models learn complex patterns of fraudulent behavior and can proactively identify risks before financial losses occur. By generating synthetic fraud scenarios, these systems continuously retrain and adapt to new threats, reducing the likelihood of false negatives and false positives. JPMorgan Chase, for example, employs advanced AI models to monitor payments, ensuring fraudulent activities are flagged early, thus improving both customer trust and institutional security.

Personalized Financial Services and Customer Engagement

Generative AI empowers financial institutions to deliver hyper-personalized services tailored to each customer's financial journey. By analyzing spending habits, income patterns, and risk profiles, AI systems generate personalized advice, investment strategies, and credit recommendations. Virtual assistants and AI-driven chatbots provide real-time guidance on queries, enhancing customer satisfaction while reducing operational costs. Morgan Stanley, for instance, uses an AI-powered assistant to process vast datasets and deliver instant, tailored investment insights to clients. This approach ensures proactive engagement, helping customers make smarter financial decisions and fostering long-term loyalty through trust and personalized service delivery.

Automating Compliance and Regulatory Processes

Financial institutions face increasing regulatory demands, making compliance both costly and complex.

Generative AI automates key compliance tasks by extracting insights from extensive legal documents, monitoring transactions for suspicious activity, and generating audit-ready reports with minimal human involvement. It streamlines KYC (Know Your Customer) and AML (Anti-Money Laundering) checks, ensuring faster onboarding while maintaining stringent compliance. AI's ability to continuously learn from new regulations makes institutions more adaptive to global mandates. By automating these processes, banks reduce errors, improve efficiency, and mitigate regulatory risks, transforming compliance from a burden into a seamlessly integrated operational function.

Optimizing Trading Strategies and Market Predictions

Generative AI revolutionizes trading by simulating dynamic market conditions and building predictive models based on vast financial datasets. These models enable institutions to assess risks, anticipate price fluctuations, and optimize real-time trading strategies with precision. Hedge funds and large investors employ AI-driven algorithms to detect hidden market opportunities, capitalize on trends, and react instantly to global events. Unlike traditional approaches, AI adapts dynamically, learning from historical and live data to refine strategies continuously. This capability ensures improved portfolio returns, risk-adjusted investments, and a significant competitive edge in high-frequency and institutional trading environments.

Streamlining Financial Document Processing

The financial industry heavily depends on documentation for loan approvals, claims, policy updates, and audits. Generative AI reduces the burden of manual handling by automating document summarization, classification, and extraction of key insights. It can transform unstructured data into structured formats, enabling faster decision-making. For example, loan applications that once required extensive review can now be processed instantly, reducing errors and operational costs. Similarly, insurance firms benefit by automating claim assessments, accelerating payouts, and enhancing customer satisfaction. By streamlining document workflows, AI not only boosts efficiency but also allows human employees to focus on higher-value strategic tasks.

Regulatory and Compliance Complexity

Financial services are among the most regulated industries globally, and integrating generative AI into these frameworks is challenging. AI models must comply with diverse regulatory requirements, including GDPR in Europe, SEC regulations in the U.S., and local financial reporting standards worldwide. A key issue is explainability—regulators require transparency in how AI-driven decisions are made, especially in sensitive processes like credit scoring or fraud detection. Black-box AI systems that cannot demonstrate accountability risk breaching compliance. Non-compliance not only invites legal penalties but also erodes market trust, damaging an institution's reputation and potentially undermining the financial system's stability.

Data Privacy and Security Risks

Generative AI requires enormous datasets, often containing highly sensitive financial records. The risk of data breaches, unauthorized access, or misuse of customer data increases significantly when such models are deployed. Compliance with strict data protection laws is mandatory, and failure to protect data can lead to severe financial and reputational consequences. While synthetic data generation can help, issues of accuracy and potential manipulation remain concerns. Strong encryption, strict access controls, and continuous monitoring are critical safeguards. Institutions must balance innovation with protection, ensuring AI systems process data responsibly while minimizing vulnerabilities to cyber threats and insider exploitation.

Lack of Explainability and Trust

One of the most pressing challenges in generative AI adoption is its black-box nature. Financial professionals often struggle to interpret the logic behind AI-generated recommendations. For critical applications like loan approvals, investment strategies, or fraud alerts, unexplained results hinder trust among customers and regulators alike. Without interpretability, decision-making transparency suffers, making it difficult to justify outcomes. This lack of clarity may cause reluctance in adoption by both employees and clients. Developing explainable AI frameworks, which clarify how conclusions are drawn, is vital. Trustworthy systems increase confidence, ensure accountability, and align innovation with ethical and regulatory standards.

Integration with Legacy Systems

Many financial institutions operate on outdated, legacy systems that lack the flexibility to support advanced AI solutions. Integrating generative AI into these infrastructures requires significant investment, technical expertise, and organizational restructuring. The process involves adapting existing banking platforms, risk management tools, and compliance software to work seamlessly with AI-driven automation. Without effective integration, AI systems risk creating operational silos, duplicating processes, and even reducing efficiency. Moreover, legacy systems often lack adequate data structures to support real-time AI operations. Overcoming these barriers is essential for ensuring that generative AI enhances productivity, streamlines operations, and provides measurable value.

Ethical Considerations and Bias

Generative AI must be implemented ethically to avoid perpetuating bias in financial decision-making. If models are trained on biased or incomplete datasets, they may reinforce discrimination in lending, hiring, or customer profiling. This can result in unfair credit denials, biased risk evaluations, or exclusion of certain demographic groups. Such outcomes not only harm individuals but also expose institutions to legal action and reputational loss. To mitigate these risks, organizations must adopt ethical AI frameworks, regularly audit models, and refine algorithms for fairness and inclusivity. Prioritizing transparency, accountability, and non-discrimination is crucial for building responsible AI in finance.

Benefits of Generative AI in Financial Services

Generative AI redefines the financial sector by automating complex processes, improving accuracy, and enhancing customer experiences.

Improved Risk Management and Fraud Detection

Generative AI is revolutionizing risk management by enabling financial institutions to analyze massive volumes of structured and unstructured data in real time. Unlike traditional systems that rely heavily on static models, AI can dynamically learn and adapt to new risk factors, providing more accurate predictions. For instance, when assessing loan approvals, generative AI identifies subtle correlations in borrower behavior, credit history, and external economic conditions that human analysts may overlook. In fraud detection, AI models recognize anomalies in transaction patterns, reducing false alarms and improving efficiency. This proactive monitoring ensures fraud is intercepted before it escalates into major financial crime.

Enhanced Customer Experience

In today's digital-first banking landscape, customer expectations revolve around speed, personalization, and accuracy. Generative AI plays a central role by powering intelligent chatbots and virtual assistants that provide round-the-clock assistance, reducing dependency on human staff. These systems can handle routine queries such as balance checks, loan eligibility, or investment options, while escalating complex issues to human agents. Moreover, AI-driven financial advisors deliver customized portfolio recommendations tailored to individual goals, income levels, and risk tolerance. This not only boosts customer satisfaction but also strengthens long-term client trust, as customers receive services aligned with their unique financial journeys.

Optimized Trading Strategies and Market Predictions

Generative AI empowers traders with sophisticated predictive analytics, reshaping investment strategies. By processing real-time and historical market data, AI generates actionable insights into stock performance, market sentiment, and global financial trends. Traders can simulate different scenarios, such as market crashes or rallies, and adjust strategies accordingly. Unlike traditional models that may lag behind sudden shifts, generative AI adapts instantly, offering portfolio managers enhanced agility. Algorithmic trading systems further benefit from AI's predictive capabilities, executing trades at optimal times to maximize returns while minimizing risks. This predictive edge ultimately results in stronger investment outcomes and reduced vulnerability to market volatility.

Automated Compliance and Regulatory Reporting

Compliance remains one of the most resource-intensive functions in financial services. Generative AI streamlines this by automating the extraction and interpretation of complex regulatory texts, ensuring institutions stay updated with changing laws. It continuously monitors transactions for suspicious activity, flagging irregularities that may require reporting. AI also generates accurate, audit-ready reports, reducing the reliance on manual effort while minimizing errors. This automation not only saves time but also significantly reduces compliance costs. By ensuring transparency and precision, generative AI helps banks and financial firms maintain trust with regulators while avoiding penalties linked to non-compliance or overlooked reporting obligations.

Cost Efficiency and Operational Productivity

Operational inefficiencies have long plagued financial institutions due to reliance on repetitive manual processes. Generative AI transforms these workflows by automating document verification, credit risk analysis, and financial modeling. By doing so, it reduces operational expenses while enabling staff to focus on more strategic, value-added tasks. Large-scale data handling, once requiring extensive manpower, can now be executed within seconds, improving both accuracy and speed. Furthermore, AI-driven automation minimizes human errors, which are costly and reputation-damaging in finance. The net result is faster turnaround times, streamlined resource allocation, and an overall boost in organizational productivity and profitability.

Scalability and Continuous Learning

Financial institutions operate in an environment characterized by constant change, from evolving customer needs to shifting regulatory frameworks. Generative AI thrives in such settings because of its ability to continuously learn from new datasets and real-time market information. Unlike static systems that require frequent manual updates, AI adapts autonomously, refining its predictions and outputs with every new input. This ensures scalability, as AI-driven tools can handle increasing volumes of data without performance loss. By keeping pace with dynamic conditions, financial institutions remain competitive, delivering adaptive, resilient, and future-ready financial services tailored to emerging market and customer demands.

Best Practices for Implementing Generative AI in Financial Services

Financial services must strike a balance between innovation, strong security, and compliance in order to successfully implement generative AI. By following best practices, organizations can efficiently manage risk and unlock value.

Regulatory Compliance and Ethical AI Usage

Implementing Generative AI in financial services requires a strong foundation of regulatory compliance and ethical considerations. Institutions must ensure all AI-driven systems adhere to global financial regulations such as GDPR for data privacy, SEC rules for transparency, and Basel III for risk management. Ethical AI usage further demands building explainability into models through tools that make AI decisions interpretable. Establishing dedicated ethics committees can help monitor and address potential biases, ensuring fairness in critical areas like loan approvals, fraud detection, and credit scoring. This commitment enhances trust among regulators, customers, and stakeholders, ensuring responsible adoption of generative AI.

Data Security and Privacy

Generative AI applications in finance depend on vast amounts of sensitive data, making security and privacy paramount. To safeguard customer and institutional information, financial firms should implement end-to-end encryption, multi-factor authentication, and advanced anomaly detection systems. Leveraging privacy-preserving techniques like federated learning can further reduce exposure risks by keeping raw data localized. Aligning with international security standards such as ISO 27001 and SOC 2 ensures robust compliance while minimizing vulnerabilities. By proactively addressing data security, financial institutions can not only mitigate cyber threats but also build customer confidence, which is essential for the large-scale deployment of generative AI systems.

Model Interpretability and Explainability

Financial services require high accountability, making model interpretability critical. Generative AI must not be treated as a black box; instead, institutions should use explainability techniques like SHAP (SHapley Additive exPlanations) and LIME (Local Interpretable Model-agnostic Explanations). These approaches help translate complex AI outputs into insights that are understandable for regulators, auditors, and business leaders. Transparent models ensure that human experts can oversee AI recommendations in areas such as risk assessments, portfolio management, and fraud detection. Explainable AI builds trust among clients and regulators, reduces operational risks, and ensures that AI insights support—not replace—human judgment in critical financial decision-making.

Seamless Integration with Financial Systems

The success of generative AI in finance hinges on its seamless integration with existing systems. Financial institutions often rely on legacy platforms, making compatibility a challenge. Deploying AI solutions through cloud-based infrastructure allows scalability and resilience, while APIs and orchestration layers enable smooth data flow between AI models and core banking systems, trading platforms, and risk management frameworks. This ensures AI-enhanced automation does not disrupt ongoing operations. Additionally, integration strategies should prioritize interoperability to support real-time decision-making and compliance tracking. By embedding AI into the financial ecosystem effectively, firms can achieve higher efficiency, agility, and customer satisfaction.

Continuous Model Improvement and Monitoring

Generative AI models in finance operate in dynamic environments, making continuous monitoring and adaptation essential. Market conditions, regulatory updates, and customer behaviors evolve rapidly, requiring AI systems to remain current and reliable. Institutions should adopt reinforcement learning to fine-tune models based on new patterns and outcomes. Regular performance audits can identify biases, inaccuracies, and compliance issues before they escalate. Automated monitoring tools should track fairness, accuracy, and transparency across models. By investing in an ongoing cycle of evaluation and refinement, financial firms ensure AI remains aligned with evolving business goals while maintaining trustworthiness and regulatory compliance.

Aligning AI with Business Strategy

Generative AI delivers maximum value when closely aligned with strategic objectives in financial services. Rather than adopting AI as an isolated technology, firms should integrate it into broader goals such as enhancing fraud detection, streamlining compliance, boosting operational efficiency, and improving customer engagement through personalized services. Clear KPIs, such as reduced operational costs, improved fraud detection rates, and higher customer satisfaction scores, should guide implementation. This ensures measurable business impact and helps refine strategies over time. By connecting AI initiatives directly to organizational priorities, financial institutions can harness AI not only as a tool but as a long-term strategic enabler.

Generative AI in Financial Services: Transforming Operations with Use Cases and Applications

Generative AI is rapidly reshaping the financial landscape by driving innovation, enhancing decision-making, and streamlining processes across risk management, customer engagement, compliance, and trading. At Tredence, we believe that successful AI deployment requires a balanced approach—one that marries transformative technology with robust security, compliance, and operational integration.

Enhanced Risk Management and Fraud Detection

Generative AI is transforming risk management in financial services by enabling advanced fraud detection and anomaly identification. Traditional rule-based systems often struggle with evolving fraud tactics, but AI models can learn from historical datasets and detect unusual transaction patterns in real time. Moreover, generative models create synthetic fraud scenarios, enhancing training datasets and improving the robustness of fraud detection systems. Continuous monitoring and reinforcement learning allow these systems to adapt dynamically, while regular performance audits ensure transparency. This proactive approach minimizes financial losses, reduces false positives, and strengthens trust among customers and regulators in highly sensitive financial environments.

Personalized Customer Engagement and Financial Services

Generative AI allows financial institutions to move from generic offerings to highly personalized customer engagement. By analyzing large volumes of structured and unstructured data—including transaction histories, investment behaviors, and customer preferences—AI can deliver tailored financial advice, personalized loan products, and dynamic portfolio management strategies. Virtual assistants powered by generative models provide real-time chat support, improving accessibility and customer satisfaction. Aligning these services with KPIs such as operational cost reduction, improved retention rates, and enhanced customer experiences ensures measurable outcomes. Ultimately, this fosters stronger client relationships, builds brand loyalty, and gives financial institutions a competitive edge in a customer-centric marketplace.

Automated Compliance and Regulatory Processes

The financial sector operates in a heavily regulated environment where compliance costs are high and errors can be costly. Generative AI streamlines compliance by automating the extraction of relevant insights from complex regulatory documents, ensuring timely adherence to evolving standards like GDPR, SEC regulations, and Basel III. AI also enhances efficiency in processes such as Know Your Customer (KYC), Anti-Money Laundering (AML) checks, and audit report generation. Integrating explainable AI ensures that all automated decisions remain transparent and traceable, mitigating regulatory risks. This approach reduces manual workload, minimizes human error, and enables institutions to remain agile in regulatory landscapes.

Seamless Integration and Scalability

Successful deployment of generative AI in finance depends on seamless integration with existing systems. Many banks and financial institutions rely on legacy infrastructure that cannot be replaced overnight. Generative AI solutions can integrate through APIs, orchestration layers, and middleware, ensuring compatibility and minimizing disruption. Cloud platforms further enhance scalability, enabling institutions to expand AI applications across departments without excessive infrastructure costs. This ensures smoother adoption and operational efficiency while retaining business continuity. By building AI systems that complement rather than disrupt, financial organizations achieve accelerated transformation with reduced risk, paving the way for sustainable, long-term technological innovation.

Data Security and Model Interpretability

Financial institutions handle highly sensitive data, making data security and model transparency essential in generative AI adoption. Advanced security practices such as end-to-end encryption, multi-factor authentication, and differential privacy protect customer information. Federated learning allows AI models to train collaboratively without directly sharing raw data, strengthening privacy. Equally important is model interpretability—using tools like SHAP and LIME ensures stakeholders understand the rationale behind AI-driven decisions. Transparent decision-making not only satisfies regulatory requirements but also enhances customer trust. Together, these measures balance technological innovation with ethical responsibility, ensuring AI-driven financial services are secure, explainable, and accountable to all stakeholders.

Financial institutions can use generative AI to combine innovation and discipline to reduce risk and unlock significant value. In order to ensure that technology powers efficiency and propels sustainable growth, we at Tredence are dedicated to helping organizations navigate this transition. The path to a competitive, flexible, and future-ready financial ecosystem is paved by adopting these integrated practices.

Examples of Generative AI in Financial Services

Generative AI is already significantly impacting the financial sector, with leading institutions deploying AI-driven solutions to improve operational efficiency, enhance customer experience, and strengthen risk management. Below are real-world examples of how financial organizations are successfully integrating Generative AI.

Fraud Detection and Security Enhancement

Generative AI is revolutionizing fraud detection and cybersecurity in the financial sector. Traditional systems rely heavily on rule-based mechanisms that often struggle to adapt to evolving fraud patterns, leading to delayed detection or high false positives. Generative AI, however, learns dynamically from massive datasets, recognizing subtle anomalies in transactions and user behavior in real time. By generating synthetic fraud scenarios, these models strengthen predictive capabilities and improve system resilience. This reduces financial risks, enhances consumer trust, and ensures proactive responses to new threats. As fraud tactics evolve, AI-driven security ensures financial systems remain adaptive, precise, and future-ready.

Global Banks

Leading global banks, such as JPMorgan Chase and HSBC, have integrated AI-powered fraud detection systems into their operations. These institutions handle millions of transactions daily, making manual monitoring nearly impossible. AI models analyze transaction histories, spending behaviors, and geo-locations, flagging irregular patterns like sudden high-value withdrawals or cross-border transfers. Generative AI enhances precision by minimizing false positives, preventing unnecessary disruptions for customers. HSBC has already reported improved fraud detection rates, while JPMorgan Chase leverages AI to process billions of data points within seconds. This enables them to protect customer assets effectively, comply with regulatory requirements, and maintain strong reputational trust.

Payment Processors

Payment processors like PayPal and Visa have become frontrunners in deploying AI for fraud prevention. Handling billions of transactions globally, these companies face constant threats from cybercriminals attempting unauthorized purchases or identity theft. Generative AI helps them simulate potential fraud scenarios, enabling real-time detection of unusual activities such as atypical purchase volumes, location mismatches, or multiple failed login attempts. By reducing fraud-related losses, they safeguard both merchants and customers while enhancing user experience with fewer false declines. Visa has publicly highlighted AI's role in preventing billions of dollars in fraudulent activity annually, showcasing how proactive security builds confidence in digital payments.

AI-Driven Customer Support

Financial service companies increasingly rely on AI-powered chatbots and virtual assistants to handle customer interactions efficiently. These AI-driven systems provide 24/7 assistance by answering questions, processing simple transactions, and offering tailored financial advice. Unlike traditional support channels that are limited by staff availability, AI assistants ensure instant responses, enhancing customer satisfaction. They also learn from consumer history, preferences, and behavioral data to deliver personalized solutions. For example, they may suggest budget plans to a customer who often overspends or recommends savings schemes based on prior investments. This constant accessibility reduces operational costs while boosting service quality.

Banking Services

In banking, AI-powered chatbots have become integral to customer engagement. Leading institutions such as Wells Fargo and Bank of America employ AI-driven assistants like Erica to provide instant financial guidance. Customers can use these chatbots to check account balances, monitor and categorize spending, and even set up bill payments. AI ensures faster query resolution, reducing the dependency on human representatives for routine inquiries. Beyond convenience, these systems provide proactive insights by analyzing transaction history for instance, warning about unusual expenses or suggesting ways to improve savings. This integration helps banks enhance efficiency, reduce wait times, and build stronger customer trust.

Wealth Management

Wealth management has been revolutionized by AI through the use of robo-advisors. Platforms like Betterment and Wealth front leverage AI algorithms to design personalized investment strategies aligned with an individual's financial goals, risk tolerance, and time horizon. These systems automate portfolio rebalancing, tax-loss harvesting, and diversification, which previously required human advisors. By analyzing market data and user inputs, robo-advisors provide cost-effective, transparent, and objective financial planning. This democratizes access to professional wealth management, enabling even small investors to benefit from sophisticated strategies. Clients enjoy round-the-clock monitoring of their investments with reduced management fees, making AI-driven wealth solutions increasingly popular.

Regulatory Compliance and Risk Management

Regulatory compliance remains a cornerstone for financial institutions, as global financial markets are governed by stringent regulations to safeguard transparency, integrity, and trust. Artificial Intelligence (AI) is revolutionizing this domain by automating traditionally manual compliance tasks, thereby reducing human errors and minimizing risks associated with regulatory breaches. AI-driven platforms can interpret complex regulatory requirements, monitor ongoing processes, and ensure that organizations stay updated with evolving guidelines. Moreover, AI aids in real-time risk assessment by analyzing patterns of non-compliance, providing predictive alerts, and helping organizations mitigate penalties. This proactive approach transforms compliance from a reactive obligation into a strategic advantage.

Audit and Compliance Automation

Audit and compliance automation through AI is reshaping how leading firms like Deloitte and PwC streamline regulatory oversight. These organizations deploy machine learning algorithms and natural language processing (NLP) tools to scan, classify, and analyze vast transaction datasets quickly and accurately. AI-powered systems not only detect anomalies and potential compliance breaches but also ensure that all activities align with evolving regulations. Additionally, automated tools generate regulatory reports in real-time, eliminating delays caused by manual compilation. This automation enhances transparency, reduces operational costs, and empowers auditors to focus on critical decision-making rather than routine checks, thus strengthening governance structures.

AML (Anti-Money Laundering) Monitoring

Anti-Money Laundering (AML) compliance is one of the most critical aspects of risk management in the financial sector. AI-driven systems developed by companies such as FICO and NICE Actimize play a crucial role in detecting suspicious activities that might indicate money laundering. These systems employ advanced analytics, graph-based modeling, and machine learning to analyze transaction flows, identify hidden relationships, and detect unusual patterns that humans may overlook. By continuously learning from new data, these tools adapt to emerging fraud tactics, ensuring financial institutions remain ahead of criminals. This proactive AML monitoring not only ensures compliance but also strengthens financial integrity.

Algorithmic Trading and Market Analysis

Generative AI is reshaping the landscape of algorithmic trading and market analysis by providing hedge funds and investment firms with unprecedented predictive capabilities. These models analyze vast amounts of structured and unstructured data, such as price fluctuations, historical market patterns, and real-time feeds, to identify profitable opportunities. Unlike traditional statistical models, generative AI can simulate multiple future scenarios, helping traders manage risks more effectively. By automating decision-making and minimizing human biases, firms enhance portfolio optimization, reduce transaction costs, and improve market timing. This data-driven approach allows for dynamic strategy adjustments in volatile markets, increasing both profitability and resilience.

High-Frequency Trading

High-frequency trading (HFT) leverages advanced AI algorithms to execute trades in milliseconds, a domain where speed translates directly into financial advantage. Firms like Renaissance Technologies and Citadel integrate generative AI with high-speed infrastructure to detect micro-market movements and capitalize on arbitrage opportunities. These systems process order books, market microstructure data, and real-time news at extraordinary speeds to ensure that profitable positions are secured before competitors react. Generative AI enhances predictive modeling, enabling the anticipation of short-lived opportunities. By minimizing latency and optimizing trade execution, AI-driven HFT strategies maximize returns while systematically mitigating exposure to adverse price movements and risks.

Market Sentiment Analysis

Market sentiment analysis powered by generative AI is becoming essential for modern financial decision-making. Platforms like Alpha-Sense integrate natural language processing (NLP) to evaluate financial reports, regulatory filings, news articles, and even social media discussions. By generating sentiment scores and trend predictions, AI offers traders and portfolio managers insights beyond numerical data. This enables early detection of shifts in investor confidence, economic policy changes, or global events impacting market dynamics. Generative models simulate potential outcomes based on sentiment fluctuations, allowing for proactive adjustments in trading strategies. This approach empowers firms to anticipate trends, reduce uncertainty, and gain a competitive edge.

Loan Underwriting and Credit Decisioning

Artificial Intelligence (AI) is reshaping loan underwriting and credit decisioning by enabling more precise risk evaluation and reducing reliance on traditional credit scores. Banks and lenders can now assess borrowers through machine learning models that analyze financial histories, spending habits, transaction data, and even behavioral indicators. This multi-dimensional analysis helps institutions identify creditworthy customers who might otherwise be overlooked due to limited or nontraditional credit histories. By minimizing manual interventions and automating data-driven insights, AI improves approval accuracy, reduces defaults, and accelerates decision-making, making credit more inclusive and accessible to broader segments of AI-Enabled Loan Approvals

society.

AI-driven underwriting systems are redefining the way financial institutions approve loans. Companies like Upstart and Zest AI leverage machine learning to evaluate borrowers' creditworthiness beyond traditional FICO scores. Their models incorporate non-traditional data points such as education, employment history, cash flow, and even digital footprint to create a holistic borrower profile. This allows lenders to extend credit to underserved populations while maintaining strong risk controls. Faster, automated approvals enhance customer experience, while reduced default rates improve profitability for banks. By using AI, lenders not only expand their market reach but also ensure fairer and more data-backed lending decisions.

Mortgage Automation

Mortgage lending has traditionally been time-consuming, with lengthy paperwork and manual verification delaying approvals. AI-powered platforms such as Blend are transforming this space by automating home loan applications and integrating directly with banks' back-end systems. These platforms streamline document collection, income verification, and compliance checks, reducing processing times from weeks to days. Borrowers benefit from seamless, digital-first experiences with greater transparency and quicker approvals. For lenders, automation minimizes errors, lowers operational costs, and improves customer satisfaction. Additionally, AI algorithms assist in detecting fraud, ensuring safer transactions. Ultimately, mortgage automation makes housing finance more accessible, efficient, and customer-centric.

Insurance Claims Processing and Risk Evaluation

Insurance companies are increasingly adopting artificial intelligence (AI) to transform claims processing and risk evaluation. Traditionally, claims handling has been slow, manual, and prone to human errors. AI-powered tools streamline this by quickly scanning documents, verifying details, and detecting inconsistencies that might indicate fraud. Risk evaluation has also evolved, with AI analyzing vast datasets such as customer demographics, driving behavior, and historical claim records to generate accurate risk profiles. This integration reduces operational costs, minimizes fraudulent payouts, and ensures fairer pricing models. Ultimately, AI strengthens customer trust through faster decisions, transparency, and personalized policy structures.

Claims Automation

Claims automation is one of the most impactful applications of AI in insurance. Companies like Lemonade have pioneered the use of AI-powered bots to process claims in just minutes, eliminating the delays of traditional manual reviews. These bots use natural language processing (NLP) to understand claim requests, computer vision to validate supporting images, and predictive models to determine eligibility. The system then either approves and settles the claim instantly or flags suspicious cases for human review. This rapid, transparent process enhances customer satisfaction, cuts administrative costs, and ensures fairness, setting new benchmarks for efficiency in the insurance industry.

Risk Modeling

Risk modeling is a core aspect of insurance, and AI has dramatically improved its accuracy. Insurers like Allstate and AXA leverage machine learning algorithms to analyze policyholder behavior, credit history, lifestyle choices, and even telematics data from connected devices. By identifying subtle patterns in large datasets, AI predicts the likelihood of accidents, health issues, or fraudulent behavior. This allows insurers to design more personalized policies, adjust premiums dynamically, and mitigate financial exposure. Furthermore, AI-driven risk modeling helps companies stay competitive by offering optimized coverage while maintaining profitability, all while providing customers with policies better suited to their actual risk profiles.

Personalized Financial Planning and Wealth Management

Artificial Intelligence (AI) is transforming the way wealth management firms and financial advisors deliver services by offering personalized financial planning and wealth management solutions. Through advanced data analytics, AI tools analyze client income, spending patterns, assets, liabilities, and financial goals to create customized plans. These solutions go beyond generic advice by factoring in real-time market trends, tax implications, and life events to generate dynamic recommendations. Clients receive continuous monitoring of their financial health, ensuring that their investments, retirement savings, and insurance needs remain aligned with evolving circumstances. This personalized approach enhances trust, financial literacy, and long-term wealth creation in Figure 3.3.

Figure 3.3: Personalized Financial Planning and Wealth Management.

AI-Driven Financial Advisory: Morgan Stanley and Goldman Sachs

Leading global financial institutions such as Morgan Stanley and Goldman Sachs are integrating AI-driven models into their advisory services to deliver tailored investment strategies. These AI systems analyze vast amounts of structured and unstructured financial data, including historical market performance, company fundamentals, and client-specific risk preferences. By doing so, they generate recommendations that balance risk and return while adapting to changing conditions. For example, clients may receive suggestions on portfolio diversification, timing of investments, or sector exposure tailored to their individual goals. This innovation not only increases advisory efficiency but also democratizes access to sophisticated financial insights.

Portfolio Optimization: BlackRock's Aladdin

BlackRock's Aladdin platform represents a pioneering example of AI-powered portfolio optimization. Aladdin leverages machine learning algorithms and predictive analytics to assess risks, forecast market movements, and optimize asset allocation for institutional investors. The system processes massive datasets ranging from economic indicators to company reports and geopolitical events to generate real-time insights. These insights enable investors to identify potential vulnerabilities in their portfolios, test multiple allocation scenarios, and make informed decisions that align with both short- and long-term objectives. By providing AI-generated risk assessments and optimization strategies, Aladdin empowers asset managers to balance growth opportunities with risk management, thereby maximizing portfolio resilience.

Retail and e-commerce: Personalization at scale

Conventional AI is similar to that trustworthy, law-abiding employee who excels at a certain task, like information classification, pattern recognition, or data analysis. It is reactive and functions within preset parameters. A summer collection with a blue theme could be created by generative AI, complete with product descriptions and marketing copy, whereas traditional AI might say that "82% of your customers like blue products." The distinction here is between creation and analysis. Conventional AI looks for patterns in data that is available or known. Generative AI produces entirely unique content with a remarkably human feel, such as text, videos, images, product designs, and customer service scripts. In retail, this point is never more evident. While traditional AI makes the most of what it already knows, generative AI imagines what is possible.

Current State of Generative AI Adoption in Retail

The stats don't lie generative AI has taken retail by storm:

Nowadays, 78% of business retailers use generative AI in at least one application that interacts with customers.

1. In the last 12 months, generative AI retail solutions have cost $18.7 billion.
2. The fashion industry pioneers' 3.2x return on investment
3. Department stores can save 47% on content creation expenses by utilizing generative AI.
4. During their shopping experience, 86% of consumers have interacted with generative AI, frequently without realizing it.
5. Compared to non-users, small to mid-size retailers that use generative AI are seeing a 31% faster growth in revenue.

The renowned shift of technology from experimental to indispensable has led to the quickest adoption in visual merchandising, customer service, and personalized marketing.

Retailers Can't Afford to Ignore This Technology

The same way that mobile commerce was ignored in 2015, generative AI will be ignored in 2025. Since you are staying the same, your competitors are already changing the way they do business. Competitive advantages are just enormous:

Speed-to-Market Acceleration

Generative AI enables retailers to compress traditional product development cycles from months to days. By using AI models to generate designs, forecast demand, and simulate customer reactions, businesses can bring new ideas to market at unprecedented speed. This acceleration means retailers can capitalize on emerging trends faster than ever, avoiding the risk of missing seasonal or viral opportunities. Prototypes, marketing visuals, and packaging can all be AI-generated, reducing delays caused by manual processes. In today's fast-paced retail landscape, speed itself becomes a competitive weapon, allowing companies to adapt to shifting consumer preferences while competitors are still planning.

Hyper-Personalization at Scale

Generative AI allows retailers to deliver hyper-personalized experiences not just for niche segments but for millions of customers simultaneously. By analyzing individual browsing behavior, purchase history, and preferences, AI can generate tailored recommendations, product bundles, and marketing messages. This personalization creates deeper customer engagement, stronger loyalty, and higher conversion rates. Instead of generic promotions, each shopper can experience a journey that feels designed uniquely for them. Importantly, this is done at scale—what once required costly manual segmentation can now be executed automatically, ensuring personalization for everyone, not just VIP customers. This transforms customer experience into a powerful growth driver.

Content Explosion

One of the most remarkable applications of generative AI in retail is its ability to produce a massive volume of creative assets without additional headcount. From product descriptions to ad copies, from social media visuals to email campaigns, AI tools can generate thousands of content variants in minutes. This ensures that marketing remains fresh, targeted, and optimized for different platforms and demographics. Retailers can now A/B test campaigns at a level previously impossible, finding the perfect tone and design for each audience. By scaling content creation so dramatically, generative AI helps brands stay ahead in crowded and noisy markets.

Cost Efficiencies

Generative AI significantly reduces the cost of producing creative assets across all disciplines—design, copywriting, video, and product concepts. Instead of relying on large teams or expensive agencies for every iteration, AI provides cost-effective solutions while maintaining high quality. This doesn't eliminate human creativity but augments it, allowing skilled professionals to focus on strategy, innovation, and oversight rather than repetitive tasks. As a result, businesses can allocate budgets more efficiently, reinvesting savings into growth initiatives or customer experience enhancements. In an industry with thin margins like retail, these cost efficiencies can make the difference between surviving and thriving.

Customer Expectations

Today's consumers no longer tolerate generic shopping journeys. They expect personalized recommendations, intuitive product discovery, and engaging digital experiences—all of which generative AI delivers. Shoppers increasingly value convenience and relevance, seeking brands that seem to "know" them. Failing to meet these expectations can lead to customer frustration, abandoned carts, and churn. Retail leaders using AI set the benchmark, and others must follow or risk irrelevance. This is not just about technology but about aligning with evolving human behavior. By embracing generative AI, retailers can meet rising expectations and build stronger, more emotional connections with their customers.

Reshaping Consumer Behavior

Beyond direct business benefits, generative AI is fundamentally reshaping how consumers behave and make purchasing decisions. As people grow accustomed to seamless AI-driven recommendations, virtual try-ons, and conversational shopping assistants, they begin to demand these features everywhere. Tolerance for static, one-size-fits-all experiences quickly diminish. Retailers who fail to integrate AI risk being perceived as outdated or disconnected from modern shopping habits. Those who lead in AI adoption become cultural trendsetters, shaping what "normal" shopping looks like for the next generation. In this sense, AI is not just adapting to consumers it is redefining them. Beyond these immediate benefits, generative AI is changing consumer behavior in a more fundamental way. Customers' patience with generic, unchanging shopping experiences is quickly eroding as they become used to AI-enhanced experiences from retail giants. The question of whether your retail company should use generative AI is no longer relevant. It's how quickly you can incorporate it before your competitive advantage completely evaporates.

Key Benefits: Transforming the Retail Landscape

Personalization at Scale: Creating Unique Customer Experiences

The era in which "personalization" meant slapping a customer's first name in an email is over. The entire personalized retail experience is being reinvented with generative AI. Consider this: 73% of consumers expect that the firms they do business with understand their individual needs. Enter generative AI your best assistant when it comes to all kinds of data that is impossible to gather manually. Major retailers like Sephora and Stitch Fix are using AI to analyze billions of data points everything from browsing history to items left in online shopping carts to build real-time personalization tools capable of being able to suggest convenient products. These systems learn as they go. Each click, purchase and return helps train the AI to get smarter about what each shopper wants, sometimes before the shopper knows it. The numbers back this up too in Table 3.2:

Table 3.2: Different Personalization at Scale.

Personalization Impact	Before GenAI	After GenAI
Conversion Rate	3.2%	7.8%
Cart Value	$64	$103
Return Rate	28%	14%

Operational Efficiency: Cutting Costs While Improving Performance

The margins in retail are extremely thin. The bottom line directly benefits from every penny that is cut out of the operation. In ways that would have seemed like science fiction only a few years ago, generative AI is reducing operating costs. Take Walmart's implementation of generative AI in-store operations, for example. They have put in place mechanisms that:

1. Adjust staff schedules according to anticipated store traffic.
2. Use visual recognition to automatically determine restocking priorities.
3. Schedules for product maintenance that anticipate equipment failure before it occurs.

But it's not just the major players. In order to compete with retail behemoths, small businesses are using inexpensive AI tools:

1. Customer support Chatbots that are truly aware of context
2. Content generation for product descriptions that is automated
3. Real-time dynamic pricing systems that change

According to a Portland boutique owner, "My AI assistant handles customer inquiries around-the-clock, composes my email newsletters, and even assists with inventory order planning." For the cost of a streaming subscription, it would be equivalent to hiring three employees."

Enhanced Decision Making Through Predictive Analytics

Generative AI has transformed decision-making in retail by replacing instinct-driven judgments with data-driven insights. Traditionally, retailers relied on past sales and manual forecasting, which often left them vulnerable to market shifts. Today, AI models analyze thousands of variables simultaneously, from consumer behavior and seasonal patterns to competitor pricing and social media trends. This predictive power allows retailers to anticipate customer demands with remarkable precision, reduce risks, and respond proactively to market changes. By adopting predictive analytics, retailers can optimize promotions, align product offerings with demand, and ultimately make smarter decisions that boost sales and profitability.

Creative Content Generation Without the Agency Price Tag

Marketing creativity in retail has always been expensive, requiring significant budgets for design agencies and production teams. Generative AI is closing this gap by automating creative content generation at scale. Retailers can now instantly create product descriptions, personalized email campaigns, social media posts, website copy, and even promotional visuals—all without agency-level costs. AI tools adapt tone and style to match brand identity while generating fresh, high-quality content faster than humans. This democratizes creativity, enabling smaller retailers to compete with giants. The result is a streamlined marketing process that saves time, reduces costs, and delivers consistent, engaging campaigns.

Streamlined Inventory Management and Supply Chain Optimization

Inventory management has always been a delicate balance in retail—excess stock leads to markdown losses, while shortages result in missed sales. Generative AI is transforming this challenge with predictive precision beyond human forecasting. By analyzing historical sales, consumer trends, supplier performance, and real-time demand signals, AI systems optimize stock levels and reorder points. Additionally, AI enhances supply chain resilience by predicting disruptions and suggesting alternate sourcing strategies. This ensures smoother logistics, reduced carrying costs, and minimized stockouts. Retailers adopting AI-powered inventory management not only achieve operational efficiency but also elevate customer satisfaction through timely product availability.

Real-World Success Stories of Generative AI in Retail

Zara Uses AI to Design New Fashion Collections

Fashion giant Zara is using generative AI to its advantage. Their design team uses AI to analyze billions of social media photos, runway shows, and street-style photos to not only follow trends but also forecast them. "Style Genesis," their AI product, is intended to help fashion designers create new patterns and color schemes that would otherwise take weeks to produce. The crazy thing is that, instead of taking six to nine months as the industry standard, Zara can now go from idea to store in as little as two to three weeks. Their summer collection for 2024. At first, designers weren't sure about the AI's suggestion to revive 70s patterns with contemporary neon accents. 85% of the items in the collection sold out in the first week, making it one of their best-selling collections ever. The designers at Zara are not afraid of their jobs. They are using AI as their creative soul mate instead. "AI takes care of the tedious tasks so our designers can concentrate on adding the human touch that makes fashion art," says Sara Martinez, Head of Design at Zara."

Amazon's AI-Powered Product Description Generator

For their marketplace sellers, Amazon's "Product Prose" AI is revolutionizing the market. Basic product specifications are cleaned up and transformed into persuasive sales copy that makes a sale! Amazon's biggest impact is being felt by small sellers. They would struggle to write engaging copy that would stand out from the clamor of the major brands. The AI now analyzes the best-performing listings in all categories and assists sellers in creating descriptions that are spot-on. Consider Jessica Chen, an Amazon seller of handcrafted jewelry. Her conversion rate increased by 43% in just two months after she shifted to AI-generated descriptions. The AI already knew what language appealed to jewelry buyers and which features to highlight. Nor is the system merely repeating specifications. It is astute enough to draw attention to specific advantages based on the product category, such as comfort and longevity for footwear, taste profiles for consumables, or technical specifications to guide electronics. Amazon claims that AI-written descriptions on its platform even outperform their in-house, manually written descriptions in terms of click-through rates by 27% and conversion rates by about 18%.

Sephora's Virtual Try-On Experience Powered by Generative AI

The "Mirror-AI" virtual try-on tool from Sephora is far superior to those awkward first-generation beauty apps. It creates realistic pictures of how makeup will look on your skin tone, face shape, and in different lighting conditions with the aid of generative AI. Thousands of actual application patterns of every product are applied circularly by this technology, which then precisely modifies them to fit the shape of your face. It's remarkable because it takes into consideration the texture, finish, and coverage of the product aspects that other virtual try-on tools completely overlook. The number of virtual try-ons on Sephora increased 600% during the pandemic, and 42% of online shoppers now use the AI tool. The accuracy is where the true magic lies. 30% of items that were virtually tried on were returned using its previous tool, with the main reason being that they "looked different than expected." That percentage was lowered to 8% by the new AI system. Client Using the app, I tried a burgundy lipstick that I never would have thought of before, wrote Marissa T. I thought it looked great because it matched my skin tone exactly. It was precisely as the AI had shown it to me when I brought it home."

Walmart's Inventory Prediction System Cutting Waste by 30%

The "Stock Sense" AI from Walmart is comparable to the wheel's invention in terms of retail inventory control. The system uses over 300 factors, including the weather, sporting events, social media trends, and, more recently, the popularity of TikTok and its hashtags, to forecast precisely which products will sell at which stores. Due to overstocking, Walmart was throwing away about $3 billion worth of food every year before putting this AI system in place. They reduced food waste by 30% and out-of-stock situations by 16% in the first year of implementation alone. The specificity of the way the AI is adjusted to hyper-local conditions is what makes their method unique. However, when Phoenix experienced a heat wave in 2024, the system automatically changed orders for meat cuts, as well as the most obvious items including fans and bottled water, as well as less obvious ones like some cosmetics and specific frozen meals that have historically sold well in hot weather in that area. The demand for some snack foods decreased by 22% during spring break weeks, whereas craft supplies increased by 35%. The system even identified that stores close to schools required varying inventory levels during these weeks. Store managers, who were initially dubious, now rely heavily on AI. As stated in the newspaper piece, a regional director at Walmart stated: "If our best managers had a crystal ball, they wouldn't know what to order."

Implementation Strategies for Different Retail Segments

E-commerce: Maximizing Online Customer Engagement

Every e-commerce player is aware of just how fiercely competitive the digital shopping market is. Astute retailers are now employing generative AI as a covert tool to break through the clutter. Consider product descriptions. No, nobody wants to read the same boring specifications on every item. Retailers, such as ASOS, are using generative AI to create unique, customized product descriptions that target different customer segments. The outcome? Conversion rates increase by 28% when the descriptions match the browsing habits of the customers. Another revolutionary feature is visual search. Customers can upload images to find similar products with Amazon's implementation. You can take a picture of something you like instead of fumbling with search terms. Then there is the revolution of chatbots. However, we're not here to talk about the obnoxious bots of the past. Using generative AI, Sephora's Beauty Bot suggests skincare and makeup products based on a user's skin type, concerns, and previous purchases. It's similar to carrying around a beauty consultant at all times. AI is also being used by some of the more astute e-commerce companies for dynamic pricing. Based on demand trends, the prices of its competitors, and the quantity of the item in question in stock, Walmart dynamically adjusts its plethora of prices. Their AI analyzes millions of data points every hour to stay competitive and increase margins. There are countless options for personalization. These days, Netflix-style "you might also like" suggestions have evolved into fully customized shopping experiences, with the interface changing entirely according to your actions.

Brick-and-Mortar: Bringing AI to Physical Retail Spaces

Physical retail is simply evolving; it is not dead. And the force behind that change is generative AI. Fitting room smart mirrors are no longer science fiction. Customers can virtually try on various outfits without changing thanks to Macy's Magic Mirror. The AI increases the size of your basket by 59% and suggests related items that match what you're trying on. Additionally, in-store navigation has improved. In contrast, Target's app uses generative AI to create customized shopping routes from your list that lead you through the store and highlight sales that are pertinent to your interests. AI-powered helpers have revolutionized customer service. Lowe's Lowe-Bot collects data on consumer purchasing patterns and inventory requirements in addition to helping customers with product information and directions. The layout of retail stores can be optimized with the help of computer vision-driven heat mapping and traffic analysis. Zara has increased sales of high-margin items by 15% by using this technology to reassign products from within its stores based on real-time customer behavior. Inventory control has also been transformed. Kroger's system reduces waste by 7% and keeps popular products in stock by using AI to predict demand patterns and reorder automatically. These technologies aren't invasive when used properly. Instead of making shopping seem impersonal or robotic, they enhance the experience.

Omnichannel: Creating Seamless Experiences Across Touchpoints

Online and offline boundaries have become indistinguishable. Since they expect the retailer to keep up, today's consumers are channel flippers and don't think twice about it. Starbucks' mobile app got this one right. Your preferences from online ordering, in-store visits, and drive-thru interactions are remembered by its generative AI engine. Even recommendations will be customized according to location, weather, and time of day. Omnichannel strategies that are successful are built on unified customer profiles. Sales representatives can readily access digital browsing history when customers visit Nordstrom's stores thanks to the company's "Customer Journey Analytics" platform, which compiles a 360-degree view of every customer. This resulted in a 23% increase in their cross-channel conversion. Another crucial element is the visibility of inventory across channels. Best Buy's AI-powered system enables features like ship-from-store fulfillment and buy-online-pickup-in-store (BOPIS) by providing real-time inventory status across all locations. Additionally, voice shopping integration is becoming more popular. As AI learns from feedback to add items to the cart via voice command, Walmart and Google Home collaborate to offer voice shopping list capabilities, gradually increasing accuracy. The most successful omnichannel deployments are imperceptible. Instead of thinking, "Oh, I'm switching from mobile to desktop to in-store," customers just shop, and the experience flows naturally.

Luxury Retail: Maintaining Exclusivity While Leveraging AI

Luxury brands face a particularly difficult challenge: how to integrate technology without sacrificing the exclusivity and individualized attention that define luxury shopping. The solution is to use AI to enhance human connections rather than to replace them. The AI-powered system used by Louis Vuitton analyzes consumer information and past purchases before sending the results to sales representatives via discreet tablets. Better insights and a human touch are still provided by the associates. Trying on from home has become more sophisticated. People can try on the newest styles from the runway without taking off their clothes thanks to Burberry's AI mirror. The system offers a futuristic experience that customers share on social media while maintaining the brand's opulent image. The scheduling of appointments has also been disturbed. In addition to scheduling appointments, Tiffany & Co.'s AI analyzes customer profiles to match them with the appropriate associate and generates customized product recommendations beforehand. The scheduling of production has grown increasingly complicated. Gucci uses artificial intelligence (AI) to forecast demand for limited-edition products and strikes the ideal balance between profit and scarcity. This has contributed to an 18% reduction in premium SMU overstock. Anti-counterfeiting and authentication technologies have both revolutionized their respective fields. Chanel's AI-powered blockchain generates a digital certificate of authenticity for customers and ensures product authenticity throughout the supply chain. The greatest luxury retailers use AI in magical rather than mechanical ways, maintaining the human touch that luxury buyers demand while opening up previously unimaginable possibilities.

Key Performance Indicators for Generative AI Projects

Generative AI ROI tracking differs from traditional tech investment tracking. You require specific metrics that demonstrate both immediate benefits and long-term impacts on the company. The best KPIs for GenAI projects in retail are:

Customer Engagement Metrics

Customer engagement metrics are crucial indicators of how effectively generative AI is improving the retail experience. By tracking metrics such as average session duration, click-through rates, and interactions with AI-generated recommendations, companies can assess whether AI-driven personalization resonates with customers. For example, an AI tool generating tailored product suggestions or creating dynamic marketing campaigns should ideally lead to deeper browsing behavior and higher content consumption. Monitoring repeat visits, interaction depth, and time spent on specific AI-powered features helps retailers understand if customers find value in these innovations. Sustained engagement signals improved user satisfaction and stronger brand loyalty over time.

Conversion Rate Changes

Conversion rate is a direct reflection of how generative AI influences customer decision-making. Retailers must measure baseline conversion rates before AI adoption and compare them to post-implementation performance across customer segments. For instance, AI-generated product recommendations, automated copywriting for promotions, or personalized shopping journeys should ideally boost the number of visitors who make purchases. Tracking these shifts segment-wise—such as new versus returning customers helps identify where AI adds the most value. A consistent uplift in conversion rates indicates that AI-generated interventions effectively reduce decision friction and motivate purchases, demonstrating clear ROI in terms of revenue growth and sales optimization.

Content Production Efficiency

Generative AI can drastically reduce the time and cost of content production in retail. By automating the creation of product descriptions, ad copy, newsletters, or promotional visuals, companies save significant resources. Tracking metrics like average turnaround time, labor hours reduced, and budget saved per content batch demonstrates operational efficiency. Retailers can also evaluate scalability—how quickly AI systems can produce thousands of product descriptions without sacrificing quality. Importantly, measuring content accuracy and brand tone alignment ensures that cost savings do not compromise customer trust. Greater efficiency not only lowers expenses but also accelerates time-to-market for campaigns and product launches.

Inventory Optimization Accuracy

Retailers face ongoing challenges with stockouts and overstock situations, both of which impact profitability. Generative AI can improve demand forecasting and inventory planning by analyzing purchasing trends, customer preferences, and seasonal variations. Inventory optimization accuracy should be tracked by measuring reductions in excess stock, fewer out-of-stock events, and higher fulfillment rates. By integrating AI-driven insights with supply chain operations, retailers can better match supply to demand. This ensures smoother logistics, reduced waste, and enhanced customer satisfaction as products remain consistently available. Higher forecast accuracy translates into direct financial gains through minimized holding costs and maximized sales opportunities.

Customer Service Resolution Rates

Generative AI chatbots and virtual assistants are increasingly deployed to enhance customer service. A critical KPI is resolution efficiency measured by average handling time and the proportion of first-contact resolutions. AI-driven support systems should reduce waiting times, provide accurate responses, and resolve common issues without escalating to human agents. Retailers can track improvements in ticket volume handled by AI, customer satisfaction scores post-interaction, and repeat inquiries on the same issue. Faster and more accurate resolutions increase customer trust and loyalty while freeing human agents to handle complex cases. Strong resolution rates indicate AI's role in creating scalable, efficient, and reliable service.

Establishing Realistic Timeframes for Return on Investment

Depending on the size of the project, the time frame for returns can be very different in Table 3.4.

Table 3.4: Key Implementation Types, Timelines, ROI, and Milestones for Generative AI Solutions in Retail.

Implementation Type	Expected ROI Timeline	Key Milestones
Customer-facing chatbots	3-6 months	30% reduction in support tickets within 90 days
Product recommendation engines	6-12 months	15-25% lift in average order value
Visual merchandising AI	9-18 months	Gradual improvement in conversion metrics
Full-scale personalization	12-24 months	Multi-phase improvements across channels

Retailers that experience the fastest returns usually start with targeted, high-impact use cases instead of rolling out the software to the whole company.

Other sectors: Entertainment, education, and beyond

The media and entertainment sector has seen substantial changes as a result of generative AI. It was previously unthinkable to dynamically produce and customize content in the media and entertainment sector. The audience's views on media and entertainment have changed as a result of generative artificial intelligence (AI). Generative AI enables people to create customized content according to the tastes and actions of customers. Here, we'll examine how generative AI is transforming entertainment and media:

Accessing Insights into Audience Preferences

Content-generating generative AI helps creators of all sizes understand what is liked, followed, and repeated by their audience. An excellent example of how artificial intelligence could be used is in the context of determining what type of content should be created or customized for which audiences. An example of this would be a video streaming platform that uses artificial intelligence (AI) and natural language processing to produce content that asks viewers questions and gives them immediate feedback on what they want to watch or do most in their spare time, as well as potential future projects.

Reimagining the Creative Process

The inherent creativity already present in the media and entertainment industries across a range of media can be strengthened and enhanced by generative AI. There is a lot of room for time, money, and effort savings, especially when it comes to repetitive tasks. Beginning with the first steps, such as storyboarding and outlining scripts, generative AI applications can add value at every stage of the creative process. An AI program might, for example, use a prompt template to generate storyboards or examine existing storyboards to recommend changes to the layout, visual narrative, and framing. Consequently, generative AI applications offer opportunities that can include video effects, music orchestration, and even editing, modifying, and replacing recorded dialogue. These opportunities are already expanding as text-to-video generation advances.

Providing Immersive and Interactive Experiences

Virtual reality (VR) and augmented reality (AR) technologies are already being used by businesses in the media and entertainment industries; the addition of generative AI can streamline and improve these initiatives. Artificial Intelligence (AI) technologies, for example, can help users create digital personas that mimic their actions and gestures in real life. This level of personalization and realism enhances the richness and interactivity of VR/AR experiences, making them more realistic and captivating. Media companies can use generative AI to create immersive experiences in the metaverse that combine elements of reality and fantasy. A VR story in which users engage with AI-generated characters is one potential result of this tactic. These artificial intelligence characters will respond to questions, engage in conversations, and even change the plot in response to the user's choices.

Transforming Content Delivery and Consumption

Generative AI is revolutionizing how businesses deliver and consumers engage with content across diverse platforms. From personalized social media posts and immersive videos to in-depth articles, AI ensures scalability while maintaining consistent quality. Companies can now reach targeted consumer groups more effectively, producing content tailored to cultural, demographic, and behavioral insights. This shift helps brands strengthen consumer relationships, expand market presence, and stay competitive. The efficiency of AI-driven workflows reduces time and costs while supporting creative teams in focusing on innovation rather than repetitive tasks. Ultimately, AI is transforming the dynamics of content ecosystems, democratizing creation, and amplifying reach.

AI-Powered Film Production

Film production is undergoing a paradigm shift with generative AI taking center stage. Tools like ChatGPT can generate detailed scripts, dialogues, camera angles, attire, and even nuanced facial expressions, streamlining creative workflows. In the near future, entire movies may be conceptualized, scripted, and partially produced by AI, drastically reducing costs and timelines. While human creativity remains essential, AI provides powerful support in ideation, visualization, and execution. Short films already demonstrate this potential, revealing a promising synergy between human imagination and machine efficiency. This evolution indicates a future where storytelling becomes more accessible, diverse, and experimental, redefining cinematic possibilities worldwide.

AI-Powered Image Generation

Generative models like Stable Diffusion, DALL·E, and Midjourney empower creators to transform simple text prompts into hyper-realistic visuals. In media and entertainment, these images enrich blogs, news articles, advertising campaigns, and social media, bringing ideas to life instantly. By minimizing the costs and time linked with traditional design, AI-generated images enable creators to focus on innovation and storytelling. These visuals also act as raw material for animation and video production, paving the way for AI-generated films and interactive media. Moreover, businesses benefit by producing compelling marketing assets that enhance engagement while maintaining creative freedom, scalability, and global aesthetic appeal.

Content Localization

Generative AI is playing a pivotal role in content localization, ensuring material resonates with diverse global audiences. Beyond mere translation, AI tailors' tone, cultural references, accents, and visual nuances to match regional contexts. Platforms like Magellan TV leverage AI tools such as AWS Polly, Transcribe, and Translate to dub and caption documentaries, extending their reach internationally. In gaming, localization enhances inclusivity by breaking down language barriers and creating immersive experiences for players worldwide. Compared to traditional manual methods, AI-driven localization is faster, scalable, and more cost-effective. Ultimately, it strengthens audience connection, improves retention, and empowers brands to expand globally with ease.

Digital Avatars and Characters

Generative AI enables the creation of lifelike digital avatars and characters, transforming industries like film, gaming, and virtual environments. These AI-driven figures reduce reliance on expensive actors, voice performers, and production teams, making content creation cost-effective and scalable. Avatars are not just realistic but adaptable, capable of responding to audience interactions in real-time. Businesses can craft unique characters for storytelling, marketing, or customer service, enhancing engagement and personalization. However, ethical considerations regarding authenticity and consumer trust remain critical. By adopting the right tools and safeguards, companies can leverage AI avatars to innovate creatively while ensuring responsible practices in entertainment ecosystems.

Education

Personalized Learning & Adaptive Tutors

AI-powered tutoring systems have revolutionized the way students learn by adapting to their individual needs. Platforms such as Khan Academy, Duolingo, and Carnegie Learning use data-driven insights to adjust lessons, exercises, and feedback according to a learner's pace and understanding. These adaptive systems identify strengths and weaknesses, offering targeted practice where it is most needed. This ensures students neither feel overwhelmed nor under-challenged, creating a balanced learning environment. Personalized learning also promotes engagement, motivation, and mastery of concepts by providing interactive and tailored educational journeys. Over time, this fosters independent learning habits and supports long-term academic success.

Reducing Educator Workload

Generative AI tools are easing the burden on educators by automating time-consuming administrative tasks such as grading, attendance tracking, and scheduling. Instead of spending hours on repetitive work, teachers can focus more on interactive instruction, mentorship, and student engagement. Automated grading systems not only provide quick feedback but also ensure consistent evaluation, while digital assistants manage records and lesson planning efficiently. This reduction in workload allows educators to invest more time in designing innovative teaching strategies and supporting students individually. Ultimately, AI serves as an assistant that enhances teaching quality while ensuring teachers maintain control over critical learning outcomes.

AI in Content Creation & Curriculum

AI is transforming curriculum design and content creation in schools. Companies like Prof Jim Inc are developing customized learning materials, including reading passages, videos, and slide decks tailored to specific grade levels. Districts such as Houston ISD are already integrating these AI-generated resources to align with educational objectives and improve classroom engagement. While the benefits include faster resource creation and more diverse content, challenges persist regarding accuracy, inclusivity, and cultural sensitivity. Teachers must review and adapt AI-generated material to ensure quality and relevance. Thus, AI acts as a supportive tool, not a replacement, enhancing creativity in education delivery.

Early AI Exposure & Ethical Learning

With AI becoming integral to daily life, children under 13 are being introduced to it at an early age through schools and at home. Parents and educators emphasize the importance of using AI responsibly, fostering creativity, problem-solving, and critical thinking alongside technical exposure. Early engagement helps young learners understand both the opportunities and limitations of AI. However, this also raises ethical concerns, including privacy, age-appropriate use, and potential biases. Regulatory discussions are increasingly highlighting the need for frameworks to protect children while encouraging innovation. Early exposure, guided by ethics, ensures future generations grow into informed and responsible AI users.

Conclusion

Generative AI is rapidly transforming industries by introducing automation, personalization, and innovation at scale. In content creation and marketing, tools like ChatGPT, Jasper, and Synthesia are enabling brands to generate high-quality text, images, and videos on demand—drastically reducing time and costs. In healthcare, AI models are accelerating drug discovery, synthesizing patient histories, and offering early diagnostic support, enhancing both efficiency and patient outcomes. The finance sector benefits through automated reporting, fraud detection, and risk modeling, reducing human error and increasing analytical depth. In retail and e-commerce, generative AI powers product recommendations, virtual try-ons, and chatbot support—creating hyper-personalized shopping experiences. Beyond these core industries, sectors like entertainment and education are adopting generative tools for scriptwriting, music generation, personalized tutoring, and curriculum design. Despite these advances, challenges remain regarding ethical AI use, data bias, transparency, and the need for human oversight. Overall, generative AI is not just augmenting existing processes—it is redefining how industries innovate, compete, and deliver value. As adoption scales, organizations must focus on responsible deployment, ensuring benefits reach both businesses and society at large.

Exercise Questions

1. What are the key benefits of generative AI in content marketing?
2. Explain how generative AI contributes to drug discovery.
3. Describe how AI is used for risk modeling in the finance sector.
4. How does generative AI personalize user experiences in retail and e-commerce?
5. Name two challenges associated with AI in education.
6. What ethical concerns arise from widespread use of generative AI?
7. Compare the use of generative AI in healthcare vs. finance.
8. How is generative AI transforming entertainment industries like filmmaking or music?
9. Discuss the role of generative AI in automating repetitive tasks.
10. What are the limitations of current generative AI systems?
11. How can businesses ensure responsible use of generative AI?
12. Predict future trends in generative AI across any one sector of your choice.

CHAPTER 4
REDEFINING EFFICIENCY AND ROI WITH GENERATIVE AI

In today's competitive landscape, businesses are under constant pressure to optimize operations, reduce costs, and deliver greater value. Traditional efficiency models—focused on labor optimization, lean management, and automation—are no longer sufficient to keep pace with the exponential growth of data, customer expectations, and market complexity. Generative Artificial Intelligence (Generative AI) has emerged as a transformative force, capable of reshaping efficiency far beyond conventional productivity improvements. By enabling machines to generate content, insights, designs, and even strategic decisions, Generative AI is redefining how organizations perceive and achieve efficiency in the digital era. Return on Investment (ROI) has historically been measured through tangible, incremental gains—such as cost savings, time reductions, or revenue growth. However, with the integration of Generative AI, the ROI framework is expanding. It is no longer limited to operational outputs but extends to creativity, innovation, and scalability. Generative AI systems allow companies to automate complex cognitive tasks, streamline knowledge creation, and deliver personalized customer experiences at scale. The result is not just faster execution but the ability to unlock entirely new revenue streams, reshaping ROI from a linear equation into a multidimensional value network. Unlike earlier waves of automation that primarily replaced repetitive or manual tasks, Generative AI introduces a layer of creative intelligence. It can generate marketing campaigns, design prototypes, draft legal documents, or even compose music—all with human-like fluency. This creative augmentation means efficiency is no longer restricted to "doing things faster" but extends to "doing things differently." The cost-to-value equation is thus redefined: companies are saving resources while simultaneously exploring innovative avenues for growth. This dual function of efficiency and creativity positions Generative AI as a catalyst for unprecedented ROI. Generative AI thrives on data, transforming it from a static resource into a dynamic asset. By analyzing vast and diverse datasets, these models can identify patterns, simulate outcomes, and propose optimized solutions that humans may overlook. This capability translates into predictive efficiency—anticipating customer needs, market shifts, or operational bottlenecks before they occur. From healthcare to finance, industries are using Generative AI to minimize trial-and-error costs, reduce risks, and accelerate decision-making cycles. Consequently, efficiency gains extend beyond operational performance into strategic foresight, creating a compounding effect on ROI. One of the most profound shifts Generative AI introduces is the democratization of personalization. Previously, tailoring experiences or products to individual needs was resource-intensive and economically unfeasible at scale. Generative AI bridges this gap by enabling hyper-personalized solutions—be it customized learning paths in education, adaptive treatment recommendations in healthcare, or individualized shopping experiences in retail. This personalization drives stronger customer engagement, loyalty, and long-term value, all of which directly enhance ROI. Efficiency, therefore, is no longer defined solely by cost minimization but by the ability to create value at scale without proportional resource expansion. Ultimately,

Generative AI compels organizations to rethink efficiency and ROI not as end goals but as dynamic, evolving outcomes. Efficiency is now about amplifying human potential, accelerating innovation, and delivering sustainable value across ecosystems. ROI, in turn, encompasses tangible financial returns, intangible brand equity, and long-term adaptability. By redefining these concepts, Generative AI is not merely a technological tool but a strategic enabler of growth, resilience, and competitive advantage. Businesses that embrace this redefinition will position themselves at the forefront of the next industrial transformation, where efficiency and ROI converge into a new paradigm of intelligent value creation.

Streamlining workflows with AI

Traditional workflow optimization has relied on automation, process redesign, and digitization. Generative AI, however, pushes efficiency beyond task-level automation into knowledge creation, contextual decision-making, and adaptive execution in Figure 4.1. It not only performs repetitive work faster but also redefines how organizations approach problem-solving, creativity, and strategic planning leading to stronger ROI through innovation-driven value creation.

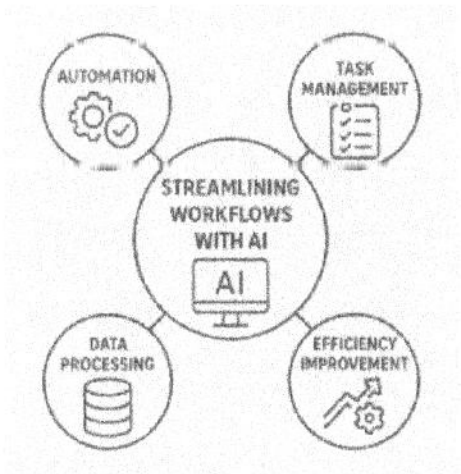

Figure 4.1: Streamlining workflows with AI.

Workflow Streamlining through Generative AI

a) Automating Knowledge Work

Generative AI significantly reduces the burden of repetitive cognitive tasks by automating knowledge work that typically requires hours or even days of effort. For instance, drafting detailed reports, legal contracts, research proposals, and policy documents can be achieved within minutes, ensuring consistency and professional quality. Automated summarization of meetings, emails, and academic articles further accelerates knowledge transfer while minimizing manual note-taking. This automation drastically cuts labor hours and reliance on outsourcing. ROI Impact: Employees regain valuable time to focus on higher-value activities, organizations save on external consulting or drafting services, and overall project cycles are shortened, boosting operational efficiency.

b) Enhancing Creativity and Innovation

Generative AI acts as a powerful catalyst for creativity, enabling organizations to move from ideation to execution at an accelerated pace. AI tools generate product design prototypes, marketing content, and customer experience simulations with remarkable speed and flexibility. In sales, e-learning, and advertising, personalization at scale becomes achievable, enhancing customer engagement. For R&D teams, AI assists in brainstorming, exploring alternative solutions, and simulating scenarios that drive innovation pipelines forward. ROI Impact: Businesses achieve faster time-to-market, capture customer attention more effectively, and establish stronger brand differentiation in competitive markets while continuously fueling a culture of innovation.

c) Process Standardization and Error Reduction

Generative AI enhances process reliability by introducing consistency and minimizing human error across critical workflows. AI-powered coding assistants ensure clean, optimized, and error-free programming. Automated compliance reporting systems generate documents aligned with regulatory frameworks, reducing the risks of non-compliance. Intelligent document classification and workflow routing streamline organizational processes, eliminating delays caused by manual mismanagement. ROI Impact: Companies benefit from fewer rework cycles, reduced error rates, and decreased regulatory penalties. This not only lowers operational costs but also builds stronger stakeholder trust, making processes more scalable and dependable across industries where accuracy is crucial.

d) Data-Driven Decision Support

Generative AI transforms raw datasets into actionable intelligence by automating dashboard creation, scenario simulations, and predictive insights. Executives no longer need to sift through complex numbers; instead, they receive curated insights tailored to departmental needs—finance gains smarter investment forecasts, HR gets workforce planning insights, and operations receive resource optimization strategies. AI simulations test multiple outcomes, helping decision-makers assess risks and opportunities with confidence. ROI Impact: Organizations can allocate resources more effectively, mitigate risks, and make well-informed strategic moves. This ensures smarter investment decisions, enhanced competitiveness, and long-term sustainability powered by data-backed intelligence.

e) Adaptive and Personalized Workflows

Generative AI enables dynamic adaptability by continuously adjusting workflows based on project complexity, deadlines, and resource availability. Employees benefit from personalized learning paths and onboarding experiences supported by AI-driven knowledge tutors. Customers experience hyper-personalized support through AI-powered chatbots and voice agents, ensuring timely and context-aware responses. These adaptive systems evolve alongside organizational needs, enhancing both internal productivity and external service quality. ROI Impact: Businesses achieve higher employee productivity, reduced training costs, and significantly improved customer satisfaction. By aligning workflows with individual requirements, organizations create a flexible ecosystem that drives sustainable growth and resilience.

Redefining ROI with Generative AI

Automating Manual Tasks Reduced Overhead and Labor Costs

Generative AI redefines cost efficiency by automating tasks that traditionally required significant human intervention. Activities like drafting reports, creating designs, processing documents, and even coding snippets can now be performed with minimal human effort. This automation reduces overhead costs, eliminates repetitive administrative workloads, and optimizes employee time for higher-value functions. For businesses, it directly translates into labor cost savings without sacrificing quality. Additionally, automation reduces dependency on outsourcing and lowers the chances of error that often increase rework costs. In essence, generative AI turns fixed operational expenses into scalable, on-demand efficiencies, making organizations leaner, faster, and more productive.

Faster Execution: Quicker Project Turnover and Delivery

Speed is a vital driver of ROI in the AI era. Generative AI tools accelerate processes like content generation, software development, design prototyping, and data analysis, reducing project completion timelines dramatically. What previously required days or weeks of work can often be accomplished in hours. Faster execution enables businesses to handle more projects within the same timeframe, directly boosting revenue and client satisfaction. This increased agility also allows firms to respond quickly to market demands, launch products faster, and capitalize on fleeting opportunities. As time-to-market shrinks, businesses gain a competitive edge while cutting opportunity costs, maximizing tangible financial returns.

Enabling New Products/Services That Didn't Exist Before

Generative AI not only optimizes existing workflows but also opens avenues for innovation by enabling entirely new products and services. For example, personalized digital assistants, AI-powered design tools, automated content platforms, and real-time language translation services have emerged only because of generative AI's capabilities. This indirect ROI is exponential, as businesses can tap into markets that were previously inaccessible. Startups and enterprises alike can prototype faster, experiment with creative offerings, and test disruptive ideas at a fraction of traditional R&D costs. These innovations not only generate fresh revenue streams but also future-proof organizations in rapidly evolving digital ecosystems.

Boosting Creativity and Innovation Pipelines

Generative AI enhances human creativity rather than replacing it. By producing drafts, designs, scenarios, and simulations, it provides a foundation on which employees can build more refined and imaginative outcomes. This collaborative AI-human dynamic boosts innovation pipelines by reducing creative blocks and accelerating idea-to-execution cycles. Teams can experiment with multiple design concepts, marketing campaigns, or product prototypes in parallel, with AI offering variations and refinements instantly. The result is a surge in creativity, broader exploration of possibilities, and reduced R&D cycles. This indirect ROI translates into stronger brand differentiation, customer engagement, and a steady influx of innovation-driven growth.

Strategic ROI (Sustainability & Scale)

Scalability Across Global Teams with Minimal Additional Cost

One of generative AI's most strategic advantages lies in its scalability. Once deployed, AI solutions can serve multiple teams, departments, and geographies simultaneously without proportionally increasing costs. Global organizations can deploy AI chatbots, design tools, or analytics engines to thousands of employees at nearly the same expense as serving a single team. This scalability minimizes duplication of resources, streamlines cross-border collaboration, and ensures consistent quality of output worldwide. By enabling seamless knowledge sharing and execution across teams, generative AI not only reduces marginal costs but also supports sustainable global growth, making it a true long-term ROI multiplier.

Sustainability Gains Through Efficient Resource Utilization

Generative AI contributes significantly to sustainability by optimizing how resources—both digital and physical are used. It reduces paper consumption through automated documentation, minimizes travel with AI-driven virtual collaboration, and optimizes energy consumption in workflows by streamlining computing tasks. In industries like manufacturing and logistics, AI-driven simulations reduce material waste by testing prototypes digitally before production. By cutting down inefficiencies and waste, organizations achieve environmental sustainability alongside financial sustainability. This dual ROI strengthens their corporate social responsibility (CSR) initiatives and brand image while also appealing to eco-conscious customers and stakeholders, making sustainability a tangible component of strategic value creation.

Enhanced Workforce Empowerment: Better Retention and Reduced Attrition Costs

Empowering employees with generative AI tools enhances job satisfaction by eliminating monotonous tasks and allowing them to focus on strategic, creative, and problem-solving activities. Workers equipped with AI support feel more capable and innovative, fostering a culture of empowerment and engagement. This directly reduces attrition costs, as satisfied employees are less likely to leave for other opportunities. Moreover, AI-driven learning assistants can help reskill employees, preparing them for evolving roles within the company. By strengthening retention and lowering recruitment costs, generative AI delivers long-term strategic ROI while simultaneously building a resilient, future-ready workforce aligned with organizational goals.

Key Business Areas Benefiting from Generative AI

The Table 4.1 highlights the prevalence rates, severity levels, and associated risk factors of neck pain observed in turban wearers within the specified age group. It provides a comparative overview of demographic variables, lifestyle influences, and coping strategies, offering valuable insights into how cultural practices intersect with musculoskeletal health. By consolidating the findings in a structured format, the table allows for easier interpretation of patterns, identification of high-risk groups, and recognition of common coping mechanisms. This structured representation serves as a foundation for drawing meaningful conclusions and proposing targeted interventions for preventive and therapeutic strategies.

Table 4.1: Key Findings on the Prevalence and Severity of Neck Pain among Turban Wearers.

Domain	Workflow Streamlined	Efficiency Gains	ROI Outcome
Healthcare	AI-generated medical reports, clinical summaries	60% faster workflows	Better patient throughput
Finance	Automated compliance, fraud	Reduced error rate	Saved regulatory penalties

	detection summaries		
Education	AI-driven tutoring, content generation	Scalable learning	Improved outcomes per student
Manufacturing	AI-based design prototypes, maintenance logs	Faster design cycles	Lower R&D and downtime costs
Marketing & Sales	Personalized campaigns, customer content	Higher engagement	Improved revenue conversion

Challenges and Considerations

Data Quality & Security

AI-generated outputs are only as good as the data they are trained and tested on. Poor-quality, incomplete, or inconsistent data can lead to inaccurate predictions, unreliable recommendations, and flawed decision-making. Ensuring data accuracy, timeliness, and completeness is critical for building trust in AI solutions. Security also plays a vital role—sensitive data must be protected through encryption, access controls, and compliance with privacy laws. Breaches or leaks not only harm individuals but can also damage an organization's reputation. Therefore, organizations must invest in robust data governance frameworks and continuous monitoring to maintain both quality and security in AI systems.

Bias & Compliance Risks

AI models inherit biases present in their training data, which can result in unfair or discriminatory outcomes. For instance, biased recruitment models may favor certain demographics, or healthcare AI may provide unequal recommendations. Such issues not only harm credibility but also pose legal and compliance risks under regulatory frameworks like GDPR or AI-specific guidelines. Transparency, fairness, and explainability are essential in mitigating these challenges. Organizations must implement bias detection tools, conduct regular audits, and ensure adherence to compliance standards. By doing so, they safeguard both ethical integrity and trust while reducing the risk of reputational and legal consequences.

Change Management

The integration of AI into workplaces often disrupts established workflows, requiring careful change management. Employees may fear job displacement, skill redundancy, or lack confidence in using AI tools effectively. Without structured training, workshops, and awareness campaigns, resistance to adoption can slow down implementation and limit the return on investment. Change management strategies should focus on communication, upskilling, and demonstrating AI as an enabler rather than a replacement. Leaders must promote a culture of collaboration where human expertise complements AI capabilities. Effective change management ensures smoother transitions, boosts employee confidence, and creates a supportive environment for AI-driven transformation.

Measuring ROI

Calculating the return on investment (ROI) for AI initiatives goes beyond simple cost savings. While automation reduces operational expenses, true value lies in measuring intangible benefits such as faster decision-making, improved customer experience, and enhanced innovation. A holistic view considers both financial and strategic impacts—like employee productivity gains or risk reduction. Establishing clear KPIs, benchmarking before implementation, and tracking long-term business outcomes are crucial. Organizations must also recognize that AI benefits may compound over time, not immediately. Measuring ROI requires a balance between short-term efficiency metrics and long-term competitive advantages, ensuring AI investments deliver sustainable business value.

Enhancing decision-making through AI-driven insights

In today's hyper-competitive environment, decision-making is no longer just about intuition or past experience. Organizations generate vast amounts of structured and unstructured data—customer interactions, financial transactions, operational logs, and market signals—that hold critical insights. Generative AI (GenAI) brings a transformative layer here: instead of merely analyzing, it interprets, predicts, and recommends. This ability shifts decision-making from reactive to proactive, directly impacting efficiency and Return on Investment (ROI).

AI-Driven Insights: How Generative AI Enhances Decisions

Data Synthesis and Pattern Recognition

Generative AI revolutionizes business intelligence by integrating data from diverse silos—finance, HR, operations, and customer service into a unified analytical framework. Unlike traditional BI tools, GenAI identifies subtle, nonlinear relationships and cross-functional patterns that humans or legacy systems might overlook. For example, linking customer complaints with sudden dips in sales and external market shifts can reveal hidden operational inefficiencies or unmet product needs. This synthesis supports proactive forecasting, sharper risk detection, and evidence-based strategy formulation. The impact is profound: organizations transition from reactive decision-making to predictive and strategic foresight, leading to competitive advantage and long-term resilience.

Scenario Simulation and Predictive Modeling

Generative AI enhances decision-making through sophisticated scenario simulation and predictive modeling capabilities. Unlike conventional forecasting methods, GenAI can generate multiple "what-if" analyses, testing business strategies against a wide range of possible futures. For instance, a retail company can explore how adjusting pricing strategies or reconfiguring supply chain routes will influence profit margins, customer loyalty, and inventory flow. By creating these dynamic simulations, leaders gain actionable insights into potential risks and opportunities before committing resources. This reduces uncertainty, minimizes costly mistakes, and empowers decision-makers to innovate with confidence, making business planning both agile and resilient in volatile environments.

Real-Time Decision Support

One of the most transformative applications of Generative AI lies in real-time decision support. By continuously processing live data streams—ranging from IoT sensors and logistics feeds to customer interaction data—GenAI delivers instantaneous insights. It can detect anomalies, predict disruptions, or recommend timely interventions. For example, in manufacturing, the system may flag machine performance deviations early, allowing preventive adjustments before downtime occurs. In retail, it might suggest stock adjustments during demand surges. This immediacy enhances operational efficiency, reduces waste, and boosts responsiveness. The result is a data-driven, always-on decision-making capability that strengthens adaptability and ensures sustained business performance.

Contextual and Personalized Insights

Generative AI goes beyond generic analytics by delivering contextual and role-specific insights tailored to business needs. It achieves this by merging internal enterprise data with external knowledge sources such as market trends, competitor strategies, and evolving regulatory frameworks. For example, marketing managers may receive targeted recommendations for campaign optimization, while finance leaders access predictive cash flow analytics rooted in real-time market dynamics. This personalization ensures insights are not only accurate but also directly actionable for each stakeholder. The outcome is faster decision-making, reduced reliance on guesswork, and more confident leadership across departments, fostering innovation and operational excellence simultaneously.

Redefining Efficiency with Generative AI

Generative AI (GenAI) is fundamentally reshaping how organizations perceive and achieve efficiency. Traditionally, efficiency meant doing the same work faster or with fewer resources. However, GenAI redefines efficiency by changing the very nature of the work being done. Instead of spending hours compiling, organizing, and analyzing data, AI systems can autonomously generate reports, provide actionable insights, and even recommend strategies. This shift empowers employees and leaders to focus on high-value tasks such as decision-making, innovation, and execution. By automating cognitive tasks once thought exclusive to human expertise, GenAI transforms efficiency from speed optimization to outcome maximization.

Automating Knowledge Work

One of the most immediate and impactful benefits of GenAI lies in automating knowledge-intensive tasks. Activities like preparing summaries, creating detailed reports, and drafting recommendations often consume significant employee time. GenAI tools can now perform these functions in minutes, analyzing large datasets, extracting key insights, and presenting them in clear, structured formats. Managers and employees no longer need to spend hours compiling or validating information; instead, they can dedicate their energy to interpreting results and making strategic decisions. This reduces bottlenecks in workflows, enhances productivity, and shifts knowledge work from labor-intensive compilation to insight-driven action.

Streamlined Workflows

Enterprises often face inefficiencies due to complex approval chains, repeated document reviews, and compliance-heavy processes. Generative AI integrates seamlessly with enterprise platforms like ERP and CRM systems to address these challenges. For example, GenAI can automatically review contracts, highlight risks, generate compliant documents, or even trigger approvals based on predefined criteria. Similarly, financial risk assessments or procurement approvals can be handled in minutes rather than days. This end-to-end automation not only reduces process delays but also minimizes human error. Organizations gain measurable efficiency by accelerating decision-making pipelines, allowing teams to achieve more in significantly less time.

Enhanced Collaboration

Cross-functional collaboration often suffers due to fragmented data, inconsistent understanding of metrics, and communication barriers. GenAI addresses these challenges by acting as an intelligent copilot. It can create interactive dashboards, simplify complex analytics into plain language, and ensure that stakeholders across departments share a common understanding of business performance. Moreover, GenAI fosters inclusivity in discussions by providing context on demand, enabling both technical and non-technical team members to participate effectively. The efficiency gain is substantial: meetings become more outcome-focused, teams align more quickly, and projects advance without the delays caused by miscommunication or lack of clarity.

Redefining ROI with Generative AI

The Figure 4.2 compares traditional ROI (Return on Investment) metrics with a redefined ROI perspective powered by Generative AI. Traditionally, ROI is measured primarily through cost reduction and productivity gains, focusing on efficiency and operational savings. In this model, innovation and customer experience often receive lower priority, as they are harder to quantify in the short term. However, with the integration of Generative AI, ROI is redefined to place greater emphasis on innovation, customer experience, and revenue growth. Generative AI enables businesses to create new products faster, deliver hyper-personalized services, and explore novel market opportunities, which drives higher long-term value. While cost reduction and productivity improvements remain part of the equation, they are now complemented by strategic and creative outcomes that expand the overall business impact. This shift reflects a transformational approach where ROI is no longer just about saving money but about unlocking new revenue streams, enhancing user engagement, and maintaining a competitive edge in rapidly evolving markets.

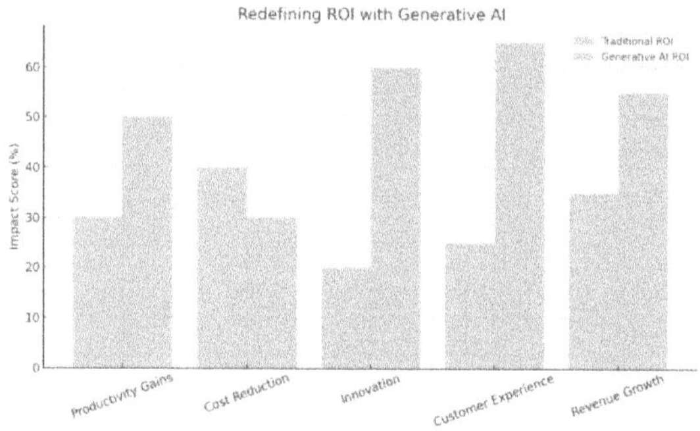

Figure 4.2: Redefining ROI with Generative AI.

Faster Time-to-Decision

Generative AI (GenAI) redefines the speed of decision-making by transforming how businesses derive insights. Traditional analytics workflows often require weeks of data collection, cleansing, and analysis before actionable outcomes emerge. In contrast, GenAI models can analyze complex datasets in near real time, uncovering patterns and recommendations almost instantly. This accelerates the ability of organizations to pivot, respond to market shifts, or adapt strategies as situations evolve. The return on investment (ROI) becomes evident through reduced latency in decision cycles, enabling companies to seize opportunities faster, outpace competitors, and enhance agility in highly dynamic business environments.

Cost Optimization

One of the strongest ROI levers of GenAI lies in its ability to optimize costs across operations. By leveraging predictive analytics, organizations can anticipate demand fluctuations, streamline supply chains, and allocate resources with precision. AI-driven insights help minimize overproduction, reduce wastage, and lower inventory carrying costs. In addition, automation of repetitive tasks reduces manual labor expenses while maintaining accuracy and efficiency. These savings translate directly into higher profit margins and smarter capital utilization. Instead of reactive adjustments, businesses adopt proactive optimization strategies, ensuring every dollar spent contributes effectively toward achieving objectives. GenAI thus turns cost reduction into a competitive advantage.

Revenue Growth

GenAI plays a pivotal role in unlocking new avenues for revenue growth. It empowers businesses to discover untapped markets, forecast emerging consumer trends, and craft hyper-personalized offerings. By analyzing customer data at scale, AI enables dynamic pricing, targeted recommendations, and tailored content delivery that enhance customer satisfaction and loyalty. This personalized engagement fosters deeper relationships, improving retention rates while simultaneously attracting new customers. Furthermore, GenAI aids in product innovation by generating ideas, simulations, and prototypes aligned with consumer preferences. The ROI impact is tangible: expanded revenue streams, increased market share, and sustainable business growth driven by AI-enabled differentiation strategies.

Risk Reduction

Mitigating risks is central to safeguarding ROI, and GenAI excels in building proactive defense mechanisms. AI-powered early warning systems can detect anomalies, predict fraud attempts, and flag compliance issues before they escalate. By continuously monitoring operations, transactions, and external conditions, GenAI minimizes exposure to financial losses, reputational damage, and regulatory penalties. Automated risk models enhance resilience by ensuring organizations remain vigilant against evolving threats. Whether in financial services, healthcare, or supply chain management, the predictive capacity of GenAI strengthens trust among stakeholders. The ROI impact manifests as reduced liabilities, preserved reputation, and greater stability, ensuring long-term sustainability in volatile markets. Mitigating risks is central to safeguarding ROI, and GenAI excels in building proactive defense mechanisms. AI-powered early warning systems can detect anomalies, predict fraud attempts, and flag compliance issues before they escalate. By continuously monitoring operations, transactions, and external conditions, GenAI minimizes exposure to financial losses, reputational damage, and regulatory penalties. Automated risk models enhance resilience by ensuring organizations remain vigilant against evolving threats. Whether in financial services, healthcare, or supply chain management, the predictive capacity of GenAI strengthens trust among stakeholders. The ROI impact manifests as reduced liabilities, preserved reputation, and greater stability, ensuring long-term sustainability in volatile markets.

Example Use Cases

Healthcare

Artificial Intelligence is transforming healthcare through AI-driven diagnostics, enabling doctors to make faster and more accurate decisions. By analyzing medical imaging, lab reports, and patient histories, AI systems detect early signs of diseases such as cancer, heart disorders, and neurological conditions. This reduces unnecessary diagnostic tests, lowers overall costs, and minimizes patient exposure to invasive procedures. AI also personalizes treatment by predicting patient-specific outcomes, ensuring targeted therapies. Beyond diagnosis, AI-powered chatbots and virtual assistants streamline patient queries and appointment scheduling, improving hospital efficiency. Ultimately, AI enhances patient care quality while enabling health providers to allocate resources more effectively.

Finance

In finance, AI is a game changer, especially in fraud detection and risk management. Traditional manual reviews are slow and prone to human error, but AI-driven fraud detection models analyze millions of transactions in real time to identify anomalies and suspicious patterns. These predictive systems trigger alerts faster than human analysts, preventing fraudulent activities before they escalate. Additionally, AI optimizes algorithmic trading, portfolio management, and credit scoring, ensuring better financial planning for institutions and individuals. By automating compliance checks, banks reduce regulatory risks. Overall, AI enhances trust, saves millions in losses, and empowers financial institutions with smarter, data-driven decision-making.

Manufacturing

Manufacturing industries benefit immensely from AI through predictive maintenance, which significantly lowers machine downtime and increases operational efficiency. AI systems analyze sensor data from equipment, detecting wear and tear patterns before failures occur. This proactive approach prevents costly breakdowns, reduces repair expenses, and extends machine life. Additionally, AI optimizes supply chains by forecasting demand, monitoring inventory, and identifying bottlenecks in production. Robotics powered by AI ensures precision, speed, and safety in assembly lines, minimizing human errors. Quality control is also enhanced with computer vision systems that identify defects in real time. The result is improved productivity, reduced waste, and higher profitability.

Retail

AI is revolutionizing retail by creating personalized shopping experiences for customers. Advanced recommendation systems analyze browsing behavior, past purchases, and preferences to suggest products, increasing both conversion rates and average order value. Retailers leverage AI-powered chatbots for 24/7 customer service, ensuring quick responses and boosting satisfaction. Inventory management also improves as AI forecasts demand and automates restocking processes, reducing overstock and shortages. In physical stores, AI enhances experiences with smart checkouts, facial recognition for loyalty programs, and dynamic pricing strategies. Personalized promotions foster customer loyalty, while predictive analytics help businesses understand evolving trends, enabling them to stay ahead in a competitive market.

Strategic Implications

Efficiency Redefined

Generative AI introduces a new dimension to efficiency by automating complex, time-consuming tasks while ensuring higher levels of accuracy and personalization. Unlike traditional automation, which focuses on repetitive rule-based processes, GenAI can handle nuanced decision-making, content generation, and adaptive learning at scale. This not only saves time and reduces costs but also frees employees to focus on high-value creative and strategic work. Efficiency is therefore redefined not just faster processes but smarter ones. Organizations leveraging GenAI see productivity gains ripple across departments, leading to more agile workflows, reduced bottlenecks, and greater alignment between resources and outcomes.

ROI Beyond Cost and Revenue

Traditional ROI calculations primarily emphasize cost reduction and revenue growth. However, Generative AI broadens this equation by introducing intangible yet critical value drivers. For instance, the ability to generate new ideas, improve customer engagement, and unlock creative possibilities becomes part of ROI measurement. The return is not just financial it encompasses improved decision-making, faster problem-solving, and innovation-led growth. Businesses can now quantify ROI by looking at productivity hours saved, knowledge creation, and even cultural transformation. This reimagined ROI framework helps organizations justify AI investments by highlighting long-term, holistic benefits alongside immediate monetary gains.

Agility as a Core Return

Agility, once seen as a qualitative advantage, is now measurable through Generative AI's impact. The technology enables businesses to adapt swiftly to changing market demands, customer preferences, and competitive pressures. AI-driven simulations, rapid prototyping, and dynamic content generation shorten response times and reduce reliance on lengthy planning cycles. This agility ensures businesses can experiment faster, pivot strategies with confidence, and seize fleeting opportunities. Measured as ROI, agility translates into reduced time-to-market, enhanced responsiveness, and minimized opportunity costs. In fast-moving industries, agility powered by GenAI is not optional it is a central return that directly drives competitiveness.

Building Resilience

Generative AI strengthens organizational resilience by anticipating risks, creating adaptive scenarios, and enhancing preparedness. For example, AI models can simulate disruptions in supply chains, economic downturns, or customer behavior shifts, enabling proactive strategies. Resilience as ROI means reducing vulnerabilities that could otherwise lead to financial and reputational losses. When disruptions occur, businesses equipped with GenAI can recover faster, maintain service continuity, and sustain customer trust. This resilience does not appear as direct revenue but is invaluable in safeguarding long-term stability. In effect, GenAI transforms resilience into a measurable and strategic component of ROI.

Innovation Capacity

One of the most profound ROI shifts with Generative AI is its role in unlocking innovation capacity. AI enables ideation at scale designing new products, creating marketing strategies, and solving complex challenges beyond human speed or scope. Innovation capacity as ROI is reflected in patents filed, new markets entered, or novel customer experiences delivered. It becomes an engine for continuous growth rather than a sporadic effort. Businesses leveraging GenAI are not only optimizing existing processes but also generating entirely new opportunities. This innovation-driven ROI positions companies to lead their industries rather than merely compete within them.

Real-world examples of ROI boosts from Generative AI

Highlighted Real-World ROI Examples

Grant Thornton & EY (Consulting Firms)

Consulting giants Grant Thornton and EY have demonstrated tangible productivity gains through generative AI. At Grant Thornton, Microsoft Copilot helped employees save an average of 7.5 hours per week, or nearly 50 minutes per day. Tasks like drafting emails, summarizing documents, and formatting reports were automated, freeing professionals for higher-value consulting activities. EY's initiative, branded as "EY.ai," empowered 5300 Oceania-based employees to save about 30 minutes weekly. Across both firms, productivity improved by roughly 20%, with close to 40% of repetitive tasks automated. These measurable benefits highlight how generative AI can redefine consulting efficiency, reduce administrative overhead, and allow firms to allocate more resources toward client-focused strategies that directly enhance revenue streams.

Headway (EdTech Startup)

Headway, a Ukrainian edtech platform, strategically integrated generative AI tools like Midjourney for creative visuals and HeyGen for video generation. This adoption revolutionized its video advertising campaigns, leading to a remarkable 40% boost in ROI. With AI-driven ad production, Headway not only optimized costs but also produced at a scale previously unattainable. In early 2024, the startup achieved 3.3 billion ad impressions, significantly strengthening its global digital presence. For a rapidly growing edtech business, this success illustrates how AI can enhance brand storytelling, increase reach, and achieve measurable financial outcomes. Headway's example underscores the transformative role of generative AI in marketing strategies for startups, proving that creative automation can deliver exponential business impact.

Grind (Coffee Retailer, Small Business Trial)

Grind, a coffee retailer participating in Google's AI pilot program, showcased how generative AI can empower small businesses. By applying AI tools in marketing campaigns, customer query handling, and business reporting, Grind tapped into efficiencies usually reserved for large corporations. Early insights revealed the potential for up to a 20% productivity increase, a substantial gain for an SME where resources are limited. AI-driven responses improved customer engagement, while automated reporting reduced operational strain on staff. For businesses like Grind, such improvements can directly translate into higher margins, better customer loyalty, and long-term scalability. This trial demonstrates how generative AI can be a true equalizer, giving small retailers a competitive edge in resource-intensive markets.

GitHub Copilot (Developer Productivity)

GitHub Copilot has emerged as a game-changer in software development productivity. In a controlled study, developers using Copilot completed coding tasks 55.8% faster than peers working without AI assistance. By suggesting context-aware code snippets, optimizing syntax, and reducing debugging cycles, Copilot drastically cut down on repetitive coding time. The tool acts like a virtual pair programmer, enabling developers to focus more on logic, creativity, and system design rather than boilerplate code. Beyond time savings, this efficiency can reduce project costs, accelerate product delivery timelines, and enhance developer satisfaction. Copilot's impact illustrates how AI is reshaping the software industry, transforming workflows, and directly contributing to higher ROI in engineering-intensive environments.

Syntea (AI-Powered Tutoring in Education)

In education, Syntea has demonstrated how AI-driven tutoring accelerates learning outcomes. University students using Syntea in distance learning settings reduced their overall study time by approximately 27%. The platform leverages generative AI to provide personalized explanations, adaptive learning paths, and instant feedback, which cut down redundant study efforts. Instead of one-size-fits-all lessons, Syntea tailors support to individual student needs, making study more efficient and effective. The time saved translates into both academic and personal gains for students, who can achieve the same outcomes in less time. For institutions, integrating such AI solutions can improve graduation rates, enhance satisfaction, and reduce instructional costs—showing education's potential ROI when adopting personalized generative AI technologies.In education, Syntea has demonstrated how AI-driven tutoring accelerates learning outcomes. University students using Syntea in distance learning settings reduced their overall study time by approximately 27%. The platform leverages generative AI to provide personalized explanations, adaptive learning paths, and instant feedback, which cut down redundant study efforts. Instead of one-size-fits-all lessons, Syntea tailors support to individual student needs, making study more efficient and effective. The time saved translates into both academic and personal gains for students, who can achieve the same outcomes in less time. For institutions, integrating such AI solutions can improve graduation rates, enhance satisfaction, and reduce instructional costs—showing education's potential ROI when adopting personalized generative AI technologies.

Broader Industry Insights & ROI Metrics

Generative AI has transitioned from experimental adoption to mainstream business value, delivering measurable ROI across industries. Early use cases demonstrate efficiency in automation, cost reduction, and employee productivity gains. Industry surveys consistently highlight that companies investing early in generative AI achieve faster returns compared to those lagging behind. The impact is not confined to one sector—it extends across development, IT operations, customer service, procurement, HR, finance, and manufacturing. Organizations are increasingly leveraging Gen AI to streamline workflows, automate documentation, enhance personalization, and drive decision-making through intelligent data insights. The broader consensus is clear: generative AI is more than a trend—it is a high-yield transformation tool reshaping business operation globally.

Snowflake Survey

According to a Snowflake survey of 3,300+ organizations, early adopters of generative AI achieved an average ROI of 41%, with 92% reporting positive returns. These results illustrate how AI delivers value rapidly across multiple business domains. Benefits are evident in software development (accelerating code generation and testing), IT operations (predictive maintenance and system monitoring), customer service (chatbots and personalized responses), procurement (automated supplier management), HR (resume screening and employee engagement), and manufacturing (quality control and predictive analytics). The survey reinforces that companies using AI strategically are moving beyond proof-of-concepts into scalable solutions. Importantly, the consistency of positive ROI across industries demonstrates that generative AI is not sector-specific but universally adaptable.

IDC (Microsoft-sponsored)

An IDC report sponsored by Microsoft revealed that generative AI provides an impressive 3.7× return for every dollar invested. This ROI multiplier positions Gen AI as one of the most lucrative technology investments available today. The industries deriving the greatest benefits include Financial Services (fraud detection, risk modeling), Media & Telecommunications (personalized content, automated editing), Mobility (autonomous systems, route optimization), Retail (personalized recommendations, demand forecasting), Energy (smart grid analytics, predictive safety), Manufacturing (supply chain automation, design optimization), Healthcare (diagnostics, documentation), and Education (adaptive learning platforms, grading automation). This broad adoption highlights that generative AI not only enhances efficiency but also creates new revenue streams. Such high returns signal a paradigm shift in enterprise value creation.

Google Cloud Survey

The Google Cloud generative AI survey found that 74% of organizations already see ROI from Gen AI adoption. More strikingly, 45% reported employee productivity at least doubled, showcasing how automation and AI augmentation free employees to focus on higher-value tasks. Furthermore, 85% observed stronger user engagement thanks to enhanced user experiences such as smarter chatbots, personalized interfaces, and intuitive recommendation systems. These statistics emphasize how Gen AI influences both internal efficiency and external customer satisfaction. By improving operational agility and strengthening customer trust, organizations are creating competitive advantages. The Google Cloud findings demonstrate that adoption is not just about cost savings—it is about amplifying productivity and engagement simultaneously.

Google Cloud ROI Summary

In addition to its survey findings, Google Cloud's ROI summary revealed that 84% of organizations successfully deployed Gen AI use cases into production within six months—a sign of rapid adoption speed. Moreover, 74% reported measurable ROI, and among those, 86% experienced annual revenue growth of 6% or more attributed directly to generative AI. These numbers suggest that Gen AI is not just an experimental tool but a scalable engine for revenue expansion. Quick conversion from concept to production is driving faster returns, while continuous improvements to AI systems amplify growth. The ability to accelerate deployment cycles while achieving top-line growth underscores why generative AI has become a boardroom priority for global enterprises.

KPMG Survey & CFO Sentiment

A KPMG survey revealed that 78% of executives in companies with $1B+ revenue expect tangible ROI from generative AI within 1–3 years, underlining high confidence among decision-makers. Key use cases include inventory management (AI-driven demand forecasts), healthcare documentation (automated clinical notes), and workflow automation (streamlining repetitive tasks). Complementing this, PYMNTS Intelligence CFO Sentiment data shows that nearly 90% of CFOs reported very positive ROI from Gen AI within just nine months, a sharp rise from only 27% earlier in the year. This dramatic shift demonstrates accelerating confidence as real results materialize. CFOs, traditionally cautious about ROI claims, are now among the strongest advocates for AI, proving that financial leadership sees direct value creation in AI investments.

ROI of Generative AI: Measuring its impact and value for any businesses

One of the most dynamic subfields of artificial intelligence (AI) that deals with the creation of content instantly is generative AI, or GenAI. Text-based content, pictures, videos, audio, and even music are all considered content in Figure 4.3. Additionally, companies in a variety of industries are progressively integrating cutting-edge GenAI services and apps into their digital ecosystem. The motivation behind adopting GenAI is to become one of the "early adopters" and enjoy the many advantages that these individuals frequently enjoy. To begin with, determining the business impact is a difficult task. AI isn't a magic bullet, though. It calls for integration, training, and technological investment. Businesses must therefore have a well-defined plan in place to gauge its effects. To ascertain whether Generative AI is yielding tangible benefits, key performance indicators (KPIs) such as cost reduction, revenue growth, efficiency enhancements, and customer satisfaction are used.

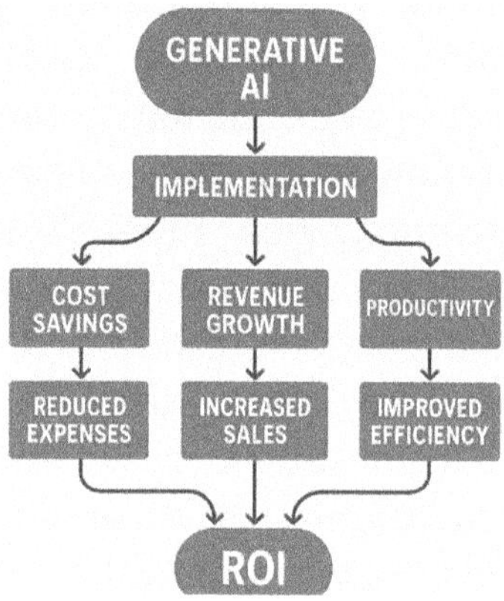

Figure 4.3: Flow chart on ROI of Generative AI to measuring its impact and value for any businesses.

Key factors driving the adoption of Generative AI

It is safe to say that generative AI technology is here to stay, given the extraordinary growth this field has experienced over the last two to three years. Here are the factors influencing its explosive growth across industries:

The Need for Increased Automation and Efficiency

One of the strongest drivers behind Generative AI adoption is the growing demand for automation and streamlined efficiency. Businesses today aim to reduce repetitive, manual tasks and accelerate workflows, which directly impacts productivity and profitability. Generative AI tools such as GitHub Copilot exemplify this shift by enabling developers to write cleaner, optimized code more quickly. The automation extends beyond software development into areas like content generation, marketing, and customer service, where GenAI can produce first drafts, suggest improvements, and respond to queries instantly. By embedding AI into critical workflows, companies save time, reduce operational costs, and minimize human errors. This efficiency ultimately enhances competitiveness, allowing organizations to bring better digital products and services to market faster.

Increased Computing Power

The exponential improvement in computing power has unlocked Generative AI's true potential. Advanced hardware like Graphics Processing Units (GPUs) and Tensor Processing Units (TPUs) have made it possible to train deep learning models with billions of parameters, something that was unimaginable a decade ago. This computational leap allows models to process massive datasets, generate human-like outputs, and adapt across multiple domains such as text, images, video, and audio. The scalability of cloud computing further complements this growth, enabling organizations of all sizes to access high-performance infrastructure on demand. These technological advancements not only reduce training times but also improve the accuracy, sophistication, and accessibility of generative models. In essence, computing power acts as the backbone that sustains GenAI's rapid advancement.

Seamless Integration into Business Workflows

Another key factor driving GenAI adoption is its ease of integration with existing business systems. Unlike earlier disruptive technologies that required heavy restructuring, Generative AI tools often embed seamlessly into current workflows, ensuring minimal downtime. For instance, conversational AI agents like Sierra can be directly integrated into websites to engage with customers, providing a more personalized and adaptive interaction compared to traditional chatbots. These tools learn from user behavior and past interactions, making them more intelligent over time. Businesses appreciate that GenAI solutions don't require exhaustive onboarding or retraining processes—employees can begin using them almost instantly. This frictionless adoption lowers barriers for companies across industries, allowing even smaller organizations to leverage AI for customer support, operations, and innovation without significant restructuring.

Market Demand and Investment are Growing

The momentum of Generative AI is further fueled by market demand and significant investments from enterprises, venture capitalists, and technology giants. As industries realize the transformative potential of GenAI in driving innovation, enhancing customer engagement, and creating new revenue streams, they are rapidly channeling resources into adoption. Forecasts suggest exponential growth of the GenAI market over the next decade, spanning applications in healthcare, finance, education, and entertainment. Companies view GenAI not just as a supportive tool but as a core technology that can secure a competitive edge. This investor confidence accelerates research, development, and deployment, creating a reinforcing cycle of innovation and adoption. The collective belief in GenAI's long-term value ensures its establishment as a cornerstone of digital transformation.

Focus on Productivity

At its core, Generative AI is about augmenting human productivity. By handling labor-intensive and time-consuming tasks such as drafting documents, analyzing data, designing creative content, or generating code snippets, GenAI frees employees to focus on high-value, strategic responsibilities. This shift doesn't just save time—it enhances the quality of decision-making, innovation, and problem-solving within organizations. Productivity gains are especially visible in knowledge-driven sectors, where professionals can rely on AI to generate quick insights or create prototypes rapidly. The outcome is a workforce that spends less time on mundane tasks and more on areas requiring human judgment, empathy, and creativity. This reallocation of human effort drives both job satisfaction and organizational performance, making productivity a central factor in GenAI adoption.

Generative AI helps (Think ROI)

Implementing GenAI apps and systems leads to increased automation, collaboration, and efficiency. Here are some of the areas where you can harness the power of GenAI and achieve great ROI.

Operational efficiency & cost savings

GenAI technology helps significantly with process or task automation and improves productivity. Some common use-cases include the following:

Automated Reports

Generative AI drastically reduces the time and effort needed to prepare detailed reports by analyzing massive datasets in seconds. Instead of manually cleaning data, applying formulas, and designing charts, AI can automatically structure insights, highlight trends, and even suggest strategic recommendations. This not only minimizes human error but also enables decision-makers to act on real-time data without delay. For example, sales teams can receive automated performance dashboards daily, and financial departments can generate expense breakdowns instantly. The result is faster reporting, higher accuracy, and significant savings in both workforce hours and operational costs.

Email Assistance

Drafting, reviewing, and refining emails can consume a surprising amount of employee time. Generative AI tools streamline this process by helping professionals quickly draft contextually relevant and polished emails. Whether it is responding to client queries, drafting proposals, or refining internal communications, AI ensures clarity, tone alignment, and efficiency. Employees save time by focusing on content quality rather than formatting or grammar. Moreover, AI tools can also summarize long email chains, extract action items, and suggest quick replies. This increases productivity, reduces communication delays, and helps organizations handle larger volumes of correspondence without increasing headcount.

AI-Assisted Coding

For software developers, Generative AI acts as a highly efficient coding partner. It can generate entire code blocks, debug errors, suggest optimal algorithms, and even refactor legacy code for improved performance. Instead of spending hours troubleshooting syntax issues or searching documentation, developers can rely on AI assistance to speed up the process. This leads to faster project delivery, lower development costs, and reduced risk of bugs reaching production. Companies benefit by shortening their product release cycles, innovating more rapidly, and ensuring better software quality. In terms of ROI, AI-assisted coding can save hundreds of developer hours annually, freeing resources for innovation.

Elevated Customer Experience (CX)

The foundation of modern business success lies in delivering an elevated customer experience (CX). Artificial intelligence has redefined how organizations interact with their clients by enabling real-time, personalized, and seamless communication. AI-powered chatbots, virtual assistants, and recommendation engines make each interaction faster, more relevant, and more convenient. Unlike traditional systems, these AI solutions are not limited by time zones or working hours, ensuring consistent service delivery. As a result, customers feel valued and supported, which strengthens loyalty and trust. Businesses adopting AI for CX not only differentiate themselves in competitive markets but also create long-term brand advocacy.

Increased Customer Engagement Levels

AI agents like Sierra, built on Agentic AI models, are transforming engagement by automating a significant portion of customer service tasks. These intelligent agents can converse naturally with customers across multiple digital channels—whether via websites, messaging platforms, or social media. They provide instant responses, escalate issues when necessary, and ensure customers always feel acknowledged. By functioning 24/7, they remove the barriers of traditional customer support, where delays often frustrate users. With AI continuously learning from interactions, businesses benefit from deeper insights into customer preferences and pain points. The outcome is higher engagement levels, more satisfied customers, and reduced operational costs.

Improved Net Promoter Score (NPS)

The Net Promoter Score (NPS) is a vital metric that reflects customer loyalty and willingness to recommend a brand. AI-driven chatbots and service assistants significantly contribute to improving NPS by creating more meaningful customer touchpoints. These tools offer proactive support, personalized problem-solving, and empathetic communication, which make customers feel valued and included. Businesses can also analyze conversational data to identify service gaps and take corrective actions quickly. As AI ensures consistency, accuracy, and responsiveness, customers are more likely to share positive experiences. Over time, this results in a higher NPS, reflecting stronger brand advocacy and sustainable business growth.

Better Conversions

Customer engagement and satisfaction directly pave the way for higher conversions. When potential buyers receive personalized recommendations and instant support, they are more inclined to trust the brand and complete their purchase journey. AI systems can analyze customer intent, suggest relevant products or services, and remove friction points, leading to shorter sales cycles. Moreover, satisfied customers are more likely to become repeat buyers, creating a compounding effect on revenue. By converting more leads into paying customers, organizations see a measurable improvement in their bottom line. Thus, AI not only enhances interactions but also drives tangible financial performance Customer engagement and satisfaction directly pave the way for higher conversions. When potential buyers receive personalized recommendations and instant support, they are more inclined to trust the brand and complete their purchase journey. AI systems can analyze customer intent, suggest relevant products or services, and remove friction points, leading to shorter sales cycles. Moreover, satisfied customers are more likely to become repeat buyers, creating a compounding effect on revenue. By converting more leads into paying customers, organizations see a measurable improvement in their bottom line. Thus, AI not only enhances interactions but also drives tangible financial performance.

Innovation & competitive-edge

The way GenAI helps teams think more clearly and create better products is one area where it has had a significant impact. Teams are freed from monotonous work by increased automation and intelligence, which frees up more time and energy for them to contribute truly valuable work. Businesses are able to decrease human error and introduce new goods and services more quickly, which ultimately gives them a competitive edge. Among the many areas in which GenAI can be extremely beneficial are:

Rapid Prototyping

Generative AI has redefined the speed and quality of rapid prototyping. Traditionally, designers and product managers would spend weeks brainstorming, sketch wireframes, and testing early concepts. Now, AI-powered tools accelerate this process by generating multiple iterations of ideas within minutes. Teams can feed in design prompts, requirements, or even rough sketches, and GenAI produces sophisticated prototypes aligned with business goals. This shortens product development cycles and allows for more experimentation without heavy costs. Ultimately, AI-driven prototyping enables organizations to quickly identify viable concepts, refine them in real time, and launch innovative solutions at the pace of market demand.

Creative Problem-Solving

One of the most impactful uses of Generative AI is in fostering creative problem-solving. Teams are no longer limited to their own brainstorming capabilities; instead, they can leverage tools like ChatGPT and others to instantly generate multiple approaches to complex challenges. For example, a manager can present a business problem and receive ten unique strategies, each grounded in different perspectives. These solutions can then be refined and customized to suit organizational context. This diversity of ideas reduces bias, broadens creativity, and helps uncover innovative solutions that might otherwise remain hidden, giving companies a sharper competitive edge.

Better Data-Driven Decision-Making

Generative AI significantly strengthens leadership's ability to make smarter, faster, and more data-driven decisions. Advanced AI models can process vast datasets in real time, providing executives with actionable insights that are both timely and accurate. Instead of relying on outdated reports or fragmented data, leaders get predictive analytics, trend forecasts, and risk assessments that inform strategy. By enabling decisions rooted in data rather than intuition, organizations reduce uncertainty, minimize risk, and increase efficiency. This analytical clarity ensures competitive positioning, as companies can act quickly on emerging opportunities, refine operational efficiency, and drive sustainable growth in a volatile marketplace.

Revenue Growth

Modern AI and GenAI tools are also being used more and more by marketing and sales teams to enhance campaign optimization, lead generation, and customer retention. Companies gauge success by using:

Sales Growth

Revenue growth through sales expansion is one of the most direct impacts of AI and Generative AI in modern businesses. By automating repetitive tasks such as scheduling, data entry, and lead qualification, AI allows sales teams to spend more time nurturing customer relationships and closing deals. Tools like conversational AI (e.g., Sierra) enhance engagement by delivering instant, personalized responses to customer queries, increasing trust and improving conversions. Predictive analytics further helps identify the most promising leads, enabling teams to prioritize effectively. Ultimately, this integration boosts efficiency, reduces costs, and translates directly into higher sales growth and overall revenue.

Customer Lifetime Value (CLV)

Customer Lifetime Value (CLV) measures the total revenue a business can generate from one customer over their entire relationship. AI and Generative AI play a key role in improving CLV by enhancing personalization, retention strategies, and post-sales engagement. By analyzing customer behavior patterns, AI-driven systems predict churn risks and recommend interventions, such as discounts or personalized offers, to maintain loyalty. GenAI-powered chatbots provide proactive support, ensuring customers feel valued long after their first purchase. This long-term engagement fosters stronger relationships, encouraging repeat sales and referrals. Higher CLV not only increases profitability but also strengthens brand sustainability in competitive markets.

Marketing Campaign Performance

Marketing campaign performance has been transformed by AI and GenAI tools that enable deep personalization at scale. Businesses can now analyze massive amounts of customer data to design campaigns that target specific preferences, behaviors, and demographics. Generative AI applications create personalized ad copy, visuals, and email content, ensuring messages resonate more effectively with each audience segment. Predictive analytics helps optimize campaign timing and budget allocation, maximizing ROI. Continuous feedback loops powered by AI track engagement, conversions, and customer sentiment in real time. This dynamic approach allows marketers to adapt strategies instantly, driving higher conversion rates and long-term revenue growth.

Conclusion

Generative AI is transforming the very fabric of how businesses operate, unlocking unprecedented levels of efficiency and ROI. As illustrated throughout this chapter, its integration into workflows significantly reduces manual intervention, enabling teams to focus on high-value tasks that drive innovation. By streamlining repetitive processes, such as content creation, customer support, and data analysis, AI not only boosts productivity but also minimizes operational costs. Furthermore, AI-driven insights empower decision-makers with real-time, data-backed intelligence—enhancing strategic planning and minimizing risks. One of the most compelling validations of GenAI's value lies in the tangible returns experienced by organizations across sectors. From marketing teams improving campaign performance through hyper-personalization to sales departments increasing conversion rates using predictive analytics, the ROI gains are both measurable and scalable. As companies increasingly embed AI across their operations, the long-term competitive advantage lies not just in adopting the technology, but in reimagining how work is done. Those who lead this transformation today will be the market leaders of tomorrow—agile, efficient, and insight-driven. Ultimately, Generative AI is not just a tool for automation—it is a catalyst for redefining the future of business performance.

Exercise question

1. Define Generative AI. How is it different from traditional AI in terms of its capabilities and business applications?

2. What does ROI (Return on Investment) mean in the context of Generative AI adoption?
3. Explain how Generative AI streamlines workflows. Provide two industry-specific examples.
4. Discuss the role of Generative AI in enhancing decision-making processes with relevant use cases.
5. How does Generative AI contribute to reducing operational costs while increasing output quality?
6. Analyze how Generative AI can transform the customer support function in an e-commerce company.
7. Imagine you are leading the marketing team of a startup. Propose a plan to integrate Generative AI for campaign personalization.
8. Compare and contrast traditional business intelligence tools with AI-driven decision-support systems.
9. Evaluate the impact of AI-powered automation on employee productivity and satisfaction.
10. How would you measure the effectiveness of GenAI tools implemented in a supply chain environment?
11. Identify one real-world company that has significantly improved ROI using Generative AI. Briefly describe their strategy and outcomes.
12. Suppose a retail company sees declining CLV (Customer Lifetime Value). How can GenAI be leveraged to improve this metric?
13. In what ways has Generative AI enabled small businesses to compete with larger enterprises?

14. Examine the risks associated with over-reliance on Generative AI for decision-making. Suggest ways to mitigate these risks.
15. Reflect on how the use of Generative AI in your field of interest or profession can redefine workflow efficiency and performance.

CHAPTER 5
ETHICAL AND SOCIETAL CONSIDERATIONS IN GENERATIVE AI

Generative Artificial Intelligence (Generative AI) has rapidly emerged as one of the most transformative technologies of the 21st century, with applications ranging from text generation and image synthesis to drug discovery and personalized education. While the creative and economic potential of these systems is undeniable, their widespread adoption has sparked critical debates surrounding ethical and societal considerations. Unlike traditional AI systems that focus primarily on prediction or classification, generative models actively produce novel content, blurring the line between human and machine creativity. This distinct capability introduces unique challenges related to authenticity, accountability, and social trust, making ethical reflection essential in shaping their development and deployment. One of the most pressing concerns in the realm of generative AI is the issue of misinformation and disinformation. Sophisticated text, video, and audio generation tools can create highly realistic but fabricated content—commonly referred to as deepfakes. These outputs can be misused to manipulate public opinion, spread propaganda, or damage reputations, leading to erosion of trust in digital media. The societal implications extend far beyond individual harm, raising questions about democratic integrity, journalistic credibility, and public safety. Addressing these risks requires not only technological safeguards such as watermarking and detection algorithms but also robust regulatory frameworks that balance innovation with protection against malicious use. Another crucial ethical dimension lies in intellectual property rights and ownership. Generative AI models are typically trained on vast datasets that often include copyrighted texts, artworks, or music without explicit consent from creators. This raises difficult questions: Who owns the content generated by AI? Should original creators be compensated when their works contribute to training data? These issues highlight tensions between technological advancement and creative labor, demanding policies that safeguard the rights of authors while enabling innovation. Moreover, the rise of AI-generated art and literature challenges traditional notions of originality, authenticity, and human creativity, prompting society to reconsider the value and definition of authorship itself. Bias and fairness also stand as central concerns in the ethical discourse on generative AI. Since these models learn from historical data, they inherently reflect and sometimes amplify societal biases present in their training sets. For instance, biased representations in text or image generation can reinforce harmful stereotypes across race, gender, or culture, perpetuating discrimination in subtle but impactful ways. Such biases do not merely manifest in creative outputs but can influence areas like hiring processes, educational tools, and healthcare applications, leading to systemic inequities. Ensuring fairness requires diverse training data, transparent evaluation standards, and ongoing monitoring to prevent discriminatory patterns from becoming embedded in everyday technologies. Beyond individual harms, generative AI has broader societal implications for labor markets and cultural dynamics. The automation of creative tasks such as writing, design, and content production threatens to displace human workers in industries traditionally considered resistant to automation. At the same time, it opens opportunities for collaboration between humans and machines, where AI enhances creativity rather than replaces it. Striking this balance is a societal challenge, as it demands rethinking educational priorities, workforce training, and economic structures to ensure inclusive adaptation to technological shifts. Furthermore, generative AI reshapes cultural consumption by influencing what people read, watch, and hear, raising concerns about homogenization of culture and the potential loss of diversity in creative expression. Lastly, questions of transparency, accountability, and governance underscore the ethical debate. Generative AI systems are often described as "black boxes," making it difficult to explain how they produce specific outputs or why errors occur. Without clear accountability, it becomes challenging to assign responsibility when AI-generated content causes harm. This opacity undermines trust, particularly in sensitive domains like healthcare, law, and education. Societal acceptance of generative AI will depend on the development of transparent systems, explainable models, and accountable governance structures that place human values at the center. Ultimately, ethical and societal considerations are not peripheral concerns but foundational to ensuring that generative AI evolves as a force for positive transformation rather than social disruption.

Managing Bias and fairness in Generative AI

Bias in Generative AI

Bias in generative AI refers to systematic patterns of unfairness in the model's outputs, often reflecting distortions from training data or design decisions. Since these models are trained on vast datasets from the internet, they can inherit existing societal stereotypes, imbalances, and prejudices. Bias manifests in different forms:

Representation Bias

Representation bias arises when certain groups, identities, or perspectives are inadequately reflected in the training data of generative AI systems. Since these models depend on massive datasets scraped from the internet, populations with limited online visibility are often overlooked. For example, underrepresentation of minority languages, cultures, or professions may cause the model to generate outputs skewed toward dominant groups. This imbalance leads to less accurate, stereotypical, or even exclusionary results for marginalized communities. Addressing representation bias requires careful dataset curation, active inclusion of diverse voices, and strategies like data augmentation to achieve more equitable model performance.

Historical Bias

Historical bias originates from pre-existing inequalities or stereotypes embedded in society and captured in datasets. Generative AI trained on such data may reinforce outdated norms, such as associating men with leadership roles and women with caregiving professions. These biases are not created by the algorithm itself but are inherited from historical contexts and social structures. For instance, biased job descriptions, gendered language, or discriminatory narratives online become part of the model's learned associations. Without intervention, AI may replicate these biases in outputs, perpetuating systemic inequities. Corrective measures include de-biasing techniques and context-aware post-processing of generated content.

Measurement Bias

Measurement bias occurs when the labels, annotations, or metrics used in training datasets contain human subjectivity or flawed assumptions. For example, annotators' cultural backgrounds may influence how emotions, sentiments, or behaviors are classified. If a dataset labels certain hairstyles, dialects, or clothing styles negatively, models trained on it may replicate these subjective judgments in generated content. This bias arises not from the diversity of data itself but from how it is quantified, coded, or interpreted. Mitigating measurement bias requires establishing consistent, transparent labeling guidelines, using multiple annotators with diverse perspectives, and validating annotations through inter-rater reliability checks.

Algorithmic Bias

Algorithmic bias results from the design choices, architectures, or optimization methods used to train generative AI. Even if data is balanced, model components like loss functions, sampling strategies, or parameter tuning may unintentionally amplify disparities. For example, generative models may prioritize producing outputs that align with the majority class, leading to neglect of minority contexts. Similarly, reinforcement through feedback loops can worsen skewed patterns, as biased outputs influence future training. This form of bias highlights that fairness is not only a data issue but also a technical one. Addressing algorithmic bias involves fairness-aware algorithms, adversarial de-biasing, and continuous auditing.

Sources of Bias in Generative AI

Bias can enter the pipeline at multiple stages:

Data Collection-Unbalanced or culturally skewed datasets

Bias often originates during data collection, when the datasets used to train generative AI systems are incomplete, unbalanced, or skewed toward specific cultures, demographics, or perspectives. If certain groups are overrepresented while others are underrepresented, the model will disproportionately learn patterns that favor the majority. For example, a text generation model heavily trained on English-language data may fail to represent non-Western cultural narratives. Similarly, image datasets dominated by lighter skin tones can cause recognition errors for darker tones. Thus, flaws at this foundational stage embed systemic bias into the AI pipeline, creating unfair outcomes across downstream applications.

Preprocessing & Labeling – Subjective or inconsistent labeling practices

Another critical source of bias emerges during preprocessing and labeling, where human annotators play a significant role. Labeling involves subjective interpretation, and inconsistencies between annotators can reinforce stereotypes or exclude nuanced perspectives. For instance, labeling emotional expressions in images may reflect cultural biases about how different groups “should” look when happy or sad. Preprocessing steps like text cleaning, tokenization, or normalization can also inadvertently strip minority language markers or dialects, reducing representational richness. Since labels serve as the ground truth for training, any subjectivity, inconsistency, or systemic bias at this stage directly influences model performance and fairness.

Model Training – Optimization objectives that ignore fairness

Even with carefully curated data, bias can arise during the training process itself. Models are often optimized to minimize overall loss or maximize accuracy without explicitly accounting for fairness across subgroups. This means a model may achieve strong aggregate performance while failing significantly for marginalized populations. Moreover, deep learning algorithms can amplify small imbalances in the data, embedding discriminatory correlations as though they are "truth." Without fairness-aware optimization techniques, such as reweighting, regularization, or adversarial debiasing, training objectives can systematically privilege efficiency and accuracy over equity, perpetuating bias that manifests later during real-world deployment.

Deployment Context – Amplifying inequalities in sensitive domains

Bias becomes particularly consequential at the deployment stage, especially in sensitive areas such as hiring, healthcare, finance, or education. Even a model with modest biases can amplify social inequalities when integrated into decision-making pipelines. For example, biased hiring models may disproportionately reject candidates from minority groups, while healthcare models trained on data from one demographic may underdiagnose diseases in others. In education, generative systems may favor dominant linguistic or cultural patterns, disadvantaging diverse learners. Without careful governance, monitoring, and feedback mechanisms, deploying biased generative AI risks not only reinforcing but also magnifying systemic inequities in society.

Fairness Challenges in Generative AI

Ensuring fairness in generative models is complex due to:

Opaque Decision-Making

Generative AI models, especially those based on deep neural networks like transformers, often function as "black boxes." Their internal decision-making processes are highly complex, involving millions or even billions of parameters that adjust during training. This makes it difficult to trace why a model produced a particular output or to explain the reasoning behind it. The opacity creates challenges when evaluating fairness because biases may be embedded within hidden layers. Without interpretability, stakeholders cannot easily audit or correct unfair tendencies, leaving users and regulators with limited trust in the fairness of these models.

Context Dependence

Fairness in generative AI is not universal; it depends heavily on the context of application. For example, in job recommendation systems, fairness may involve ensuring equal opportunities across demographic groups, while in creative writing, fairness might concern avoiding harmful stereotypes or exclusion of certain cultural narratives. The standards of fairness vary drastically between sensitive domains like healthcare or recruitment and less critical areas like entertainment. This context dependence complicates the establishment of universal fairness guidelines. Models must be tailored to specific use cases, making fairness a moving target rather than a fixed standard.

Global Sensitivities

Fairness in generative AI must account for cultural, social, and demographic differences across societies. What is considered fair in one country may be seen as biased or insensitive in another. For instance, gender roles, racial identities, or religious representations differ globally, and generative models trained on datasets from one region may inadvertently marginalize or misrepresent others. This global sensitivity requires AI developers to incorporate diverse datasets, consult cultural experts, and adapt fairness metrics regionally. Failure to do so risks reinforcing cultural hegemony, erasing minority perspectives, and propagating unfair or offensive outputs worldwide.

Trade-offs

Striving for fairness in generative AI often involves trade-offs with other performance goals like accuracy, efficiency, or creative diversity. For example, applying strict fairness constraints may reduce a model's ability to generate highly personalized outputs, leading to less accurate recommendations. Similarly, ensuring balanced representation across groups might limit the diversity of generated content. These trade-offs force designers to prioritize ethical considerations over technical optimization, which can be controversial. Balancing fairness with innovation requires careful decision-making, as overemphasis on either side may compromise user trust, societal acceptance, or the model's overall utility.

Strategies for Managing Bias

Several methods are used to reduce and manage bias:

Data-Centric Approaches

Balanced Dataset Curation

Balanced dataset curation is the foundation of managing bias in machine learning systems. By ensuring fair representation across gender, ethnicity, geography, and socio-economic status, models are exposed to diverse patterns and contexts rather than skewed distributions. For example, an image recognition system trained mainly on Western datasets may fail when applied in Asian or African contexts. Actively sourcing varied data reduces such blind spots, promoting inclusivity and fairness. Moreover, balancing involves not just quantity but quality, ensuring that minority groups are represented accurately without stereotypes. This approach directly improves generalization, trust, and equitable decision-making in AI systems.

Bias Detection Tools

Bias detection tools are essential for auditing datasets and model outputs to uncover hidden unfairness. These tools rely on statistical audits, fairness metrics, and explainability frameworks to detect disparities in prediction accuracy across demographic groups. Metrics such as demographic parity, equalized odds, and disparate impact help identify whether certain groups are systematically disadvantaged. Visualization dashboards and model explainability techniques make the detection process more transparent, empowering researchers to take corrective measures. Regular use of these tools ensures ongoing monitoring, since bias may creep in during data collection, model updates, or deployment. Thus, detection is a proactive defense mechanism.

Synthetic Data Generation

Synthetic data generation is a powerful strategy to counter bias, particularly when real-world datasets are limited or imbalanced. Using techniques such as data augmentation, generative adversarial networks (GANs), or large-scale simulations, researchers can create counterfactual or balanced samples to improve fairness. For instance, if a dataset underrepresents women in leadership roles, synthetic examples can balance representation without compromising privacy. Synthetic data also enables testing models under rare or extreme scenarios, enhancing robustness. While care must be taken to avoid introducing artificial distortions, synthetic generation remains a flexible and scalable solution for improving inclusivity and mitigating bias in AI systems.

Model-Centric Approaches

Fairness-Aware Training Objectives

Fairness-aware training objectives involve integrating additional loss functions, constraints, or penalties into the learning process to minimize bias. Instead of only focusing on accuracy or prediction error, the model is trained to balance performance with equitable treatment of different demographic groups. This can be achieved by penalizing outcomes that disproportionately disadvantage protected attributes such as gender, race, or age. For example, a classification system could include a fairness constraint ensuring equal false-positive rates across groups. These objectives guide the model toward producing predictions that not only maximize utility but also align with ethical standards and fairness goals.

Adversarial Debiasing

Adversarial debiasing uses adversarial networks to minimize the model's reliance on sensitive attributes. In this approach, the main predictive model is trained alongside an adversary whose task is to predict protected attributes (like gender or ethnicity) from the model's outputs or latent features. The predictor tries to maximize performance, while the adversary tries to expose bias. The training process encourages the predictor to generate representations that hide sensitive information, making it harder for the adversary to succeed. As a result, the model learns to reduce discriminatory signals, leading to more equitable decision-making while maintaining accuracy.

Regularization & Fine-Tuning

Regularization and fine-tuning play a crucial role in reducing bias in model-centric approaches. Regularization techniques, such as adding constraints to model weights or applying dropout, help prevent the model from overfitting biased patterns in the data. Fine-tuning further enhances fairness by retraining the model on curated or rebalanced datasets that better represent minority groups. This may include data augmentation or transfer learning methods to ensure equal performance across subpopulations. By iteratively adjusting parameters and retraining, the model improves its generalizability, reduces bias amplification, and produces outputs that are fairer while maintaining strong predictive power.

Post-Processing Approaches

Output Filtering

Output filtering is one of the most direct post-processing strategies applied to generative AI models. It acts as a safeguard layer that screens generated content before it reaches the user. The system evaluates outputs against predefined rules, ethical guidelines, and safety filters to detect harmful, offensive, or biased material. This can include filtering hate speech, misinformation, violent imagery, or personally identifiable information. Modern implementations often use keyword-based scanning, toxicity classifiers, or fairness detection tools. The main advantage is reducing risks of reputational harm and ensuring compliance with ethical standards. However, excessive filtering can cause over-censorship, reducing creativity and usefulness.

Re-ranking Techniques

Re-ranking techniques enhance fairness and inclusivity by adjusting the priority of generated results after the initial AI output. Instead of presenting results exactly as the model produces them, a secondary system re-orders them to achieve balance or mitigate bias. For example, in job recommendation systems, re-ranking may ensure representation across gender, ethnicity, or educational background, preventing systemic discrimination. This approach helps address unconscious biases embedded in training data. Techniques often involve fairness constraints, diversity scoring, or probabilistic weighting to rebalance the results. While re-ranking improves equity and user trust, it must carefully balance fairness with accuracy, ensuring relevance is not compromised.

Human-in-the-Loop Review

Human-in-the-loop (HITL) review combines the efficiency of AI with the judgment and ethical reasoning of human experts. In this approach, AI generates content or recommendations, but sensitive or high-stakes outputs are reviewed, validated, or modified by humans before release. This is common in domains such as healthcare, legal analysis, or policy-making, where errors or bias could have serious consequences. Experts provide oversight, identify nuanced risks, and improve contextual accuracy. Human involvement also creates accountability and transparency in decision-making. Although HITL increases operational costs and slows automation, it significantly strengthens trustworthiness, ethical compliance, and safety in AI-assisted workflows.

Fairness Evaluation Metrics

Evaluating fairness requires quantitative and qualitative checks:

Demographic Parity

Demographic parity is a fairness criterion that ensures equal outcome distribution across different demographic groups, such as gender, race, or age. In practice, this means that the probability of receiving a favorable outcome like being approved for a loan or admitted to a program should be the same for all groups, regardless of sensitive attributes. For example, if 60% of men are accepted into a hiring pipeline, demographic parity requires that approximately 60% of women should also be accepted. While this ensures equity in representation, critics argue it may ignore performance differences and potentially reduce decision-making efficiency.

Equalized Odd

Equalized odds is a fairness metric that focuses on ensuring similar error rates across demographic groups. Specifically, it requires that both true positive rates and false positive rates remain consistent across groups. For instance, in a medical diagnosis model, equalized odds would mean that women and men with a disease are equally likely to be correctly identified (true positive), and those without the disease are equally unlikely to be falsely diagnosed (false positive). This criterion is often stricter than demographic parity because it accounts for both outcomes and errors, ensuring models don't disproportionately harm any group through mistakes.

Calibration

Calibration as a fairness measure ensures that predicted outcomes maintain consistency across different subgroups. A model is considered calibrated if, for any given prediction score, the actual probability of the outcome occurring is the same across groups. For example, if an AI model predicts a 70% likelihood of loan repayment, then approximately 70% of applicants should repay, regardless of gender, race, or age. Calibration focuses on fairness in probabilities rather than outcomes or error rates. It is particularly valuable in decision-support systems, where stakeholders rely on consistent probability estimates, but it may conflict with other fairness criteria like equalized odds.

Qualitative Audits

Qualitative audits complement quantitative fairness metrics by examining model outputs for social biases, stereotyping, or harmful content. These audits involve human reviewers analyzing generated text, images, or decisions to identify patterns of exclusion, toxicity, or subtle discrimination. For example, in a generative AI system, a qualitative audit might reveal that job-related prompts produce gender-biased role assignments or that image generators reinforce racial stereotypes. Unlike numerical fairness metrics, qualitative audits provide contextual insights and help identify fairness gaps not easily captured by statistics. They are crucial for ensuring ethical AI use, especially in applications where societal and cultural impacts matter..

Governance, Transparency, and Regulation

Bias and fairness management goes beyond technical fixes it requires governance and accountability:

Documentation Practices

Strong governance in AI requires transparent documentation that explains the foundations of models and datasets. Tools like model cards and data sheets provide detailed descriptions of training objectives, evaluation metrics, data sources, and intended use cases. They also highlight risks, limitations, and biases that may arise during deployment. Transparency reports serve as a bridge between developers, regulators, and end users by outlining how decisions are made and how errors are mitigated. These practices not only enhance accountability but also allow external reviewers, policymakers, and the public to critically evaluate AI systems in real-world contexts.

Ethical Guidelines

Governance frameworks must be rooted in clear ethical principles that guide both development and deployment of AI. Organizations should adopt AI ethics charters that set boundaries on acceptable applications, define safeguards for human rights, and prevent harmful uses such as surveillance abuse or discriminatory profiling. Ethical guidelines encourage teams to integrate fairness, inclusivity, and sustainability at every design stage. Moreover, having explicit codes of conduct ensures that employees and stakeholders understand their responsibilities. Such frameworks also create a culture of responsible innovation, where the pressure to release AI quickly does not override moral obligations to society.

Regulatory Compliance

To ensure accountability, AI systems must align with legal and policy frameworks that enforce fairness, safety, and reliability. For instance, the EU AI Act categorizes AI applications based on risk, imposing stricter requirements for high-risk uses such as healthcare, employment, or law enforcement. Regulatory compliance demands rigorous testing, audits, and reporting mechanisms to confirm adherence to data protection laws, cybersecurity standards, and consumer rights. By embedding compliance processes into the development lifecycle, organizations reduce reputational risks and legal penalties. Beyond law, aligning with international guidelines like OECD or UNESCO recommendations further strengthens trust in global AI ecosystems.

Stakeholder Involvement

Effective governance extends beyond engineers and policymakers; it must involve a broad coalition of stakeholders. Communities affected by AI decisions, ethicists, social scientists, and domain experts should be engaged in the design, evaluation, and deployment stages. This participatory approach ensures that AI systems reflect diverse perspectives and respect cultural, ethical, and societal values. Involving stakeholders also helps identify potential harms early, such as reinforcing stereotypes or excluding marginalized groups. Collaborative governance builds legitimacy and fosters public trust, demonstrating that AI is being developed not just for efficiency or profit but also for the collective good of society.

Data Privacy and Ethical Dilemmas

Generative AI (e.g., GPT, DALL·E, Stable Diffusion) has revolutionized content creation, enabling machines to generate text, images, audio, and code. However, its development and deployment raise serious ethical and data privacy concerns. These issues stem from the nature of data collection, model training, output generation, and societal impact. A comprehensive, structured explanation of Data Privacy and Ethical Dilemmas in Generative AI, covering key issues, dilemmas, and implications:

Data Privacy Challenges

Training Data Sourcing

Generative AI models rely on massive datasets often collected by scraping public and semi-public online platforms. While this provides the necessary scale for training, it also introduces serious privacy risks. These datasets may unintentionally contain copyrighted texts, sensitive government information, or personally identifiable information (PII) such as addresses, emails, and even medical data. When this data is fed into training pipelines without strict curation, the AI may later generate outputs that resemble private conversations, health records, or legal documents. Such risks highlight the urgent need for stricter sourcing policies, data cleaning, and transparent documentation of dataset composition.

Data Ownership

Data ownership remains a major unresolved issue in generative AI. When datasets are compiled from millions of online sources, the question arises: who truly owns the information? Is it the original author, the platform hosting the content, the company creating the dataset, or the AI developer? This ambiguity creates complex legal and ethical challenges around intellectual property rights. Artists, writers, and researchers often discover that their work has been used to train AI without permission. This raises concerns about exploitation, fair compensation, and accountability, ultimately fueling debates on licensing, copyright, and ethical use of digital content.

Unintentional Memorization & Leakage

One of the most alarming risks in generative AI is unintentional memorization of training data. Large models sometimes store and reproduce sensitive information verbatim, including phone numbers, social security details, passwords, or confidential business records. This happens because overfitting or improper dataset filtering can cause models to "remember" exact text sequences. When prompted in specific ways, the AI might leak this information, posing major threats to individual privacy and corporate security. Such leaks erode trust in AI systems, making robust data sanitization, differential privacy methods, and controlled evaluation critical to preventing inadvertent disclosure of private information.

User Data in Interactions

Chat-based generative AI systems often log user input under the guise of improving future performance. While this helps refine responses, it creates ethical dilemmas when sensitive information such as financial details, health conditions, or personal identifiers is stored without explicit consent. Users may unknowingly share private data, assuming interactions are confidential. If these logs are reused in training, analyzed by third parties, or breached, it can result in significant privacy violations. To mitigate this, AI developers must adopt transparent data-use policies, minimize storage, anonymize logs, and seek informed consent before collecting or reusing user-provided information.

Ethical Dilemmas in Generative AI

Bias and Fairness

AI models are trained on vast datasets collected from real-world sources such as text, images, and social interactions. These datasets inevitably contain human biases—racial, gender, cultural, or political—that the model may unknowingly absorb. For example, language corpora often reflect historical inequalities or stereotypes, leading models to favor certain groups or perspectives over others. Fairness in AI requires recognizing that models are not "neutral" mirrors of knowledge but are shaped by the quality and diversity of their data. Addressing bias involves careful dataset curation, balanced representation, bias-detection metrics, and continuous evaluation to ensure inclusivity in AI-driven decision-making.

Ethical Dilemma: Neutrality vs. Reality

One of the most pressing ethical questions in AI development is whether systems should generate neutral content or reflect reality with all its inherent biases in Table 5.1. If an AI tries to stay neutral, it risks producing overly sanitized or unrealistic responses that may overlook social context. On the other hand, mirroring real-world biases can reinforce harmful stereotypes and deepen inequalities. Ethical frameworks, transparent guidelines, and stakeholder input are crucial to strike a balance between truthful representation and social responsibility.

Table 5.1. Ethical Dilemma of Neutrality vs. Reality in AI Systems.

Aspect	Neutrality	Reality (Reflecting

	(Sanitized Output)	Biases)
Definition	AI generates balanced, neutral, and "safe" responses without leaning toward any bias.	AI mirrors real-world data, including its social, cultural, and political biases.
Advantages	- Prevents reinforcement of harmful stereotypes. Safer for diverse audiences. Maintains ethical responsibility.	Provides authentic reflections of society. Maintains contextual accuracy. Avoids oversimplification or "sugarcoating."
Disadvantages	Risk of producing overly sanitized or unrealistic content. May ignore real social context. Can seem detached from reality.	May reinforce harmful stereotypes. Can deepen inequalities. Risks normalizing discriminatory patterns.
Impact on Society	Promotes inclusivity but may feel artificial or incomplete.	Provides realism but risks perpetuating systemic biases and injustices.
Stakeholders' Concern	Users may demand truthful representation beyond "political correctness."	Developers and policymakers worry about ethical and legal implications.
Key Requirement	Ethical frameworks, transparency, and stakeholder	Same requirement—clear guidelines and interventions to prevent harm.

	participation to balance both sides.	

Example: Stereotypical Roles in Professions

When prompted with professions, AI systems sometimes default to biased associations—for instance, assuming doctors are male and nurses are female, or linking leadership roles to Western names while assigning service roles to non-Western names. These outputs reveal how training data encodes subtle stereotypes. While such examples may seem minor, they can perpetuate harmful narratives about gender, race, or culture at scale. Addressing this issue requires active interventions such as bias correction techniques, diverse training datasets, and human oversight. Ultimately, ensuring fair and accurate representations helps AI contribute positively to societal progress rather than reinforcing outdated roles.

Misinformation & Deepfakes

Generative AI can create convincing but false content:

Deepfake Videos

Deepfake videos represent one of the most alarming uses of generative AI. By replacing faces or altering voices in videos with precision, deepfakes create convincing but fabricated footage. Such manipulations can be weaponized for political propaganda, character assassination, cyber fraud, or non-consensual exploitation. Unlike traditional photo editing, deepfakes mimic real human expressions and speech patterns, making them extremely hard to detect. This undermines trust in video evidence, which historically has been considered credible proof. While detection tools are improving, the sophistication of deepfakes continues to outpace defenses, posing ethical, legal, and technological challenges worldwide.

Fake News Articles

Generative AI can also automate the creation of fake news articles that mimic journalistic styles. These articles can spread disinformation quickly, amplifying false narratives across social media. AI-generated fake news can look polished, include fabricated quotes, and exploit trending topics to maximize reach. The consequences extend beyond misleading individuals—fake news can destabilize communities, fuel polarization, and influence elections. The low cost and high efficiency of AI-driven content generation make it an attractive tool for malicious actors. Combating fake news requires stronger fact-checking systems, literacy programs, and responsible AI deployment to maintain credibility in the digital information space.

Synthetic Voices

Another dimension of AI-driven deception lies in synthetic voices. With only a few seconds of audio, AI can clone someone's voice, enabling impersonation in phone scams, fraud, or identity theft. Unlike text or images, voices carry emotional authenticity, making such fabrications more persuasive and dangerous. Criminals can exploit synthetic voices to trick family members, mislead employees, or bypass security systems. On the positive side, voice synthesis has beneficial applications in accessibility and entertainment. However, its misuse raises urgent questions about authentication and safeguards. Developing watermarking, verification technologies, and regulations is essential to prevent harm while enabling positive use cases.

Dilemma: Balancing Freedom of Creativity with Harm Prevention

The rise of generative AI creates a dilemma between promoting creativity and preventing harm. On one side, AI enables filmmakers, educators, and artists to innovate with unprecedented tools. On the other, it equips malicious actors with powerful means to deceive and exploit. Striking a balance requires multi-stakeholder collaboration—governments, tech companies, educators, and civil society must work together to establish ethical frameworks. Restrictions must not stifle innovation, yet safeguards must limit abuse. Solutions may include digital watermarks, stricter platform policies, legal accountability, and digital literacy initiatives. Ultimately, the challenge lies in fostering responsible innovation while safeguarding truth, trust, and human dignity.

Autonomy vs. Control

A pressing dilemma in generative AI is balancing creative freedom with the responsibility to prevent harm in Table 5.2. On one hand, giving AI systems and creators full autonomy fosters innovation, artistic expression, and transformative applications across industries. On the other hand, unchecked use risks misuse in spreading disinformation, reinforcing biases, or generating harmful content. Establishing strict control could stifle creativity, while excessive freedom might escalate societal risks. Thus, the challenge lies in designing governance frameworks, ethical guidelines, and responsible AI policies that maintain innovation while safeguarding against malicious intent. This balance is central to ensuring trust, accountability, and sustainable AI growth.

Table 5.2: Balancing Autonomy and Control in Generative AI, Key Dimensions, Benefits, Risks, and Governance Considerations.

Aspect	Autonomy	Control
Definition	Granting AI systems and creators freedom to innovate and operate with minimal restrictions.	Imposing strict rules, filters, and governance to limit potential harm or misuse of AI systems.
Advantages	Encourages innovation, artistic creativity, and rapid development of transformative applications.	Ensures safety, prevents harmful outputs, reduces spread of disinformation and bias.
Risks/Concerns	Can lead to misuse, unethical content generation, bias amplification, or disinformation spread.	May stifle creativity, slow down innovation, and limit potential breakthroughs.
Impact on Society	Promotes openness and democratization of technology but raises security and ethical concerns.	Promotes trust, accountability, and safer deployment but risks over-regulation and censorship.
Governance	Requires self-	Requires policies,

Need	regulation, ethical guidelines, and transparent AI design principles.	monitoring systems, and enforceable legal frameworks.
Ideal Balance	Freedom with responsibility – encourage innovation while embedding safeguards and oversight.	Balanced regulations that protect users without halting progress or creativity.

Intellectual Property & Plagiarism

Intellectual property (IP) refers to creations of the mind, such as inventions, artistic works, and literary writings, that are protected by legal rights like patents, copyrights, and trademarks. Plagiarism, on the other hand, occurs when someone presents another person's work or ideas without proper acknowledgment, passing them off as their own. In the digital era, the boundaries between originality and copying have blurred, especially with vast information availability. Protecting IP is crucial to encourage creativity and innovation, while avoiding plagiarism safeguards academic honesty, professional integrity, and fair recognition of authorship in both educational and professional contexts.

AI Outputs & Copyrighted Works

Artificial Intelligence systems trained on massive datasets often generate outputs that resemble copyrighted materials, such as songs, artworks, or written texts. This resemblance is not always intentional but results from the patterns AI learns during training. While some argue this is similar to human inspiration, others see it as a violation of creative ownership. Musicians, authors, and artists worry that AI may dilute originality, exploit their creative labor, or undermine their economic rights. As AI-generated content grows, questions of ownership, licensing, and ethical usage become increasingly complex, demanding clearer legal frameworks and accountability standards.

Ethical Dilemma: Inspiration, Transformation, or Theft

The core ethical dilemma lies in determining whether AI-generated content should be viewed as genuine inspiration, creative transformation, or outright theft. When AI reuses learned patterns to create something new, it can resemble the way humans draw inspiration from existing works. However, without attribution or consent, it risks being categorized as plagiarism or infringement. If the transformation adds originality and value, it may qualify as innovation; but if it merely replicates, it borders on theft. Striking a balance requires rethinking authorship, fair use, and responsibility in the age of machine creativity, ensuring both progress and ethical fairness.

Accountability & Responsibility in AI

If AI causes harm (e.g., defamatory text, harmful medical advice): Artificial intelligence systems have immense potential, but they also carry risks when misused or when their outputs lead to harmful consequences. For example, an AI generating defamatory text could damage reputations, while harmful medical advice could directly endanger lives. The challenge lies in determining accountability—should it rest with the developers who designed the system, the users who applied it, or the AI as an independent entity? Since AI lacks legal personhood, it cannot be directly held accountable. This creates a significant gap in liability and responsibility, leading to ethical and legal debates across governments, industries, and academia.

Accountable

Accountability in AI is a layered question. Developers are often considered responsible because they design the algorithms, set model boundaries, and decide how much transparency or bias mitigation is applied. However, users also play a crucial role, as misuse, overreliance, or applying AI outputs without human oversight can amplify harm. Holding AI itself accountable remains legally impossible, since it has no legal identity or intent. Therefore, accountability often becomes a shared responsibility: developers must ensure ethical design and guardrails, while users must exercise judgment, cross-check outputs, and adhere to regulations in sensitive domains like healthcare, law, or finance. Currently, legal frameworks are unclear. Presently, global legal systems are struggling to keep pace with AI development. Most jurisdictions lack clear laws assigning liability when harm arises from AI outputs. In the European Union, the proposed AI Act attempts to classify risks and place obligations on developers and deployers, but it is still evolving. In the U.S. and many other regions, liability often defaults to existing product liability or negligence frameworks, which may not fully capture the complexities of autonomous AI behavior. The absence of standardized laws creates uncertainty, leaving victims of AI harm with limited recourse and stakeholders without definitive guidelines for accountability.

Regulatory and Governance Concerns

Generative AI raises serious regulatory and governance concerns because its development and deployment often outpace existing laws. Policymakers struggle to balance innovation with accountability, as AI can create outputs with legal, ethical, and societal implications. Governance frameworks must address transparency, explainability, and accountability of AI systems, particularly in high-stakes domains like healthcare, finance, and law enforcement. A major challenge lies in regulating models trained on massive, opaque datasets that may contain biased or copyrighted content. Without clear rules, organizations risk legal disputes, reputational damage, and public distrust. Therefore, robust governance is essential for responsible AI adoption.

Compliance with Privacy Laws

Compliance with privacy laws is one of the most pressing issues in deploying generative AI. Frameworks such as the General Data Protection Regulation (GDPR) in Europe, HIPAA in the United States, and the EU AI Act impose strict obligations on organizations handling personal data. Generative AI models often scrape large-scale datasets from public and private sources, making it difficult to verify whether data was obtained with proper consent. Furthermore, these models may inadvertently reproduce sensitive information. Ensuring compliance requires data governance practices like anonymization, robust consent management, and strict data access controls to avoid violations and penalties. GDPR, HIPAA, and the EU AI Act demand strict rules on:

Data Minimization

Data minimization is a core principle in privacy regulations that requires organizations to collect and process only the data necessary for a specific purpose. Generative AI often contradicts this principle because it relies on vast datasets for training, many of which include redundant or irrelevant information. This creates challenges in justifying the proportionality of data collection under GDPR and similar laws. By reducing the scope of data used, organizations can lower risks of breaches, protect user rights, and increase trust. Techniques like synthetic data generation, federated learning, and selective dataset curation can help align AI development with minimization standards.

Consent

Obtaining informed consent is a cornerstone of ethical and lawful data usage under regulations like GDPR and HIPAA. For generative AI, ensuring valid consent is complex, as data often originates from secondary sources or web scraping where individual permissions were never sought. Moreover, users typically lack visibility into how their data may be reused for training purposes. To comply, organizations must implement transparent consent mechanisms that clearly explain the scope, purpose, and potential risks of data usage. Failure to secure proper consent exposes companies to regulatory fines, litigation, and reputational harm, making it a critical governance priority.

Right to be Forgotten

The right to be forgotten, enshrined in GDPR, empowers individuals to request deletion of their personal data. Generative AI presents unique challenges in honoring this right because once data is embedded into a model's parameters, it becomes nearly impossible to extract specific information. Users may demand erasure, but retraining entire models is costly and often impractical. This tension highlights a gap between legal requirements and technological feasibility. Research into machine unlearning and model editing is ongoing, aiming to enable selective data removal without full retraining. Until solutions mature, AI providers must carefully weigh compliance risks and obligations.

Opaque Training Datasets

Opaque training datasets are a central problem in generative AI governance. Many large-scale models are trained on datasets aggregated from diverse online sources without full documentation or transparency. This lack of clarity creates difficulties in verifying compliance with data protection laws, assessing bias, or identifying potential copyright violations. Moreover, the opacity undermines accountability, as stakeholders cannot trace harmful outputs back to their data origins. Regulators increasingly demand dataset transparency and documentation to evaluate risks. To address this, organizations must adopt practices like data lineage tracking, model cards, and dataset documentation to ensure trust, accountability, and compliance.

Transparency & Explainability

Transparency and explainability are essential in artificial intelligence because they allow users, developers, and stakeholders to understand how and why a system arrives at certain conclusions. In the absence of transparency, AI systems may function effectively but leave critical gaps in accountability. For example, when a decision directly impacts healthcare, hiring, or finance, stakeholders need to know the logic and processes behind the output. Explainability ensures that AI is not just a technical tool but also a trustworthy partner, fostering ethical alignment, regulatory compliance, and societal acceptance. Without transparency, trust in AI-driven solutions remains fragile.

Models Operate as "Black Boxes."

Most advanced AI models, especially deep learning architectures, function as "black boxes" due to their complex internal computations that are not easily interpretable by humans. These models can involve millions of parameters and nonlinear transformations, making it extremely difficult to trace how input data translates into an output. While black-box systems may achieve high accuracy, their opacity raises concerns in sensitive fields like law enforcement, medicine, and education. Users cannot fully validate or challenge outcomes when they lack insight into model reasoning. This black-box nature highlights the need for interpretability tools and transparent design practices in AI development.

One of the central challenges in AI adoption is that users often struggle to understand why the system produced a particular output or recommendation. For instance, a medical diagnosis tool might suggest a condition without clarifying the contributing symptoms or test results. Similarly, a loan approval system might reject an application without explaining the risk factors. This lack of interpretability reduces user confidence and restricts the opportunity for feedback or correction. Providing clear reasoning pathways through explainable AI (XAI) techniques—empowers users to question, validate, or improve system outputs, ensuring fairness, accountability, and trust in AI applications.

Users Cannot Always Know What Data Influenced It

AI systems learn and make decisions based on massive datasets, but users often have no visibility into what data shaped the model's behavior. This lack of clarity raises concerns about hidden biases, outdated information, or skewed representations within the training data. For example, if an AI model reflects discriminatory patterns in hiring, users cannot easily trace whether biased historical records influenced the decision. Without insight into training datasets, it becomes challenging to audit or improve the system. Therefore, transparency about data provenance, quality, and relevance is crucial for building ethical, reliable, and socially responsible AI.

Lack of Explainability Undermines Trust and Ethical Accountability

When AI outputs cannot be explained or justified, trust in the system diminishes, and its ethical accountability is questioned. This issue becomes critical in high-stakes decisions, such as medical diagnoses, criminal sentencing, or financial lending, where consequences are significant. A lack of explainability prevents users from challenging errors, addressing bias, or holding developers accountable. It creates a gap between technological efficiency and human values, eroding confidence in AI adoption. Ethical frameworks emphasize the need for transparent and explainable systems to ensure fairness, respect human rights, and support responsible innovation. Explainability thus becomes a cornerstone of trustworthy AI.

Global vs. Local Laws

Artificial Intelligence is developing at a global scale, but the laws governing it differ widely across regions in Table 5.3. Global standards emphasize principles like fairness, accountability, and transparency. However, local laws adapt these principles to cultural, political, and economic contexts. This divergence creates a regulatory mosaic that companies must navigate. A model trained and deployed in one jurisdiction may be compliant there but fall short elsewhere. Global alignment is still in its infancy, making it difficult to establish universally accepted standards. The lack of harmonization pushes organizations to adopt flexible frameworks that can accommodate multiple legal environments simultaneously.

Table 5.3: Comparison of Global vs. Local Laws in Artificial Intelligence Regulation.

Aspect	Global Laws/Standards	Local Laws/Regulations
Scope	Emphasize broad principles such as fairness, accountability, transparency, and ethical AI.	Adapt principles to specific cultural, political, and economic contexts.
Consistency	Aim for universal alignment, but still in infancy; no binding uniform rules.	Differ widely across regions (EU, US, China, India, etc.), leading to diverse legal landscapes.
Compliance Challenge	Global standards provide high-level guidelines for responsible AI.	A model compliant in one jurisdiction may violate requirements in another.
Flexibility	Promote frameworks that are broad and adaptable across countries.	Require companies to customize compliance for each region's specific law.
Impact on Organizations	Encourage global collaboration and shared ethical	Create a regulatory mosaic, forcing companies to navigate multiple overlapping

	vision.	or conflicting laws.
Future Outlook	Moving slowly toward harmonization and common standards.	Continue to evolve rapidly, influenced by national interests and priorities.

Different regions (EU, US, China, India) have contradictory AI regulations

The European Union (EU) follows a precautionary approach with its AI Act, classifying AI systems by risk level and imposing strict requirements on high-risk applications. The United States leans toward innovation-driven policies, favoring voluntary guidelines and sector-specific rules. China emphasizes state control, prioritizing national security, data sovereignty, and censorship, while actively investing in AI for governance and industry. India is adopting a balanced model—promoting AI innovation while highlighting ethics, data protection, and inclusivity. These contradictory regulatory styles create compliance challenges for companies working across borders, as they must tailor their systems and processes to satisfy diverse and sometimes conflicting rules.

Raises dilemmas in cross-border AI deployment

Deploying AI across multiple jurisdictions raises dilemmas in governance, ethics, and compliance. A healthcare AI tool, for example, may meet safety requirements in the EU but lack approval in the US due to differing certification processes. Data localization rules in China may restrict global data sharing, while the US may demand transparency that conflicts with local secrecy laws. These contradictions complicate scaling AI products, increasing costs and legal risks. Businesses must decide whether to design region-specific versions of their systems or limit operations to certain geographies. Ultimately, the fragmentation of AI governance slows global adoption and innovation.

Societal and Human Impact

Labor Displacement

Generative AI has rapidly transformed the landscape of creative and technical industries by automating tasks such as content writing, graphic design, coding, and even music composition. While this advancement boosts efficiency and lowers costs, it simultaneously displaces a significant portion of the workforce whose livelihoods depend on these skills. The ethical dilemma arises in weighing economic progress against social welfare. Should society prioritize productivity and innovation at the expense of creative employment? Critics argue that unchecked automation widens income inequality and undermines human dignity, whereas proponents highlight new opportunities in AI supervision, curation, and strategy.

Manipulation and Influence

Generative AI has introduced new challenges in information authenticity by enabling the creation of highly convincing but potentially misleading content. Deepfakes, fabricated news articles, and algorithmically tailored propaganda can manipulate public perception, influence elections, and destabilize trust in democratic systems. Unlike traditional misinformation, AI-generated media is scalable, personalized, and difficult to distinguish from reality. The ethical concern centers on the erosion of democratic integrity and informed citizenship. Should governments regulate AI-driven content generation, or should digital literacy be prioritized to empower individuals against manipulation? The balance between free expression and safeguarding public trust remains highly contested.

Human-AI Dependency

As generative AI tools become integral to daily life—assisting in writing, decision-making, and problem-solving humans risk becoming overly reliant on them. While these tools enhance productivity, constant dependence may erode essential cognitive skills such as critical thinking, creativity, and independent problem-solving. Over time, individuals may outsource judgment to algorithms, diminishing human agency and resilience. The ethical dilemma revolves around whether AI's role should be consciously limited to preserve human autonomy. Should policies encourage AI as a supplement rather than a replacement? Striking the right balance between augmentation and dependency is vital to ensure that human ingenuity continues to thrive.

Mitigation Strategies

Data Privacy Protection

Protecting data privacy in generative AI requires robust mechanisms that minimize direct exposure of sensitive information. Differential privacy introduces controlled statistical noise into datasets, ensuring individual-level details remain hidden while preserving aggregate trends. Federated learning further enhances protection by training models across distributed devices, allowing data to stay local without centralized collection. This approach prevents raw data from leaving user environments, drastically reducing the risk of breaches. Additionally, anonymization techniques—such as de-identification and pseudonymization—must be strictly enforced during dataset preparation. Collectively, these methods ensure that user information remains secure while enabling effective AI model training.

Ethical Frameworks

Adopting strong ethical frameworks ensures AI development aligns with human values. Organizations should embrace guidelines focusing on fairness, accountability, and transparency, minimizing potential harm caused by biased or opaque systems. Fairness ensures equitable treatment across diverse populations, while accountability places responsibility on developers and organizations for system outcomes. Transparency involves open communication about model design, datasets, and limitations. Establishing AI ethics committees within organizations is critical for regular oversight, ethical reviews, and decision-making. Such committees can guide responsible innovation, prevent misuse, and align AI with societal expectations, ensuring trustworthiness and sustainability in real-world applications.

Model Governance

Effective model governance is essential for maintaining trust and reliability in generative AI systems. Regular audits should be conducted to detect bias, assess fairness, and ensure safety compliance across models. These audits must include independent evaluations, statistical tests, and bias-detection tools. Documentation plays a critical role—model cards and data sheets provide structured information about datasets, training processes, performance, limitations, and intended use.

Open, accessible documentation enables transparency, helping users and regulators understand the scope and risks of deployed models. Governance frameworks also involve clear accountability structures, monitoring tools, and mechanisms to ensure compliance with evolving legal and ethical standards.

Content Moderation

As generative AI produces vast amounts of digital content, robust moderation practices are vital. Watermarking and labeling AI-generated content make it distinguishable from human-created material, reducing risks of misuse. These markers support authenticity checks, protecting users from deception. Detection mechanisms for deepfakes and misinformation are equally important, employing forensic analysis and machine learning classifiers to identify manipulated media. Automated flagging systems combined with human review teams ensure balanced moderation. Such systems prevent harmful outputs, reduce misinformation spread, and uphold societal trust in digital ecosystems, particularly in domains like journalism, education, and social media platforms where credibility is critical.

Legal & Policy Interventions

Legal and policy frameworks provide essential safeguards for responsible AI deployment. Stronger intellectual property (IP) protections are necessary to address challenges of ownership, copyright infringement, and misuse of AI-generated works. Policymakers must adapt existing IP laws to cover emerging scenarios unique to generative models. International cooperation is equally crucial, as AI systems operate across borders, requiring harmonized regulations. Global agreements can ensure consistent standards for safety, fairness, and accountability while reducing regulatory loopholes. Such collaborations enable effective governance, support ethical innovation, and establish a legal environment where creativity, security, and human rights are equally protected.

Societal Impact: Job Evolution and skill requirements

Generative AI is reshaping the job market by transforming traditional roles and creating new ones that demand a blend of technical expertise, creativity, and ethical awareness. While some routine and repetitive tasks are being automated, opportunities are growing in areas such as AI model development, data curation, prompt engineering, and AI ethics oversight. This shift requires workers to adapt by acquiring advanced digital literacy, problem-solving skills, and domain-specific knowledge to collaborate effectively with AI systems. Moreover, soft skills such as critical thinking, adaptability, and cross-disciplinary collaboration are becoming equally essential, ensuring that human talent complements rather than competes with AI capabilities.

H1 – Automation of micro-tasks (now)

The first horizon of change in work is marked by the automation of micro-tasks through AI tools. Activities such as drafting emails, summarizing documents, cleaning data, generating test cases, preparing meeting notes, and creating code scaffolding are now completed faster with AI assistance. Rather than eliminating jobs, the biggest impact lies in compressing task time. Routine tasks that once consumed hours can now be accomplished in minutes, leading to a 20–60% time savings. This shift frees employees to focus on higher-value responsibilities like problem-solving and creativity, setting the stage for new ways of working rather than widespread displacement.

H2 – Human–AI teaming (0–3 years)

The second horizon highlights the growing partnership between humans and AI systems. In the near future, Retrieval-Augmented Generation (RAG) and agentic AI systems will be embedded across daily tools. Domain experts will not just execute tasks but act as AI conductors, curating prompts, shaping policies, and managing relevant data flows. This collaboration transforms expertise into orchestrating efficient, safe, and high-quality outputs with AI as a co-worker. As a result, shared KPIs across organizations will evolve—quality, safety, and cost-efficiency will not be limited to technical teams but will become cross-functional priorities, redefining teamwork, accountability, and the distribution of responsibilities.

H3 – Job creation (3–7 years)

The third horizon represents the longer-term outcome: job creation in entirely new domains. Professions will emerge around AI safety, governance, evaluation, and the management of synthetic data, alongside operational roles like model operations (ModelOps), AI user experience (UX), and multimodal content design. These roles will attract talent laterally from software development, research, design, compliance, and operations, offering diverse career pathways. Just as the internet created web developers and digital marketers, AI will give rise to new professions requiring both technical literacy and domain expertise. Rather than eroding the workforce, this horizon reshapes the labor market by unlocking fresh opportunities.

Sectors

Software/IT

In Software and IT, generative AI is reshaping workflows by automating tasks such as transforming specifications into code, running tests, managing migrations, and handling repetitive refactoring. Developers increasingly focus on higher-level architecture and integration while leaving routine coding to AI-assisted systems. New roles like LLMOps specialists, retrieval engineers, and evaluation engineers are emerging to ensure model accuracy, safety, and performance. FinOps functions are also expanding, where engineers optimize cost, latency, and resource allocation for large-scale AI deployments. Human expertise remains critical in supervising AI outputs, ensuring code quality, and managing system-level innovation beyond automated programming.

Marketing/Communications

In marketing and communications, AI streamlines creative ideation, generating advertising copy, localizing campaigns for different markets, and producing endless variations of assets at scale. Generative tools free teams from repetitive execution, allowing professionals to focus on brand voice, long-term strategy, and decision-making. AI can test message resonance across different demographics quickly, but human oversight ensures authenticity and emotional connection. Content versioning for multiple formats—social, print, digital—is now largely automated, yet approvals and ethical considerations remain in the human domain. The shift repositions marketers as curators, strategists, and brand guardians while AI takes over bulk production and micro-optimization tasks.

Design/Media

In design and media, AI accelerates tasks like storyboarding, concept art creation, and layout exploration. Designers now rely on prompt engineering and chained tools to rapidly generate prototypes and visual options. Instead of spending hours on initial drafts, creative professionals invest more time refining, curating, and guiding AI outputs to align with brand and artistic vision. Quality gates and rights management become crucial, as AI-generated assets often raise intellectual property and licensing issues. Human oversight ensures originality, compliance, and contextual appropriateness. The sector is transitioning from manual asset creation to orchestration of AI workflows, where creativity meets governance.

Finance/Legal

Finance and legal fields are experiencing a profound shift as AI assists in drafting documents, reviewing contracts, detecting anomalies, and monitoring regulatory compliance. Algorithms can flag suspicious activities, generate risk reports, or summarize complex policies at remarkable speed. However, explainability and auditability are paramount, meaning human experts must validate all AI-driven outputs. While AI reduces clerical burden and accelerates research, humans remain central to judgment-heavy decisions, negotiations, and client interactions. Lawyers, auditors, and financial analysts increasingly act as supervisors and interpreters of AI-driven insights, ensuring compliance, fairness, and accountability in environments where precision and trust are critical.

Healthcare

In healthcare, AI is streamlining documentation, coding, triage assistance, and patient education. Systems can auto-generate clinical notes, prepare insurance codes, and support medical staff in decision-making by surfacing relevant patient histories. Patient-facing chatbots provide education, follow-up reminders, and preliminary triage, improving accessibility. Yet clinicians remain central, validating outputs, correcting errors, and ensuring patient safety. Privacy and governance frameworks are strict, as healthcare data requires the highest security standards. AI's role is supportive rather than substitutive, giving doctors and nurses more time for direct patient care. The focus is on responsible augmentation of clinical workflows rather than full automation.

Education

In education, AI powers courseware generation, personalized tutoring, and formative feedback at scale. Intelligent systems create lesson plans, quizzes, and interactive exercises aligned to curriculum requirements, freeing educators from repetitive administrative design. AI tutors offer individualized support, adapting explanations to student learning styles and pacing. Educators, however, shift focus toward pedagogy, critical thinking development, and assessment integrity, ensuring students do not misuse AI. Another priority is teaching AI literacy—helping students understand, evaluate, and responsibly use these tools. Far from replacing teachers, AI transforms them into learning facilitators who integrate automation into a human-centered educational experience.

HR/Operations

In HR and operations, AI handles tasks like drafting job descriptions, generating interview guides, and building employee-support chatbots. It accelerates policy creation, ensures compliance consistency, and enhances onboarding experiences. Generative tools also provide predictive analytics for employee performance and retention, giving HR professionals more strategic insight. The role of HR evolves toward AI-augmented people analytics, where data-driven decisions complement traditional human judgment. By automating repetitive documentation and communication, professionals gain more time for empathetic engagement, talent development, and organizational culture-building. This marks a shift from administrative burden to strategic influence, reshaping HR as both people-centric and technologically empowered.

Manufacturing/Supply Chain

In manufacturing and supply chain management, AI integrates predictive maintenance, vision-based inspections, and intelligent text generation for work instructions. Generative models analyze procurement data, detect inefficiencies, and recommend supply adjustments. Combined with IoT and robotics, these tools enable seamless coordination of automated production lines and logistics systems. Workers transition into supervisory roles, overseeing AI-driven diagnostics and robotic operations while ensuring safety and compliance. The convergence of generative AI with industrial systems creates faster responses to disruptions and demand fluctuations. Human expertise remains critical in strategic planning, ethical oversight, and complex problem-solving beyond automated prediction and optimization.

Technical foundations

Large Language Models (LLMs) are built on deep learning architectures that process sequential data using billions of parameters trained on massive datasets. Their technical foundation lies in the Transformer architecture, which leverages self-attention to capture long-range dependencies. Unlike older models like RNNs or LSTMs, Transformers parallelize computations, making training scalable. Key advancements include pretraining on diverse corpora followed by fine-tuning for specific tasks, enabling zero-shot and few-shot learning. Optimization techniques such as Adam, gradient clipping, and mixed precision accelerate training while reducing costs. Hardware accelerators like GPUs and TPUs, along with distributed training strategies, make modern LLM development feasible.

LLM fundamentals

LLM fundamentals involve several core mechanisms. Tokenization breaks text into manageable units (tokens), which the model interprets numerically. Context windows define how much text an LLM can consider at once, limiting reasoning depth. Temperature and top-p control randomness: higher values increase creativity; lower values enforce precision. System prompts establish global behavior, while user prompts provide task-specific input. Tool use and functions extend models by integrating APIs or external knowledge bases for reasoning beyond training data. Agents build on this by combining planning, memory, and tool orchestration, enabling autonomous workflows such as answering multi-step queries or executing tasks across applications.

RAG

Retrieval-Augmented Generation (RAG) enhances LLMs by grounding responses in external data. Chunking strategies split documents into optimal segments for retrieval, balancing completeness with granularity. Embeddings convert chunks into dense vectors, enabling semantic similarity search via vector databases like FAISS or Pinecone. Retrieved results are ranked by relevance, sometimes reranked using cross-encoders for improved precision. Freshness ensures the system retrieves up-to-date data, critical for time-sensitive queries. Citations add transparency by linking generated outputs back to original sources, increasing trust. Overall, RAG reduces hallucinations and extends LLMs' effective context window, combining generative fluency with retrieval accuracy for robust applications.

Evaluation

Evaluating LLMs requires combining automated metrics with human judgment. Task-gold design involves creating reliable ground-truth datasets to benchmark performance. Automated metrics vary by task: Exact Match (EM) and F1 for question answering, Precision/Recall for information extraction, pass@k for code correctness, and Precision@k/Recall@k for retrieval tasks. Operational metrics include latency at p95/p99 (tail response times), cost per task, and hallucination rates, which measure factual inaccuracies. Human evaluation complements these by assessing fluency, coherence, and appropriateness in real contexts. Together, these methods ensure balanced evaluation across quality, efficiency, and safety, providing a holistic view of an LLM system's reliability.

Data

High-quality data is the backbone of effective LLMs. Data cleaning removes noise, duplicates, and inconsistencies, while labeling provides supervised signals essential for fine-tuning. Weak supervision uses heuristics or distant labels to scale annotations when gold data is scarce. Provenance and lineage ensure transparency, tracking data origins and transformations, which is vital for compliance and debugging. Personally Identifiable Information (PII) handling requires anonymization, redaction, or encryption to safeguard privacy. Governance enforces ethical, legal, and organizational standards for data use, preventing bias and misuse. Collectively, these practices improve model robustness, fairness, and trustworthiness while aligning data pipelines with responsible AI principles.

Ops

Operationalizing LLMs involves ensuring stability, reliability, and safety at scale. Observability tracks metrics, logs, and traces to monitor system health. Canarying gradually rolls out updates to a subset of users, limiting risks. Feature flags allow toggling new features on/off without redeployment, while rollback mechanisms restore stable versions if failures occur. Offline vs online evaluation parity ensures models tested in lab conditions perform equally in production. Caching reduces latency and cost by reusing frequent responses. Guardrails enforce constraints—such as blocking unsafe outputs or enforcing formatting—ensuring outputs remain aligned with user expectations, compliance requirements, and ethical guidelines in real-world deployment.

Optimization

Optimizing LLMs balances performance with efficiency. Prompt compression reduces redundant tokens, lowering costs and latency. Retrieval pruning selects only the most relevant context in RAG pipelines, minimizing noise. Few-shot prompting offers quick adaptability, but fine-tuning provides deeper task alignment; hybrid approaches often balance flexibility and control. Parameter-efficient fine-tuning methods like LoRA and PEFT update small subsets of weights, reducing compute needs. Quantization compresses weights into lower-bit formats for faster inference on limited hardware. Distillation transfers knowledge from large teacher models to smaller student models, preserving performance while reducing footprint, enabling deployment across devices with constrained resources.

Multimodal basics

Multimodal AI integrates text, images, audio, and video. Image generation, often guided by conditioning inputs like text prompts or sketches, enables creative and practical applications. Optical Character Recognition (OCR) extracts text from images, powering document digitization and accessibility. Automatic Speech Recognition (ASR) transcribes spoken language into text, while Text-to-Speech (TTS) synthesizes natural audio from written input, enabling conversational AI. Video captioning unites vision and language models to describe dynamic visual content, supporting accessibility and content indexing. Together, these capabilities extend LLMs beyond text-only tasks, enabling richer interactions and applications across healthcare, education, media, and human-computer interaction.

Safety, Ethics, and Compliance

Safety, ethics, and compliance form the foundation of trustworthy AI development. Safety ensures that systems are reliable, robust, and minimize unintended harms in real-world environments. Ethics emphasizes fairness, transparency, and accountability, guiding developers to align technology with human values and societal well-being. Compliance ensures adherence to relevant legal frameworks, regulatory standards, and organizational policies. Together, these pillars create guardrails for responsible innovation, preventing misuse and reinforcing public trust. In practice, this involves proactive risk assessments, adherence to international standards, and embedding ethical principles into every stage of system design, deployment, and monitoring for continuous improvement.

Harm Taxonomies

Harm taxonomies categorize risks such as misinformation, bias, privacy breaches, or physical harm, providing structured ways to anticipate threats. Red-team methods stress-test systems by simulating adversarial attacks, ensuring resilience under hostile conditions. Safety policies define organizational commitments and enforcement mechanisms. Bias detection and mitigation strategies identify discriminatory patterns in datasets or outputs, enabling corrective interventions. Privacy by design embeds user data protection into every architectural decision, reducing exposure risks. Audit logs provide traceability for accountability, while incident response frameworks ensure rapid containment and recovery after failures or misuse. Together, these practices operationalize AI safety and governance at scale.

Familiarity with High-Level Frameworks

High-level frameworks such as the NIST AI Risk Management Framework (AI RMF) provide standardized approaches to managing AI risks. They outline principles for trustworthy systems, including fairness, transparency, accountability, and resilience. Familiarity with such frameworks enables teams to align practices with recognized industry benchmarks, ensuring interoperability and regulatory compliance. Internal governance playbooks extend these guidelines into organizational contexts, offering step-by-step policies, escalation protocols, and monitoring mechanisms. This dual familiarity ensures both external compliance and internal operational efficiency. Together, they provide a comprehensive foundation for ethical AI governance and sustainable adoption within businesses and institutions.

Problem Framing

Problem framing is the skill of clearly defining the scope, objectives, and constraints of a challenge before attempting solutions. In AI development, poor framing can lead to irrelevant or harmful outcomes, while good framing ensures alignment with stakeholder needs and organizational goals. It involves clarifying the "why," "what," and "for whom" of a problem, identifying assumptions, and avoiding overly narrow or biased perspectives. By framing problems effectively, teams can focus efforts on impactful use cases, allocate resources wisely, and avoid misaligned outputs. This skill ensures that AI systems are purpose-driven, context-sensitive, and capable of delivering meaningful results.

KPI Design

Key Performance Indicator (KPI) design is central to measuring the success of AI projects. Effective KPIs translate abstract goals into quantifiable metrics that guide experimentation and evaluation. They must balance technical accuracy with human-centered impact, ensuring that models not only perform well statistically but also create value for end users. Poorly designed KPIs can incentivize harmful shortcuts or neglect crucial outcomes like fairness or safety. Good KPI design involves consultation with stakeholders, alignment with business objectives, and incorporation of ethical considerations. Well-chosen KPIs enable continuous learning, informed decision-making, and accountability across the AI lifecycle.

Experimentation

Experimentation drives iterative learning in AI development. By designing controlled experiments, teams can test hypotheses, validate assumptions, and compare competing approaches. Structured experimentation prevents premature conclusions, allowing evidence-driven decisions instead of guesswork. Key techniques include A/B testing, randomized controlled trials, and ablation studies, depending on the context. Beyond technical validation, experimentation supports understanding of human factors such as usability, adoption, and unintended effects. A culture of experimentation encourages innovation while reducing risk, since failures become learning opportunities. By systematically testing and refining ideas, organizations build more reliable, scalable, and impactful AI systems over time.

Stakeholder Communication

Stakeholder communication ensures that technical teams, executives, regulators, and end-users share a common understanding of AI systems. Effective communication translates complex technical insights into accessible narratives, fostering trust and collaboration. It involves transparency about limitations, uncertainties, and trade-offs while also highlighting opportunities and benefits. Regular updates, clear documentation, and participatory feedback loops strengthen engagement across diverse audiences. Poor communication can lead to mistrust, misaligned expectations, or resistance to adoption. Skilled stakeholder communication thus balances detail with clarity, enabling informed decisions, smoother change management, and broader acceptance of AI innovations across organizational and societal contexts.

Domain Expertise

Domain expertise anchors AI solutions in real-world contexts. While technical skills enable model development, domain expertise ensures that models address practical, relevant, and context-sensitive challenges. It provides insights into data quality, feature relevance, regulatory considerations, and stakeholder needs specific to an industry or sector. For instance, in healthcare, domain experts guide compliance with safety standards and medical ethics, while in finance, they ensure regulatory adherence and risk awareness. Without domain expertise, AI risks being technically sound but socially irrelevant or even harmful. Integrating domain knowledge with AI methods creates systems that are both powerful and responsible.

Change Management

Change management focuses on preparing organizations and people to adopt and adapt to AI-driven transformations. It involves anticipating resistance, addressing cultural concerns, and ensuring smooth integration of new tools into workflows. Effective strategies include training programs, transparent communication, and participatory decision-making, which build user confidence and reduce fear of displacement. Change management also emphasizes aligning technology with organizational values and long-term goals, ensuring sustainable adoption. Without it, even the most advanced AI systems risk rejection or underuse. Successful change management creates a culture of adaptability, where employees see AI as an enabler rather than a threat.

Critical Thinking and Evidence-Based Judgment

Critical thinking and evidence-based judgment are essential to making sound decisions in AI projects. Critical thinking challenges assumptions, questions data quality, and tests logical consistency, preventing blind reliance on algorithms. Evidence-based judgment emphasizes decisions grounded in empirical findings rather than intuition or hype. Together, they enable balanced evaluation of trade-offs, uncertainties, and potential biases. These skills are vital when interpreting experimental results, setting policies, or responding to ethical dilemmas. In rapidly evolving fields, they help distinguish genuine breakthroughs from overpromises. Ultimately, combining critical reasoning with evidence ensures AI solutions are robust, fair, and aligned with real-world needs.

Role-wise skill checklists

Engineers (SW/LLMOps)

Engineers in software and LLMOps require strong programming fundamentals, particularly in Python, C++, and frameworks like PyTorch or TensorFlow for building scalable AI systems. They must master distributed computing, data pipeline orchestration, and deployment tools such as Docker, Kubernetes, and cloud services (AWS, GCP, Azure). Core responsibilities include optimizing inference speed, fine-tuning models, monitoring drift, and ensuring reproducibility. Skills in CI/CD, prompt engineering, and API design are crucial for seamless integration. Additionally, engineers need debugging, profiling, and benchmarking expertise to maintain system reliability. Collaboration with researchers, PMs, and governance teams ensures products remain efficient, ethical, and production-ready.

AI PMs (Product Managers)

AI product managers must combine technical fluency with strategic vision to align AI capabilities with business needs. They require knowledge of ML workflows, model limitations, and metrics like precision, recall, or fairness indicators to make informed trade-offs. Key skills include stakeholder communication, backlog prioritization, and roadmap planning. They must bridge engineers, designers, and governance teams, ensuring features are user-centered and compliant with regulations. AI PMs must also assess feasibility of fine-tuning, scaling, or integrating external APIs. Strong analytical and documentation skills help define success metrics, while awareness of emerging AI trends ensures long-term competitiveness in fast-evolving markets.

Designers/Content

Designers and content specialists shape how users interact with AI systems. They must balance creativity with usability, ensuring AI-driven features are intuitive and trustworthy. Skills include prompt design, UX/UI prototyping, multimodal interaction design, and accessible content creation. A strong grasp of human-centered design principles is vital to mitigate bias and ensure inclusivity. They must also collaborate with engineers to fine-tune AI responses for tone, clarity, and accuracy. Content professionals should understand generative models, localization challenges, and ethical storytelling. Visual designers, meanwhile, require expertise in Figma, Adobe tools, and interaction testing to deliver cohesive experiences that enhance user engagement.

Governance/Safety

Governance and safety professionals ensure AI systems comply with ethical standards, legal regulations, and organizational values. They require deep understanding of responsible AI frameworks, fairness audits, bias detection, and interpretability tools (e.g., SHAP, LIME). Skills in drafting policies, risk assessments, and incident response protocols are crucial. They must be adept at red-teaming models, monitoring for harmful outputs, and implementing guardrails such as content filters or classifier-based moderation. Collaboration with cross-functional teams ensures safe deployment without stifling innovation. Knowledge of evolving global AI regulations (e.g., EU AI Act, US guidelines) equips them to anticipate compliance risks and safeguard public trust.

Building Trust in AI systems

Building trust in AI systems especially in Generative AI (GenAI) is critical for widespread adoption in education, healthcare, governance, business, and daily life. Trust is multidimensional, involving technical robustness, ethical alignment, and social acceptance. Below is a detailed breakdown:

Transparency and Explainability

Transparency

Transparency in AI refers to the principle that users should be able to clearly understand how an artificial intelligence system functions. This involves disclosing the data sources that power the system, the training processes undertaken, and the inherent limitations it may possess. When organizations adopt transparent practices, users gain visibility into what influences the outputs, reducing ambiguity and suspicion. Transparency also includes communicating potential risks, biases, and uncertainties in a straightforward manner. By providing this clarity, AI developers enable users to make informed choices about trusting and using the system. Ultimately, transparency builds accountability, reliability, and long-term trust.

Explainability

Explainability goes hand in hand with transparency but focuses on making AI decisions understandable to humans in practical terms. For example, if an AI generates an image, predicts disease risk, or suggests a financial decision, it should be possible to explain why it made that choice. This is crucial in sensitive domains like healthcare, finance, and law where outcomes must be justified. Explainability ensures that users are not left guessing about "black box" outputs but can trace decisions to logical factors. Achieving explainability not only cnhances trust but also allows stakeholders to evaluate fairness, safety, and accountability in AI-driven processes.

Techniques for Interpretability

To achieve interpretability, researchers and engineers have developed various techniques that shed light on model reasoning. For instance, attention visualization in transformer models reveals which parts of the input data the model focused on when generating an output. Similarly, saliency maps highlight important pixels in an image that influenced a classification. Post-hoc explanation models like LIME (Local Interpretable

Model-agnostic Explanations) and SHAP (Shapley Additive Explanations) further break down predictions to human-understandable contributions of features. These tools are vital in ensuring that complex deep learning models remain accessible to non-expert users. Interpretability bridges the gap between algorithmic complexity and human comprehension.

Documentation and Openness

Openly documenting datasets, training pipelines, biases, and model architectures fosters confidence in AI systems. Such documentation enables peer review, auditing, and collaborative improvement. By being explicit about potential biases in data or acknowledging weaknesses in model design, developers demonstrate responsibility and integrity. Public model cards and datasheets for datasets have become industry standards to encourage openness. This not only improves trust but also ensures compliance with ethical and legal standards. For users, documentation provides clarity about how to responsibly apply AI tools. For developers, it creates a foundation for accountability and continuous innovation, enhancing the credibility of AI adoption.

Reliability and Robustness

Reliability and robustness are critical qualities in Generative AI, ensuring that the models consistently perform as expected across diverse scenarios. A reliable system delivers outputs that align with user expectations and task requirements, regardless of input variations. Robustness complement's reliability by preparing the model to handle unpredictable or challenging conditions without degrading performance. Together, they create a trustworthy AI system capable of functioning under real-world constraints. For example, a text generator must consistently produce coherent, contextually appropriate content, while an image model must maintain quality across different resolutions and prompts. These factors directly influence user trust and adoption.

Robustness Testing

Robustness testing evaluates how Generative AI models respond to unusual, distorted, or malicious inputs. Techniques such as adversarial attacks, noisy data injection, and perturbations are commonly used to expose model weaknesses. By systematically testing vulnerabilities, researchers can strengthen defenses and prevent failures that may arise in deployment. For instance, adversarial examples in image generation may lead to distorted outputs, while slight changes in phrasing may confuse text-based models. Conducting robustness tests ensures the AI can withstand manipulation attempts or unexpected variations, thereby enhancing security, performance stability, and practical usability in critical applications such as healthcare and finance.

Generalization Beyond Training Data

Generative AI systems must generalize well to remain reliable in real-world applications. Generalization refers to a model's ability to perform accurately on unseen data that differs from its training set. Without this, models risk overfitting, becoming too dependent on training patterns, and failing when exposed to new situations. Stability under distribution shifts when real-world data diverges from training data is equally vital. For example, a chatbot trained only on formal English must still perform reasonably when encountering slang, abbreviations, or cultural nuances. Strong generalization builds user confidence, as it demonstrates that the AI is not limited to narrow, predefined conditions.

Benchmarks for Measuring Reliability

To ensure reliability, standardized benchmarks are used to evaluate Generative AI models across tasks. For image generation, the Fréchet Inception Distance (FID) measures similarity between generated and real images. In text generation, the BLEU score assesses how closely outputs align with reference sentences, while TruthfulQA evaluates factual accuracy and resistance to misinformation. These benchmarks provide quantifiable metrics that researchers and developers can use to compare performance, track improvements, and identify weaknesses. They also help maintain transparency in AI research by offering consistent evaluation criteria. Ultimately, benchmarks are vital tools for validating that generative models achieve reliable and trustworthy outcomes.

Bias, Fairness, and Inclusivity

Bias

Generative AI models are trained on vast internet-scale datasets that inevitably contain the biases present in society. These biases may be related to race, gender, age, culture, or ideology, and they can manifest in subtle or overt ways through the system's outputs. For example, biased language in training data can lead to AI-generated content that reinforces harmful stereotypes or excludes marginalized voices. Left unchecked, these biases undermine trust, credibility, and ethical use of AI. Addressing bias requires continuous monitoring, testing, and improvement, since no dataset is fully neutral and AI systems inherently reflect the data, they learn from.

Fairness

Ensuring fairness in Generative AI requires deliberate effort throughout the development lifecycle. This involves curating balanced datasets, applying bias detection metrics, and implementing algorithmic debiasing strategies to minimize discrimination. Fair AI systems must provide consistent outcomes across diverse groups without privileging one population over another. For instance, fairness can be measured by evaluating model accuracy across different demographic segments. Techniques such as adversarial debiasing, reweighting datasets, or fairness-constrained optimization are often employed. Developers, policymakers, and ethicists must collaborate to create accountability frameworks, so that fairness becomes a measurable, enforceable principle in AI development and deployment.

Inclusivity

Inclusivity in Generative AI extends beyond fairness and bias correction—it emphasizes designing systems that respect and reflect diversity in language, culture, gender, ability, and accessibility. A truly inclusive AI should understand multilingual contexts, represent non-Western cultures accurately, and adapt outputs for people with disabilities. This ensures that AI technologies do not just serve privileged populations but are beneficial to everyone. Inclusivity requires active engagement with diverse communities during design and testing. It also involves embedding accessibility features like text-to-speech, screen reader compatibility, and adaptive interaction modes to bridge gaps for underrepresented or differently-abled user groups.

Example: A practical example of fairness, bias mitigation, and inclusivity in Generative AI is the development of medical tools. Imagine a diagnostic AI model designed to assist doctors. If it is trained mostly on data from one region or ethnicity, it may fail to perform accurately for others, leading to health inequities. For instance, a skin cancer detection tool trained primarily on lighter skin tones could misdiagnose darker skin tones. To ensure fairness, the dataset must include balanced medical images across ethnicities, genders, and age groups. Such inclusive design guarantees that the AI supports equitable healthcare outcomes globally.

Safety and Risk Mitigation

Safety and risk mitigation are central to building trust in Generative AI (GenAI) systems. Users need assurance that these systems won't generate content that is harmful, offensive, or misleading. Since GenAI models operate on probabilistic patterns, there is always the chance of unintended or risky outputs. Establishing strong safety frameworks ensures that AI aligns with ethical standards, minimizes misuse, and protects diverse groups of users. Risk mitigation strategies also extend to anticipating adversarial use cases, such as generating misinformation or biased content. Without robust safety measures, trust erodes, reducing adoption and credibility of GenAI across critical industries.

1. Trust requires confidence that GenAI won't produce harmful, offensive, or misleading outputs. For GenAI systems to gain wide acceptance, users must believe they are reliable and safe. Confidence stems from knowing that the system avoids producing harmful, offensive, or misleading outputs that could compromise user dignity, security, or decision-making. This confidence is built through transparency in model development, consistent monitoring, and accountability mechanisms. Trust is not automatic—it evolves as users experience the model's outputs and see evidence of safeguards in action. In sensitive areas like education, governance, or mental health, ensuring outputs remain respectful and accurate is

essential.Ultimately, confidence in AI safety builds the foundation for sustainable trust.

2. Safety layers like reinforcement learning with human feedback (RLHF), red-teaming, and content filters prevent toxic or unsafe outputs. Multiple layers of safety are required to prevent AI from generating toxic or unsafe outputs. Reinforcement Learning with Human Feedback (RLHF) enables models to learn acceptable boundaries from human evaluations, aligning responses with societal values. Red-teaming where experts deliberately try to break the system uncovers vulnerabilities before deployment, ensuring risks are addressed proactively. Content filters add another protective layer by detecting and blocking inappropriate outputs in real time. These layered strategies collectively reduce the chances of harmful interactions slipping through. By combining human oversight, adversarial testing, and automated filtering, GenAI systems become more resilient and trustworthy for widespread adoption.

3. Guardrails against hallucinations (fabricated but plausible outputs) are vital in high-stakes domains like law or healthcare. Hallucinations when AI produces fabricated but convincing outputs pose a serious threat, especially in high-stakes domains like law, healthcare, and finance. A hallucinated legal precedent or misdiagnosis can lead to severe consequences, including wrongful judgments or medical harm. Guardrails such as fact-checking modules, domain-specific fine-tuning, and integration with verified databases help reduce these risks. Human-in-the-loop oversight also ensures that critical decisions are reviewed by experts before application. In professional contexts, accuracy is

paramount, and hallucinations must be minimized through rigorous design and continuous monitoring. Strong guardrails not only prevent errors but also preserve user trust in AI-assisted decision-making.

Accountability and Governance

Accountability and governance are cornerstones of building trust in artificial intelligence systems. Users are more willing to adopt and rely on AI when they are confident that there are clear mechanisms to identify who is responsible for errors, misuse, or unintended consequences. Without accountability, AI deployment can feel opaque, leaving individuals vulnerable to harm without recourse. Strong governance ensures that responsibility is not diffused but rather clearly assigned to developers, organizations, and decision-makers. Transparent governance mechanisms also serve as deterrents against unethical use, creating a culture of responsibility that safeguards both users and society at large.

Users trust systems when there is clear accountability for errors or misuse

Trust in AI systems is inseparable from accountability because people need to know that when things go wrong, someone can be held answerable. For instance, if an autonomous vehicle makes an incorrect decision, users expect clarity on whether the manufacturer, software developer, or operator is accountable. Establishing such responsibility frameworks reduces fear of untraceable harm and ensures fairness. Clear accountability also empowers users to report concerns without hesitation, knowing that corrective mechanisms exist. By building accountability into design and deployment, organizations send a strong message that user welfare is prioritized, which fosters long-term confidence and adoption of AI systems.

Governance frameworks define responsibility

Governance frameworks like the EU AI Act, OECD AI principles, and UNESCO's AI ethics guidelines serve as global anchors for responsible AI adoption. These frameworks set out clear principles on transparency, fairness, human rights, and explainability, defining the duties of both governments and organizations. For example, the EU AI Act classifies AI systems by risk categories and mandates stricter oversight for high-risk applications. Similarly, the OECD principles emphasize accountability, robustness, and respect for democratic values. Such frameworks provide structured pathways for regulation, compliance, and redress, ensuring that AI does not evolve in a regulatory vacuum but within a defined ethical boundary.

Organizations should implement AI audit trails, usage monitoring, and ethical review boards

Practical accountability in organizations requires more than policy it needs mechanisms like AI audit trails, monitoring tools, and ethical review boards. Audit trails help track decisions made by AI systems, providing transparency when evaluating why an error occurred. Usage monitoring ensures that AI models are not misused beyond their intended scope, protecting users from harmful applications. Ethical review boards bring interdisciplinary expertise to evaluate AI deployments before and during use, considering fairness, bias, and societal impact. Together, these measures create an organizational culture where accountability is proactive rather than reactive, reducing risks while enhancing trust among users, regulators, and stakeholders.

Human-in-the-loop oversight ensures decisions are reviewable and correctable

Despite advances in automation, human-in-the-loop oversight remains vital for accountability and governance. By ensuring that humans can intervene in, review, and correct AI decisions, organizations prevent blind reliance on machine outputs. This oversight is particularly important in sensitive domains like healthcare, law, and finance, where algorithmic mistakes can carry severe consequences. Human involvement not only allows ethical judgment but also builds user confidence that AI systems are not operating in a vacuum. Additionally, reviewable decision-making enables error correction and continuous improvement, ensuring systems evolve responsibly. In this way, human oversight acts as both a safety net and an ethical compass for AI governance.

Security and Privacy

Trust is broken if AI mishandles sensitive data: Artificial Intelligence systems operate on vast amounts of data, much of which may be sensitive, personal, or confidential. If AI mishandles this information, whether through improper storage, unauthorized access, or misuse, it directly undermines user trust. Once trust is lost, adoption slows down, and skepticism grows regarding AI technologies. Mishandling may occur in various forms, such as accidental data leaks, unethical data sharing, or biased inferences that expose private attributes. Therefore, strict governance, transparent handling practices, and robust monitoring are essential.

Trust in AI is fragile, and mishandling sensitive data can irreversibly damage the credibility of organizations.

Differential privacy, federated learning, encryption, and secure multi-party computation can safeguard user data: To preserve user privacy in AI systems, advanced privacy-preserving technologies play a crucial role. Differential privacy ensures that statistical outputs remain useful while concealing individual identities. Federated learning allows models to be trained locally on user devices, avoiding centralized data storage and reducing exposure risks. Encryption protects data during storage and transmission, ensuring that only authorized parties can access it. Secure multi-party computation enables multiple parties to collaborate on computations without revealing their private inputs. Together, these techniques form a comprehensive framework that safeguards sensitive information, allowing AI to function effectively while minimizing the risks of data breaches.

Users should know how their data is stored, anonymized, and used in model fine-tuning: Transparency in AI data management is essential for building user confidence. Users must be clearly informed about how their data is collected, stored, and protected from unauthorized access. Anonymization should be a standard practice, ensuring that personal identifiers are removed before analysis or model training. Moreover, when data is used for fine-tuning models, organizations should disclose the process, purpose, and safeguards in place. Providing clear, understandable policies enables users to make informed decisions and reinforces trust. Ethical responsibility requires that organizations treat user data with care and clarity, making privacy practices a visible part of AI deployment.

Data poisoning and model theft must be actively prevented: As AI adoption grows, threats like data poisoning and model theft have become major concerns. Data poisoning occurs when malicious actors manipulate training datasets to corrupt model behavior, leading to biased or harmful outcomes. Model theft involves unauthorized extraction of trained models, which can compromise intellectual property and expose vulnerabilities. Preventing these risks requires robust monitoring of data pipelines, adversarial testing, and employing watermarking or fingerprinting techniques to secure model ownership. Additionally, continuous auditing and cybersecurity practices are vital. Without strong defenses, attackers can exploit weaknesses, threatening both AI reliability and the safety of individuals who rely on it.

Ethical and Societal Alignment

AI must reflect ethical principles such as beneficence (do good), non-maleficence (do no harm), justice, and autonomy. In GenAI, ethical trust relates to ensuring that art, literature, or media generated by AI respects intellectual property rights. Systems aligned with societal values—like reducing misinformation, supporting sustainability, and improving accessibility—earn stronger long-term trust.

Conclusion

The exploration of ethical and societal considerations in Generative AI highlights the importance of balancing innovation with responsibility. Managing bias and ensuring fairness remain crucial, as unchecked bias can perpetuate inequality and erode trust. Addressing data privacy and ethical dilemmas requires not only robust technical safeguards but also legal and policy frameworks that protect individual rights while supporting innovation. The societal impact of Generative AI is equally profound—reshaping job markets, redefining skills, and creating opportunities for new forms of human–machine collaboration. Preparing for this transformation demands continuous upskilling, adaptability, and policies that safeguard workers during transitions. Building trust in AI systems emerges as the foundation for sustainable adoption. Transparency, explainability, accountability, and human-centered governance are indispensable in ensuring that AI remains an empowering tool rather than a disruptive threat. Ultimately, the lessons from these discussions point toward a future where Generative AI can be harnessed ethically, inclusively, and responsibly. By embedding fairness, safeguarding privacy, anticipating social shifts, and reinforcing trust, society can ensure that AI technologies serve humanity's collective good while minimizing potential harms. This integrated perspective underscores the critical role of ethics in shaping AI's transformative journey.

Exercise Questions

1. What types of biases can appear in Generative AI systems, and how do they impact users?
2. Explain strategies for identifying and reducing bias in training datasets.
3. Discuss how fairness can be evaluated and measured in Generative AI applications.
4. Provide examples where lack of fairness in AI has caused real-world challenges.

5. What are the major privacy concerns when using user data in training Generative AI?
6. Compare techniques such as differential privacy and federated learning in protecting data.
7. Describe an ethical dilemma in AI deployment and propose a balanced resolution.
8. Should Generative AI systems always disclose when content is AI-generated? Why or why not?
9. How might Generative AI reshape traditional job roles in creative industries?
10. Identify new skills that professionals must develop to remain competitive in the AI-driven workforce.
11. What policies could governments adopt to mitigate job displacement caused by AI?
12. Discuss the positive and negative societal impacts of Generative AI on employment.
13. Why is explainability important for building trust in Generative AI?
14. Discuss the role of regulations and governance frameworks in enhancing AI trustworthiness.
15. Suggest ways to design human-centered Generative AI systems that prioritize user control and safety.

CHAPTER 6
IMPLEMENTING GENERATIVE AI IN YOUR BUSINESS

Generative Artificial Intelligence (Generative AI) has quickly evolved from a niche research concept into a transformative force reshaping industry worldwide. By enabling machines to generate new content whether it be text, images, code, or even product designs—Generative AI empowers businesses to innovate at a pace never seen before. Unlike traditional AI, which mainly classifies or predicts outcomes, Generative AI creates entirely new possibilities. For companies, this means unlocking new ways of engaging with customers, streamlining operations, and gaining competitive advantages in increasingly dynamic markets. Implementing Generative AI in business is not merely a technology upgrade it is a strategic move that determines long-term competitiveness. Early adopters are already leveraging AI to automate routine tasks, personalize marketing campaigns, optimize supply chains, and design new products. This adoption accelerates decision-making while reducing costs, but more importantly, it allows organizations to reimagine what value they can deliver to their customers. For businesses seeking growth, integrating Generative AI is becoming as essential as adopting the internet was two decades ago. The real power of Generative AI lies in its versatility. In retail, AI-driven chatbots can provide personalized shopping recommendations; in healthcare, it can assist with drug discovery and medical imaging analysis; in finance, it can detect fraud and create predictive investment models; and in education, it can generate adaptive learning materials tailored to individual learners. Each application enhances efficiency and customer satisfaction while opening new business models. This cross-industry adaptability makes Generative AI a universal catalyst for innovation. While the benefits are compelling, implementing Generative AI is not without challenges. Businesses must address critical issues such as data quality, infrastructure readiness, and integration with existing systems. Moreover, ethical concerns surrounding bias, intellectual property, and transparency cannot be overlooked. A poorly planned implementation may lead to mistrust among customers, regulatory penalties, or ineffective outcomes. Thus, businesses need a clear roadmap that balances technical capabilities with governance frameworks to ensure sustainable and responsible AI adoption. Successful integration of Generative AI requires more than technology it demands the right ecosystem. This includes skilled professionals who understand both the technical and business aspects of AI, partnerships with technology providers, and investment in cloud platforms or AI infrastructure. Moreover, fostering a culture of innovation where employees view AI as a tool for augmentation rather than replacement is crucial. Businesses that align their people, processes, and platforms with AI adoption are more likely to achieve measurable outcomes and maintain long-term scalability. Ultimately, implementing Generative AI is about future-proofing the business. Organizations that take proactive steps today will be better positioned to respond to market shifts, changing consumer behaviors, and technological disruptions tomorrow. The path forward involves starting small through pilot projects learning from outcomes, and scaling responsibly. With the right vision and execution, Generative AI can move from being an experimental tool to becoming the backbone of next-generation enterprises, enabling them to innovate, compete, and thrive in the digital age.

Steps to Adopt Generative AI tools

Identify Business Use Cases

Before selecting any tool, start by identifying high-impact areas where generative AI can add value. These may include:

Customer Service

Generative AI can revolutionize customer service by offering intelligent chatbots and virtual assistants that provide quick, consistent, and personalized responses to customer queries. Unlike traditional bots limited to pre-set rules, generative AI enables conversational flexibility, allowing it to understand context, detect sentiment, and provide human-like interactions. This reduces response time, enhances customer satisfaction, and frees up human agents for more complex issues. Additionally, these assistants can operate 24/7, ensuring customers always have access to support. Over time, they learn from interactions, improving accuracy and relevance, making them valuable tools for scaling customer service while controlling costs.

Content Creation

Content generation is one of the most powerful use cases for generative AI, as businesses rely heavily on constant content creation for digital presence. AI can draft marketing copy, write engaging blogs, produce video scripts, and generate compelling product descriptions tailored for different platforms. By analyzing customer preferences, market trends, and brand tone, generative AI produces high-quality, consistent, and scalable content quickly. This reduces time and cost while allowing creative teams to focus on strategy and innovation. It also supports personalization, enabling businesses to deliver targeted content that resonates with different customer segments, boosting engagement, conversion, and overall brand visibility.

Data Analysis & Summarization

Generative AI significantly enhances data analysis and summarization by transforming raw datasets into clear, actionable insights. Instead of manually analyzing large volumes of data, AI can quickly process information, highlight patterns, and auto-generate detailed reports or concise executive summaries. This allows decision-makers to focus on strategy rather than routine interpretation tasks. Generative AI can also summarize lengthy documents, meeting transcripts, or research papers, saving professionals considerable time. With natural language generation, reports are not just factual but also presented in easy-to-understand formats. This improves productivity, supports informed decision-making, and ensures stakeholders always have access to clear, reliable insights when needed.

Product Design & Prototyping

Generative AI can transform product design and prototyping by helping businesses rapidly visualize ideas and explore variations. Using advanced models, AI can create multiple prototypes based on a single concept, allowing teams to test aesthetics, functionality, and user preferences at scale. Designers can input rough sketches or descriptions, and AI generates realistic renderings or 3D models. This accelerates innovation cycles, reduces prototyping costs, and helps identify the most promising ideas early in the process. Moreover, AI-driven design fosters creativity by suggesting alternatives humans may not consider, leading to innovative, user-friendly products that align with evolving market demands and trends.

Code Generation and Debugging

Generative AI is reshaping software development through automated code generation and debugging. Tools like GitHub Copilot assist developers by writing code snippets, completing functions, and offering solutions in real time based on natural language prompts. This not only speeds up development but also reduces repetitive tasks, allowing programmers to focus on architecture and innovation. AI tools can also detect bugs, suggest fixes, and optimize code, thereby improving quality and reducing errors. For new programmers, these tools act as intelligent mentors, providing guidance and best practices. Overall, AI-powered coding accelerates project delivery, improves reliability, and enhances developer productivity significantly.

Assess Technical Readiness and Resources

Once use cases for Generative AI are clearly defined, the next critical step is to assess the technical readiness and resources of your organization. This involves carefully evaluating whether your existing infrastructure, data pipelines, workforce capabilities, and compliance measures can support AI integration at scale. Businesses often underestimate this step and face challenges later during deployment, such as system incompatibility, lack of skills, or poor-quality data. A thorough readiness check ensures smoother adoption, reduces risks, and helps allocate investments wisely. Below, we break this assessment into four dimensions: data readiness, talent, tool compatibility, and security & compliance.

Data Readiness

High-quality data is the backbone of any AI initiative. To successfully fine-tune or contextualize models, organizations must first verify whether they have access to sufficient volumes of relevant and reliable data. Poorly structured, incomplete, or biased data can lead to inaccurate model outputs and undermine business outcomes. Data readiness involves checking for proper labeling, preprocessing pipelines, and real-time accessibility. It also requires evaluating data governance frameworks to ensure consistent updates and scalability. If gaps exist, strategies such as data augmentation, partnerships for external datasets, or improved collection mechanisms must be implemented to prepare a solid foundation for AI systems.

Talent

Even the most advanced tools fail without skilled professionals to guide their use. Organizations must assess whether their teams possess adequate expertise in AI, machine learning, or data science to build, deploy, and maintain models effectively. Talent readiness includes evaluating technical roles such as ML engineers, data scientists, and AI strategists, as well as domain experts who can contextualize AI outcomes. If gaps are found, businesses should consider structured training programs, partnerships with external consultants, or new hiring initiatives. A balanced approach that combines upskilling existing employees with acquiring specialized talent ensures sustainable AI adoption and long-term capability building.

Tool Compatibility

Seamless integration with existing platforms is another key factor in readiness. Businesses must evaluate whether their systems and software environments are compatible with modern AI ecosystems like OpenAI, Google Vertex AI, or Amazon Bedrock. Tool compatibility includes checking APIs, cloud infrastructure, data pipelines, and orchestration frameworks for smooth interoperability. If legacy systems pose limitations, organizations may need to modernize infrastructure or adopt middleware solutions. A future-ready architecture that supports flexible scaling, multi-cloud strategies, and plug-and-play integrations will ensure that AI adoption remains cost-effective, scalable, and adaptable to evolving technological landscapes.

Security & Compliance

AI deployment introduces sensitive data handling responsibilities that must align with strict industry regulations. Organizations must assess whether their infrastructure can safeguard data privacy, ensure secure storage, and comply with frameworks like HIPAA, GDPR, or local regulatory standards. This involves encryption protocols, access controls, audit trails, and data residency checks. Beyond legal compliance, ethical considerations such as fairness, transparency, and accountability also play a role in maintaining trust. Establishing a strong governance model ensures that AI systems operate responsibly, avoiding penalties, reputational risks, and customer mistrust while meeting both industry and societal expectations.

Choose the Right Generative AI Tools and Platforms

Selecting the right Generative AI tools and platforms is a crucial first step in successful adoption. Organizations must evaluate tools based on their specific requirements, including business use cases, ease of integration with existing systems, scalability for future growth, and licensing costs. While some tools offer broad capabilities, others are designed for niche applications, so aligning them with business needs ensures efficiency and ROI. Additionally, businesses must weigh factors such as long-term vendor support, availability of documentation, community strength, and training resources. A well-chosen platform can significantly reduce operational challenges and maximize the benefits of AI adoption.

Text Generation Tools

For text generation, popular platforms include OpenAI's GPT-4, Anthropic's Claude, and Google's Gemini. These large language models are widely adopted due to their ability to generate human-like, contextually appropriate text for diverse applications. GPT-4 is highly versatile, supporting tasks like drafting emails, generating reports, and creating conversational agents. Claude emphasizes ethical AI and safety in responses, making it a preferred choice for businesses with high compliance needs. Google Gemini integrates well with Google's ecosystem, benefiting organizations using Google Workspace. Choosing the right text generation tool depends on priorities like performance, cost-effectiveness, and alignment with organizational workflows.

Image Generation Tools

When it comes to image generation, tools like DALL·E, Midjourney, and Stable Diffusion are widely recognized for their creativity and versatility. DALL·E is known for its strong integration with OpenAI's ecosystem and its ability to generate unique visuals from detailed text prompts. Midjourney is preferred for artistic, highly stylized images, making it popular among designers and marketers. Stable Diffusion, on the other hand, provides more control through open-source flexibility, allowing customization for specific business or research applications. Organizations should evaluate these tools based on output quality, scalability for high-volume use, integration options, and licensing models to ensure long-term sustainability.

Code Generation Tools

For code generation, GitHub Copilot and Amazon's CodeWhisperer are among the most effective solutions. GitHub Copilot, powered by OpenAI Codex, seamlessly integrates into popular IDEs and supports developers by suggesting code snippets, reducing repetitive tasks, and speeding up development cycles. It is especially useful for enhancing productivity in collaborative environments. Code-Whisperer, developed by Amazon, emphasizes integration with AWS services, making it suitable for cloud-centric projects. Both tools support multiple programming languages and can reduce errors by providing contextual recommendations. The right choice depends on whether the focus is on broader development needs or cloud-specific integrations for enterprise projects.

Custom Models

For organizations with unique requirements, custom models such as Hugging Face Transformers or fine-tuned BERT and GPT variants offer greater flexibility. Hugging Face provides a vast library of pre-trained models that can be adapted for tasks ranging from natural language processing to multimodal applications. Fine-tuning models like BERT or GPT allows organizations to train on domain-specific datasets, ensuring outputs align closely with specialized industries such as healthcare, finance, or law. While this approach requires more resources and expertise, it provides higher levels of control, personalization, and accuracy, making it ideal for businesses with proprietary or sensitive data needs.

Decide whether you want:

API-based solutions (quick deployment, minimal maintenance)

API-based solutions are best suited for businesses that want to quickly integrate generative AI capabilities without heavy infrastructure investment. These solutions provide ready-made functionalities like natural language processing, image generation, or chatbot services, which can be deployed using simple API calls. Since the provider handles updates, scaling, and bug fixes, organizations experience minimal maintenance overhead. This makes it a cost-effective and time-efficient option, particularly for startups and small enterprises. However, API-based solutions may limit customization and require sending data externally, which might raise privacy concerns. They are ideal for rapid prototyping, customer-facing tools, and scaling quickly.

On-premise or private-hosted LLMs (more control, data security)

On-premise or private-hosted LLMs are designed for organizations that prioritize control, security, and customization over ease of deployment. By hosting AI models on their own servers or private cloud, businesses can ensure sensitive data never leaves their environment, meeting strict compliance and regulatory requirements. This approach allows tailoring of models to specific use cases, performance tuning, and integration with proprietary datasets. However, the setup and maintenance costs are higher, as it requires dedicated infrastructure, technical expertise, and continuous monitoring. Despite higher complexity, this model is preferred by enterprises in sectors like healthcare, finance, and government where data security is critical.

Vertical-specific AI tools (marketing, legal, HR, etc.)

Vertical-specific AI tools are specialized applications built to address challenges within a particular industry. For example, marketing-focused AI may analyze customer data for campaign optimization, while legal AI tools streamline contract review and compliance checks, and HR-focused AI enhances recruitment or employee engagement. These solutions are tailored to domain-specific workflows, making adoption smoother and results more relevant compared to generic AI tools. They often come pre-trained with industry-specific data, reducing the need for extensive fine-tuning. While they may lack flexibility outside their niche, vertical AI tools offer immediate value by solving well-defined business problems effectively and efficiently.

Develop and Test AI Solutions in a Pilot Program

Start small

The first step in implementing AI is to begin with small-scale proof of concept models. These models act as early experiments to test whether the AI idea has practical value in the business context. By starting small, organizations minimize risks while learning how the technology behaves. A PoC allows stakeholders to observe initial results, measure feasibility, and evaluate if the solution solves the intended problem. This stage is crucial to demonstrate tangible outcomes without committing excessive resources. It helps identify gaps early, refine ideas, and set the foundation for larger implementations with confidence and clarity.

Pilot Scope

Defining a clear pilot scope ensures the project remains manageable and focused. Selecting one specific use case allows teams to concentrate resources and attention on testing AI in a controlled environment. This could involve automating a single process, such as document classification, or applying predictive analytics to a targeted dataset. Limiting scope prevents unnecessary complexity while enabling measurable results. A well-designed pilot creates realistic conditions without exposing the business to large-scale risks. This focused testing builds a learning ground to understand the AI system's potential impact, scalability, and how well it integrates into current workflows.

Train or fine-tune models using domain-specific data if necessary

Generic AI models often lack the context required for specialized industries or organizations. To achieve better accuracy and relevance, training or fine-tuning models with domain-specific data becomes essential. For example, in healthcare, using patient records and clinical guidelines improves diagnostic models, while in finance, historical transaction data strengthens fraud detection. Fine-tuning allows models to adapt to business-specific terminology, processes, and requirements. This step ensures outputs are meaningful and aligned with real-world challenges. Tailoring AI through specialized data enhances trust, performance, and reliability, providing solutions that address actual business needs rather than generic assumptions.

Involve stakeholders in evaluating outputs for accuracy, tone, and bias

Stakeholder involvement is critical in validating AI solutions. Subject matter experts, end-users, and business leaders must evaluate outputs for accuracy, tone, and potential bias. This collaborative review helps detect flaws that technical teams might overlook, such as cultural sensitivity, industry jargon, or unintended ethical issues. By including diverse perspectives, organizations ensure that AI outcomes align with both technical standards and human expectations. Stakeholders provide valuable feedback on how results feel in practice, whether they are usable, trustworthy, and ethically sound. This participatory evaluation fosters adoption, accountability, and confidence in the AI system's fairness and reliability.

Collect feedback on utility, speed, user experience, and errors

Gathering feedback is a vital part of the pilot phase, as it helps assess how AI performs in real use. Users and stakeholders should comment on utility—whether the solution solves their problem—along with speed and efficiency. User experience plays a big role, as even accurate outputs may fail if the interface feels complex or inconvenient. Feedback also highlights errors, gaps, and limitations, providing opportunities for refinement. Continuous input enables developers to iterate quickly and improve models. This process ensures that the AI solution evolves based on actual business requirements and user expectations rather than assumptions.

AI's reliability, performance, and ROI before scaling

The pilot stage is not just about testing functionality—it is about building confidence for future investment and scale. By systematically assessing reliability, performance, and return on investment (ROI), businesses can determine whether AI delivers measurable value. If the pilot demonstrates cost savings, efficiency improvements, or enhanced decision-making, leaders gain evidence to justify expansion. Conversely, identifying weaknesses early prevents wasted resources on ineffective solutions. This structured evaluation creates a roadmap for scaling AI across more use cases. Ultimately, the pilot acts as a safety net, ensuring AI adoption is practical, impactful, and aligned with organizational goals.

Address Governance, Ethics, and Compliance

As you deploy, put governance frameworks in place:

AI Ethics

AI ethics form the backbone of trustworthy generative AI deployment. Organizations must ensure that AI outputs are fair, unbiased, and respectful, avoiding toxicity or harmful stereotypes. This involves continuous monitoring of models for bias, using diverse training datasets, and conducting fairness audits to detect unintended discrimination. AI should promote inclusivity and transparency, ensuring that generated content aligns with ethical principles and organizational values. Regularly revisiting ethical guidelines helps address emerging challenges as AI evolves. By embedding ethical considerations into every stage of AI use, companies not only build trust among stakeholders but also protect their reputation and societal responsibility.

Human-in-the-Loop

A critical element of governance in generative AI deployment is the human-in-the-loop approach. While AI can generate content and insights at scale, the ultimate responsibility must rest with human decision-makers. Humans act as quality gatekeepers, reviewing AI outputs for accuracy, context, and alignment with company goals. This approach reduces risks of misinformation, bias, or inappropriate outputs. By combining human judgment with AI efficiency, organizations ensure that automated systems remain accountable and reliable. Human oversight also encourages responsible adoption, as employees remain engaged in evaluating outputs, correcting errors, and ensuring that technology complements human expertise rather than replacing it.

Data Privacy

Protecting user data is fundamental to responsible AI governance. Organizations must anonymize and secure personal information before using it in AI systems to reduce risks of exposure or misuse. Role-based access controls should be implemented to ensure only authorized personnel can access sensitive data, thereby minimizing insider threats. Encryption during storage and transmission strengthens privacy protection. Regular audits, penetration testing, and compliance with data protection regulations reinforce this security framework. By prioritizing privacy, companies build trust with customers and employees while ensuring legal and ethical integrity. Strong privacy measures not only protect individuals but also safeguard the organization's reputation.

Compliance

Generative AI must operate within the boundaries of existing laws and regulations to avoid legal liabilities. Aligning practices with frameworks such as GDPR in Europe or HIPAA in healthcare ensures that data protection and user rights remain intact. Compliance also extends to intellectual property, ensuring that generated outputs do not infringe on copyrights or trademarks. Organizations should establish internal audit mechanisms to verify adherence to local laws and corporate policies. By proactively addressing compliance, companies reduce regulatory risks and penalties while fostering an environment of accountability. Strong compliance frameworks also create competitive advantages by demonstrating reliability and integrity.

Internal AI Use Policies

Developing comprehensive internal policies on AI use is crucial for organizational governance. These policies should define acceptable applications of generative AI, outline ethical standards, and provide clear guidelines for employees. Training programs can help staff understand responsible use, potential risks, and how to escalate issues when AI outputs are questionable. Policies must cover areas such as intellectual property, data handling, and accountability for misuse. Encouraging transparency in AI adoption ensures employees remain vigilant and aligned with company objectives. Well-defined internal policies not only protect organizations from risks but also cultivate a culture of responsible, innovative, and ethical AI use.

Scale Across Teams and Monitor Continuously

Once pilot results are validated, expand adoption:

Train employees on how to effectively use and monitor AI tools

Once the pilot stage demonstrates successful results, scaling across teams requires structured training programs. Employees must be guided not only on how to use AI tools but also on interpreting their outputs correctly. Training should emphasize understanding limitations, ethical considerations, and best practices for leveraging AI insights in decision-making. Workshops, hands-on practice sessions, and role-based learning modules help teams adapt faster. Additionally, developing AI literacy across the workforce ensures confidence in adoption and reduces resistance. By building capability, organizations empower employees to monitor AI-driven processes effectively and ensure accuracy, fairness, and compliance in daily workflows.

Integrate AI into workflows using APIs, webhooks, or custom dashboards

After training, AI systems must be seamlessly embedded into business operations. APIs and webhooks allow real-time data transfer between platforms, enabling smooth automation of tasks. For example, customer support teams can integrate AI chatbots into CRM systems, while finance departments can use AI dashboards to monitor transactions. Custom dashboards provide centralized visibility, allowing employees to interact with AI outputs intuitively. Integration ensures AI becomes a natural extension of existing tools rather than an isolated solution. This alignment reduces redundancy, enhances efficiency, and allows for consistent usage across departments, ensuring the organization extracts maximum value from AI investments.

Track KPIs

To justify scaling AI across teams, organizations must monitor its performance through key performance indicators (KPIs). Metrics like employee productivity, operational cost reduction, customer satisfaction, and turnaround time highlight tangible benefits. Advanced analytics can also measure adoption rates and error reductions. Tracking KPIs ensures accountability and helps leadership evaluate return on investment. Importantly, KPIs must be tailored to each department's objectives customer-facing teams may focus on satisfaction scores, while logistics may track efficiency gains. By continuously monitoring results, businesses can identify whether AI is driving meaningful improvements, enabling data-driven adjustments to strategies and processes where necessary.

Continuously Improve

AI adoption is not a one-time event but an ongoing process. Once deployed, models, prompts, and data inputs must be refined to align with evolving business needs. For generative AI, prompt engineering can improve relevance and clarity of outputs, while machine learning models may need retraining with updated datasets. Regular evaluation prevents performance degradation and ensures adaptability to changing market conditions. Feedback loops from employees and customers play a critical role in fine-tuning. Organizations that commit to continuous improvement create resilient AI systems that consistently deliver high-quality outcomes and remain competitive in dynamic business environments.

Establish AI Center of Excellence (CoE)

To ensure long-term success, organizations should establish an AI Center of Excellence (CoE). A CoE acts as a governance and innovation hub, responsible for developing best practices, monitoring compliance, and ensuring responsible AI usage. It centralizes expertise, provides advisory support to departments, and standardizes frameworks for AI adoption. The CoE also fosters cross-functional collaboration, helping identify new use cases and accelerating innovation. By defining ethical guidelines and addressing risks like bias or misuse, it builds organizational trust in AI. Ultimately, a CoE ensures scalability, consistency, and sustainable growth, making AI an integral and well-governed part of business strategy.

Stepwise Framework for Implementing Generative AI in Business

To successfully implement generative AI in a business setting, organizations must adopt a structured approach that begins with identifying value-driven use cases and extends through to ethical deployment and scaling. Each step from assessing technical readiness to selecting appropriate tools, conducting pilot testing, establishing governance, and finally scaling ensures that AI integration aligns with strategic goals while minimizing risk. This roadmap not only supports operational efficiency and innovation but also reinforces trust, compliance, and long-term impact across business functions in Table 6.1.

Table 6.1: Stepwise Framework for Implementing Generative AI in Business – Focus Areas and Expected Outcomes

Step	Focus Area	Outcome
Identify Use Cases	Pinpoint AI opportunities	Business alignment
Assess Readiness	Infrastructure, people, compliance	Risk mitigation
Choose Tools	Select models/platforms	Fit-for-purpose tech
Pilot AI Solutions	Test and validate	Evidence of value
Set Governance	Ethical and legal compliance	Trust and safety
Scale & Monitor	Roll out AI with controls	Sustained impact

Building a Culture of Innovation

Building a culture of innovation is essential for successfully implementing Generative AI (GenAI) in any business. This is not just about integrating a technology it's about reshaping mindset, workflows, leadership, and values to drive continuous innovation through GenAI tools. Below is a detailed, multi-dimensional explanation of how to embed a culture of innovation in your organization while adopting Generative AI.

Visionary Leadership & Commitment from the Top

Leadership must champion AI innovation not only in words but through action. This includes:

1. Articulating a clear AI-powered innovation vision.
2. Allocating budget, time, and people for pilot and scaled initiatives.
3. Encouraging experimentation by removing the fear of failure.
4. Acting as role models by using GenAI tools in strategic decision-making.

A committed leadership drives trust, inspires action, and anchors innovation in organizational priorities.

Establish an AI Center of Excellence (CoE)

A formal AI CoE institutionalizes innovation:

Defines standards, frameworks, and policies for AI use

An AI Center of Excellence (CoE) plays a crucial role in standardizing how artificial intelligence is implemented across an organization. By defining clear frameworks, best practices, and policies, the CoE ensures that AI projects follow consistent methodologies, thereby improving quality and efficiency. These guidelines address aspects such as data governance, model development workflows, compliance requirements, and performance benchmarks. Establishing uniform standards also minimizes risks, prevents duplication of efforts, and helps teams adopt proven practices. This structured approach creates a reliable foundation for scaling AI initiatives, ensuring long-term sustainability while aligning innovation with business goals and regulatory obligations.

Identifies high-value use cases for Generative AI

The AI CoE serves as a strategic unit that evaluates and prioritizes opportunities where Generative AI can deliver maximum value. It systematically scans across business functions, identifies repetitive or knowledge-intensive tasks, and determines areas where AI can enhance productivity, creativity, or decision-making. By aligning these use cases with organizational priorities, the CoE ensures that resources are invested wisely. High-value use cases might include content automation, customer support augmentation, product design, or predictive insights. This proactive approach ensures that AI adoption is purposeful, measurable, and tied directly to business outcomes, enabling both quick wins and long-term competitive advantages.

Creates reusable assets (e.g., prompt libraries, APIs)

To accelerate adoption and reduce redundant efforts, the CoE develops reusable assets that can be shared across teams. These assets may include prompt libraries for Generative AI, pre-trained models, APIs, reusable datasets, and standardized templates. Such resources lower the barrier to entry, allowing teams with limited technical expertise to leverage AI effectively. By centralizing and curating these tools, the CoE ensures consistency, security, and scalability in deployment. This also fosters collaboration, as teams can build on existing assets rather than starting from scratch. Ultimately, reusable AI components drive efficiency, reduce costs, and accelerate innovation cycles across the organization.

Promotes ethical, secure, and explainable AI use

A key responsibility of the AI CoE is to ensure that innovation is pursued responsibly. It establishes ethical guidelines to address issues such as data privacy, bias mitigation, transparency, and explainability in AI models. Security measures are enforced to protect sensitive data and prevent misuse of AI tools. By embedding responsible AI principles into every stage of development, the CoE builds trust with stakeholders, employees, and customers. It also provides training and awareness programs to help teams understand the ethical implications of Generative AI. This commitment ensures that AI adoption not only drives innovation but also upholds societal and organizational values. The CoE acts as a central engine powering decentralized innovation across teams. While the CoE provides a centralized framework and resources, its ultimate role is to empower teams across the organization to innovate independently. By offering tools, guidelines, and expertise, it enables departments to adapt AI solutions to their unique needs while still maintaining alignment with enterprise standards. This balance of centralization and decentralization ensures agility without sacrificing control. Teams can experiment, deploy, and scale AI-driven solutions faster, knowing they have the backing of a robust support system. Thus, the CoE functions as the engine that fuels a culture of continuous innovation, driving AI adoption at scale across the enterprise.

Foster a Culture of Experimentation and Learning

GenAI thrives in an experimental environment:

Encourage low-risk pilots with iterative feedback loops: Generative AI adoption becomes sustainable when organizations encourage low-risk pilots that provide a safe environment for experimentation. Instead of immediately deploying large-scale solutions, small and controlled experiments allow teams to test hypotheses, validate assumptions, and refine models before committing significant resources. Iterative feedback loops, where outcomes are evaluated, discussed, and improved upon, help ensure continuous learning. This minimizes risk while maximizing innovation potential, as mistakes can be corrected early without major consequences. Such pilots also build organizational confidence in AI, fostering a mindset that values gradual progress and evidence-based decision-making rather than rushing to untested large-scale implementations.

Reward curiosity and learning from failure: A true culture of experimentation requires redefining how success is measured. Instead of penalizing failures, organizations must reward curiosity, risk-taking, and the lessons extracted from unsuccessful attempts. Recognizing the value of failed experiments communicates that every attempt contributes to progress, reducing fear and encouraging bold ideas. Celebrating employees who ask unconventional questions, explore new datasets, or challenge existing assumptions strengthens organizational resilience. Leaders play a crucial role in modeling this behavior by openly sharing their own learning experiences. By framing failure as a stepping stone rather than an endpoint, companies accelerate innovation and empower employees to engage more creatively.

Promote cross-functional hackathons or innovation days focused on AI-driven ideas:

Cross-functional hackathons and dedicated innovation days create powerful opportunities to generate AI-driven ideas. These events bring together diverse teams engineers, data scientists, marketers, HR professionals, and designers to collaborate on real-world challenges. The mix of perspectives ensures solutions are practical, human-centered, and aligned with business goals. Hackathons encourage rapid prototyping under time constraints, sparking creativity and teamwork. They also uncover hidden talent within the organization and give employees a platform to showcase skills beyond their daily roles. When leadership supports and implements outcomes from such events, it reinforces the belief that experimentation has tangible value, motivating employees to engage deeply with AI.

Celebrate small wins and rapid prototypes, not just final deliverables: Acknowledging incremental progress is vital for sustaining momentum in AI innovation. Organizations should celebrate small wins such as a working prototype, a model improvement, or a creative automation idea. Highlighting these achievements keeps teams motivated and emphasizes that progress is not only measured by the final product but also by milestones reached along the way. Rapid prototypes, even if imperfect, provide valuable proof-of-concept and help secure buy-in from stakeholders. By recognizing these early efforts, leadership reinforces a growth mindset, encourages continued exploration, and ensures that innovation remains an ongoing journey rather than a one-time destination or rigid end goal.

This supports a "fail-fast, learn-faster" culture needed for innovation at speed: The ultimate aim of fostering experimentation and learning is to build a "fail-fast, learn-faster" culture. In the rapidly evolving AI landscape, speed matters, and organizations cannot afford to cling to outdated ideas or fear mistakes. By embracing rapid cycles of trial, error, and adaptation, businesses enhance their agility and responsiveness. This culture ensures that every failure shortens the path to success, as insights gained inform the next iteration. Employees feel empowered to test bold ideas without hesitation, leading to breakthrough innovations. Over time, this mindset transforms AI adoption into a core strength, positioning organizations as leaders in digital transformation.

Upskill Employees in AI Literacy and Creative Confidence

People are at the heart of any transformation. Upskilling them empowers participation:

Conduct training programs in GenAI tools

Training programs are the foundation for equipping employees with AI literacy. By offering structured workshops on generative AI tools such as ChatGPT for text generation, GitHub Copilot for coding assistance, or Midjourney for design creativity, organizations enable employees to experience AI practically. These programs should combine theory with hands-on exercises, allowing employees to solve real work problems using AI. When individuals learn how to navigate tools, they gain confidence and overcome resistance to new technologies. Continuous training also ensures teams remain updated with rapidly evolving AI advancements, making them more capable of leveraging technology for innovation and productivity.

Teach prompt engineering, data awareness, and AI safety practices: Prompt engineering is a core skill that maximizes the value of generative AI. Employees must learn to design effective prompts that deliver accurate and context-appropriate results. Alongside this, developing data awareness ensures employees understand the importance of clean, unbiased, and secure data feeding AI systems. Teaching AI safety practices such as responsible usage, bias mitigation, and compliance with ethical guidelines further creates a responsible workforce. Together, these competencies empower employees to not only use AI effectively but also safeguard the organization from risks. This comprehensive approach builds both technical and ethical confidence in adopting AI responsibly and sustainably.

Nurture creative thinking and problem-solving abilities: AI can enhance human potential, but creativity and problem-solving remain uniquely human strengths. Organizations must design programs that encourage employees to think beyond standard solutions, using AI as a collaborator rather than just a tool. By fostering brainstorming sessions, hackathons, and innovation labs, employees can learn to pair their creativity with AI's generative power. This synergy helps them reimagine processes, design new products, or develop novel services. Encouraging divergent thinking alongside AI also nurtures resilience, adaptability, and innovation. When creative confidence is combined with AI capabilities, employees are better prepared to lead transformational change rather than simply react to it.

Encourage use of AI to automate routine tasks so employees can focus on high-value innovation: Automation is one of AI's strongest advantages. By encouraging employees to use AI for repetitive tasks such as drafting reports, summarizing documents, coding snippets, or processing data, organizations free up valuable human time. This shift enables employees to redirect their energy toward critical thinking, strategy, and innovation. Routine automation not only improves efficiency but also enhances job satisfaction by removing mundane work. Employees can then focus on designing creative solutions, building stronger customer relationships, and driving business growth. This balance of automation and human ingenuity creates a workplace where innovation thrives and employees feel empowered to contribute strategically.

Integrate GenAI into Business Workflows & Decision-Making

To sustain a culture of AI-driven innovation, GenAI must be woven into everyday workflows:

Use APIs, webhooks, or custom dashboards to embed AI

Integrating Generative AI seamlessly into existing business tools ensures adoption without disrupting employee workflows. By leveraging APIs and webhooks, organizations can connect AI engines directly with platforms like CRMs, ERPs, or communication tools, enabling real-time insights and automation. Custom dashboards further centralize these AI functions, allowing employees to access intelligent suggestions, predictive analytics, or automated responses without leaving their primary work environment. This reduces friction, improves efficiency, and promotes consistent usage. By embedding AI where employees already spend time, businesses encourage natural adoption, making AI an invisible yet powerful productivity enhancer rather than an additional task to manage.

Redesign workflows to include human-AI collaboration loops

To maximize the potential of Generative AI, workflows must be intentionally redesigned for collaborative efficiency between humans and AI. Rather than replacing human judgment, AI can act as a first-pass creator—drafting reports, analyzing data, or generating design prototypes. Humans then refine outputs with domain expertise, contextual knowledge, and critical thinking. This loop ensures speed and scalability from AI, while maintaining creativity, accuracy, and ethical oversight from people. By structuring workflows around this iterative exchange, businesses establish a partnership model where AI augments, not replaces, human effort. This collaborative framework fosters trust, accelerates productivity, and consistently produces high-quality outcomes.

Empower teams with self-service AI capabilities—removing IT bottlenecks

A major barrier to AI-driven innovation is over-reliance on IT departments for access and deployment. By offering self-service AI platforms, employees can independently experiment, analyze, and automate tasks within their roles. Tools such as AI chatbots, drag-and-drop model builders, or no-code automation environments democratize AI usage, enabling non-technical staff to benefit directly. Removing bottlenecks accelerates adoption, reduces organizational silos, and sparks creativity across teams. When employees can explore use cases on their own, innovation becomes decentralized and inclusive. This empowerment nurtures a sense of ownership, where individuals contribute directly to AI-driven transformation without waiting for centralized technical approvals.

Innovation becomes continuous when AI is part of the operational fabric

The true cultural shift happens when AI is no longer seen as a project but as an ingrained component of everyday business operations. By embedding Generative AI into decision-making, communication, and process execution, innovation becomes a continuous cycle rather than sporadic bursts. Employees consistently leverage AI for insights, optimization, and creativity, turning it into a daily habit. Over time, this fosters a culture of experimentation and agility where improvements are constant. AI transforms into a foundational layer of the organization's ecosystem, ensuring that the business evolves dynamically, adapts to changes, and continuously discovers new opportunities for growth and efficiency.

Adopt Agile Governance with Guardrails

Adopting agile governance with guardrails ensures that organizations can innovate rapidly without sacrificing oversight. Unlike rigid governance, agile governance provides a flexible framework that adapts to the pace of experimentation while still setting clear rules. It enables decision-making to remain swift, decentralized, and responsive to changing needs. Guardrails such as security protocols, ethical boundaries, and compliance standards act as invisible support, allowing teams to explore new ideas safely. This balance encourages both creativity and accountability. By combining agility with strong governance, businesses create an environment where innovation thrives without slipping into chaos or regulatory risks.

A culture of innovation doesn't mean a free-for-all: While innovation is essential, it cannot be equated with unstructured or careless experimentation. A culture of innovation must operate within defined parameters to prevent disruption, misuse of resources, or harmful outcomes. Innovation without discipline often leads to wasted efforts, ethical concerns, or even regulatory violations. Leaders must instill a mindset where creativity coexists with responsibility, ensuring that all experiments serve strategic goals. Structured frameworks, check-ins, and accountability mechanisms ensure that innovation adds value. This prevents the "free-for-all" mentality and aligns creative ideas with organizational purpose, making innovation sustainable, impactful, and beneficial for long-term growth.

Implement agile governance frameworks that support experimentation while maintaining security, privacy, and compliance: An effective governance framework balances innovation with compliance by providing a flexible yet structured approach. Agile governance allows experimentation through rapid iteration, pilot projects, and adaptive feedback loops. At the same time, it ensures that essential safeguards like security, privacy, and regulatory compliance—are never compromised. This duality is critical in industries such as healthcare, finance, or education, where innovation must not endanger sensitive data or trust. Organizations can deploy agile governance through lightweight approval processes, sandbox environments, and compliance checkpoints embedded in workflows. This ensures that experimentation remains safe, controlled, and strategically aligned with business and legal requirements.

Define ethical guidelines and responsible AI policies: As businesses adopt advanced technologies like AI, ethical guidelines are crucial to prevent misuse and unintended harm. Defining responsible AI policies ensures transparency, fairness, and accountability in model development and deployment. These guidelines should address issues like bias, explainability, and human oversight, while aligning with international AI ethics standards. Ethical policies set expectations for developers, users, and stakeholders, ensuring trust and credibility. They also create a moral compass for innovation, encouraging technology that benefits society while minimizing risks. A well-documented ethical framework transforms innovation from being merely profit-driven to being socially responsible and sustainable in the long term.

Use monitoring tools to audit model usage, output quality, and potential biases: Continuous monitoring ensures that innovation remains reliable, trustworthy, and free from harmful consequences. Organizations should deploy tools to track how models are being used, evaluate their performance, and detect issues like drift, errors, or biases. Monitoring tools provide valuable insights by flagging anomalies, identifying unfair outcomes, and ensuring compliance with internal and external standards. Automated auditing systems can produce reports for regulators, management, and stakeholders, enhancing transparency. By embedding real-time feedback loops, businesses can correct problems early and avoid reputational or legal damage. This proactive approach builds confidence in both experimental and production-level deployments of innovative systems.

Well-designed guardrails create a safe space for innovation: Guardrails serve as protective boundaries that encourage innovation without fear of crossing into unsafe or unethical territory. They establish rules, best practices, and oversight mechanisms that enable teams to experiment boldly while remaining secure and compliant.

Instead of restricting creativity, guardrails empower innovators by reducing uncertainty and offering clarity about what is permissible. This assurance fosters psychological safety, encouraging teams to push boundaries without worrying about unintended risks. In essence, guardrails act as enablers, not barriers, of creativity. With well-designed boundaries, organizations can sustain innovation at scale while maintaining trust, accountability, and long-term success.

Promote Cross-Functional Collaboration & Idea Sharing

Innovation with GenAI is not siloed it thrives in collaboration:

Build cross-disciplinary squads (tech + marketing + ops + HR) to ideate GenAI applications: Cross-functional squads bring together individuals from diverse backgrounds such as technology, marketing, operations, and human resources, creating a melting pot of ideas and expertise. By combining technical know-how with market insights, operational understanding, and people-centric perspectives, organizations can identify GenAI applications that are both innovative and practical. These squads can work in agile frameworks, rapidly prototyping and testing concepts before scaling. The diversity of thought helps uncover blind spots, align innovations with customer and organizational needs, and foster a culture where every department actively contributes to shaping the GenAI journey. This synergy accelerates adoption and impact.

Create knowledge-sharing platforms (wikis, forums, demos): Knowledge-sharing platforms such as internal wikis, discussion forums, or demo sessions act as collaborative ecosystems where employees can document, exchange, and refine GenAI-related ideas. These platforms ensure that innovations are not confined to isolated teams but are accessible to the entire organization. Wikis can store best practices, tutorials, and use cases, while forums facilitate open discussion on challenges and opportunities. Demo sessions encourage hands-on learning, allowing teams to showcase prototypes or experiments. Over time, these platforms serve as a living repository of institutional GenAI knowledge, fostering transparency, continuous learning, and collective problem-solving across departments.

Encourage customer-facing teams to surface pain points that GenAI can solve: Customer-facing teams such as sales, support, and service have direct insights into recurring customer challenges, inefficiencies, and unmet needs. Encouraging these teams to actively share pain points creates a feedback loop where GenAI solutions are rooted in real-world problems rather than hypothetical scenarios. For instance, customer service teams might highlight repetitive inquiries that can be automated through AI-powered chatbots, while sales teams might point to lead qualification challenges that GenAI models can streamline. By capturing and channeling this frontline knowledge, organizations can prioritize high-impact initiatives, ensuring GenAI solutions deliver tangible value and enhance customer satisfaction and loyalty.

Blending diverse perspectives leads to richer, more relevant GenAI use cases: Innovation flourishes when multiple perspectives converge. By blending the analytical skills of technologists, the creativity of marketers, the efficiency mindset of operations, and the empathy-driven approach of HR, organizations unlock GenAI applications that are not only technically sound but also strategically aligned. Diverse perspectives help avoid narrow solutions, broaden the scope of ideation, and ensure inclusivity in design. Such collaborative thinking often reveals unexpected synergies for example, linking workforce upskilling with AI-driven personalization or combining predictive analytics with customer engagement strategies. This fusion of insights results in richer, more relevant, and sustainable GenAI use cases that drive long-term transformation.

Align GenAI Strategy with Long-Term Business Goals

Innovation must serve the larger strategy:

Use GenAI to enhance strategic priorities

Generative AI should be seen as an enabler of existing strategic priorities rather than a standalone trend. By carefully mapping AI initiatives to business goals, organizations can unlock real value. For example, enhancing customer experience through personalized interactions, improving product development with AI-driven prototyping, or boosting employee productivity with intelligent assistants directly supports long-term growth. Instead of experimenting randomly, leaders must ensure each GenAI use case clearly ties back to core objectives. This approach ensures investments in AI deliver measurable outcomes while reinforcing competitive differentiation and sustainability rather than becoming isolated experiments.

Evaluate new business models enabled by GenAI

Generative AI not only supports existing strategies but also opens opportunities for entirely new business models. Organizations can explore AI-powered services, such as automated consulting platforms or content creation tools, which provide scalable offerings at lower costs. Personalization at scale is another transformative area, allowing businesses to deliver unique experiences tailored to each customer in real-time. By evaluating such opportunities, companies can move beyond incremental gains and redefine industry standards. Strategic leaders should regularly assess market trends, competitive dynamics, and customer expectations to decide how GenAI-enabled innovations can complement or even reshape their long-term revenue streams.

Continuously align AI roadmaps with business transformation goals

AI roadmaps must evolve hand-in-hand with broader business transformation agendas. Technology adoption without alignment risks creating silos or fragmented solutions. A successful strategy involves setting clear milestones, integrating GenAI into digital transformation roadmaps, and continuously monitoring progress against evolving business objectives. For instance, if the company shifts toward sustainability, AI use cases should be evaluated for their role in optimizing energy consumption, reducing waste, or supporting ethical innovation. By embedding flexibility and alignment checks into AI planning, leaders ensure that GenAI remains a dynamic driver of transformation instead of stagnating as a one-time project.

Innovation as a driver of sustainable competitive advantage

The ultimate purpose of aligning GenAI with long-term goals is to transform innovation into a source of sustainable competitive advantage. Organizations that view AI merely as a shiny technology risk wasting resources and losing strategic direction. True value arises when AI capabilities become deeply embedded in business processes, culture, and customer journeys. By combining technological adoption with strategic foresight, companies can consistently stay ahead of competitors, deliver differentiated experiences, and adapt quickly to changing markets. This disciplined alignment ensures that GenAI is not just a passing trend but a cornerstone of long-term resilience, growth, and market leadership.

Overcoming challenges in AI integration

Lack of Strategic Alignment

Challenge: Businesses often jump into GenAI without aligning it with core strategic goals. This leads to disjointed use-cases and wasted resources.

Solution:

To effectively implement Generative AI (GenAI) within an organization, it is essential to begin by clearly defining the specific business objectives that GenAI is intended to support. These objectives may include enhancing customer service through automation, generating dynamic content, or delivering personalized experiences at scale. Once these priorities are established, a well-structured GenAI strategy roadmap should be developed, ensuring it is aligned with the company's broader digital transformation goals. This roadmap will help maintain focus and continuity as the organization scales its GenAI initiatives. Furthermore, involving both technical experts and business stakeholders throughout the planning and deployment phases is crucial. This cross-functional collaboration ensures that the implementation is not only technically sound but also aligned with business metrics, thereby maximizing return on investment (ROI) and ensuring the initiative delivers tangible value across the organization.

Data Quality and Availability

Challenge: GenAI models rely heavily on large volumes of high-quality data. Many organizations struggle with siloed, outdated, or unstructured datasets.

Solution:

To successfully implement Generative AI in business processes, it is crucial to first conduct a comprehensive data audit to evaluate the current state of data infrastructure, identify gaps, and determine readiness for AI integration. Once the audit reveals deficiencies or inconsistencies, organizations must implement robust data cleaning, labeling, and enrichment pipelines to ensure the input data is accurate, consistent, and contextually rich—crucial for training effective GenAI models. For domains or scenarios where data is sparse or imbalanced, businesses can leverage synthetic data generation using GenAI to simulate underrepresented use cases and enhance model generalizability. Throughout this process, it is essential to ensure strict compliance with data governance and privacy regulations such as GDPR and HIPAA, embedding ethical standards and legal safeguards into every stage of data handling and AI deployment.

Model Selection and Customization

Challenge: Off-the-shelf models may not align with industry-specific needs or internal policies.

Solution:

When evaluating generative AI deployment strategies, organizations must carefully weigh their options between open-source models, commercial APIs, and custom fine-tuned solutions. Open-source models such as LLaMA and Mistral offer greater transparency and flexibility, often preferred by teams with in-house expertise and a need for customization. On the other hand, commercial APIs like those offered by OpenAI or Anthropic provide easy-to-integrate, scalable solutions with strong support and high performance out of the box, though they often come with limitations in customization and data privacy concerns. For organizations with highly specific needs, building or fine-tuning custom models using domain-specific data ensures higher relevance, contextual accuracy, and potentially superior performance in niche tasks. Regardless of the choice, it is essential to prioritize models that strike a balance between predictive accuracy, interpretability, and resource efficiency ensuring the solution is not only effective but also explainable and sustainable within operational constraints.

Infrastructure and Integration Complexity

Challenge: Implementing GenAI requires significant infrastructure and compatibility with existing IT ecosystems.

Solution:

To successfully implement Generative AI solutions at scale, businesses should leverage cloud-based platforms such as Azure OpenAI and AWS Bedrock, which provide robust infrastructure for hosting large language models with scalability, flexibility, and security. These platforms allow organizations to deploy AI models without the need for extensive in-house hardware, enabling seamless access to cutting-edge capabilities. Additionally, investing in ML Ops (Machine Learning Operations) pipelines is essential for managing the full AI lifecycle — including deployment, monitoring, and version control. This ensures that models remain reliable, up-to-date, and easy to maintain across various environments. Furthermore, integrating Generative AI into existing enterprise tools via APIs or low-code/no-code connectors can accelerate adoption and maximize value. This approach allows teams to embed AI-powered functionalities into workflows such as CRM, ERP, and collaboration platforms without needing deep technical expertise, fostering innovation and efficiency throughout the organization.

Talent and Skill Gap

Challenge: Many organizations lack internal expertise to develop, manage, or even evaluate GenAI models.

Solution:

To effectively integrate artificial intelligence into business operations, organizations must prioritize the development of internal capabilities and strategic hiring. A foundational step involves upskilling existing teams through targeted AI training programs such as Prompt Engineering, AI Literacy, and Machine Learning Operations (ML Ops). These initiatives empower employees to understand and leverage AI tools, ensuring smoother adoption and innovation from within. Simultaneously, businesses should consider hiring or contracting specialized talent including AI experts, data scientists, and GenAI engineers, whose technical proficiency can accelerate project execution and solution deployment. To bridge the gap between technology and business needs, it is essential to form cross-functional teams that blend domain-specific experts with technologists. This interdisciplinary approach fosters collaboration, aligns AI efforts with real-world applications, and drives value creation across all functions.

Ethical and Responsible AI Usage

Challenge: Generative AI can amplify biases, create misinformation, or violate IP/data privacy.

Solution:

To ensure ethical and trustworthy use of artificial intelligence, organizations should adopt a Responsible AI framework that emphasizes fairness, transparency, and accountability at every stage of development and deployment. This includes proactively using bias detection tools during model training and ongoing output monitoring to identify and mitigate discriminatory patterns or unintended consequences. Furthermore, establishing dedicated AI ethics committees and review boards is essential for overseeing critical deployments and ensuring that AI systems align with societal values, legal standards, and organizational goals. Such comprehensive governance helps foster trust in AI technologies and ensures they are used responsibly and equitably.

Security and IP Protection

Challenge: GenAI models might inadvertently leak proprietary data or expose systems to adversarial threats.

Solution:

To ensure the safe and responsible deployment of generative AI systems, it is essential to implement robust security measures at multiple layers. First, enterprises should deploy advanced security protocols such as data encryption and strict access control mechanisms to protect sensitive data and prevent unauthorized usage. Additionally, continuous monitoring of model outputs is critical to detect potential risks like prompt injection attacks or inadvertent data leakage, which can compromise system integrity or user confidentiality. To further safeguard intellectual property and maintain trust, techniques such as differential privacy and model watermarking should be implemented. These strategies not only protect the output from misuse or reverse engineering but also ensure compliance with data privacy standards and enable traceability of AI-generated content.

Change Management and Resistance

Challenge: Employees may fear AI replacing their jobs or disrupting workflows.

Solution:

To successfully implement Generative AI (GenAI) within an organization, it's essential to foster a culture of augmentation rather than automation. This means emphasizing how GenAI enhances human capabilities instead of replacing them. By positioning AI as a collaborative partner, employees can view it as a tool that streamlines tasks, boosts creativity, and supports decision-making. Offering hands-on training sessions and AI co-pilot tools further empowers users, making them feel supported and in control rather than threatened. It's equally important to clearly communicate the tangible benefits GenAI brings to the table—whether through improved efficiency, better insights, or new service opportunities—along with highlighting the emergence of new roles and career paths evolving with AI integration. This approach ensures employee buy-in, reduces resistance, and paves the way for a smooth and impactful GenAI adoption.

Evaluation and ROI Measurement

Challenge: Businesses struggle to measure the real impact of GenAI on operations or revenue.

Solution:

To effectively implement Generative AI (GenAI) within a business environment, it's crucial to define key performance indicators (KPIs) that will measure its impact. These KPIs may include efficiency gains, cost savings, user engagement metrics, or creative throughput, depending on the specific goals of the deployment. Establishing these measurable outcomes helps in setting clear expectations and tracking success over time. To ensure the effectiveness of GenAI-driven changes, businesses should employ A/B testing methodologies. This allows comparison between traditional and GenAI-enhanced processes or interfaces, enabling data-driven decisions about what changes are genuinely beneficial. Moreover, it's essential to develop a continuous feedback loop by monitoring real-time usage data, collecting stakeholder input, and assessing system performance regularly. This iterative feedback mechanism ensures that the AI deployment remains aligned with user needs and business objectives, facilitating timely adjustments and sustained improvements.

Scalability and Maintenance

Challcngc: Early prototypes may not scale across departments or customer segments.

Solution:

To successfully integrate generative AI into business operations, it is advisable to start with pilot projects in isolated domains where the impact can be measured and controlled. This approach allows for low-risk experimentation and clearer assessments of value. Once these pilots demonstrate success, the implementation can then scale horizontally across other functions and departments. Crucially, the deployment should be planned with a mindset of continuous improvement this includes iterative updates to the models, regular retraining based on new data, and proactive incorporation of user feedback to refine system behavior. To maintain consistent model performance over time and prevent degradation, organizations must also deploy model observability tools. These tools help monitor data and concept drift, provide insights into model decisions, and ensure that performance metrics remain aligned with business objectives.

Conclusion

Implementing Generative AI in a business setting requires more than just acquiring tools—it demands a strategic vision, organizational readiness, and a commitment to innovation. By following structured steps such as identifying use cases, selecting suitable AI models, ensuring ethical compliance, and integrating AI into existing workflows, businesses can unlock the transformative potential of GenAI. Building a culture of innovation is central to this process. Employees must be encouraged to experiment, fail fast, and learn continuously. Leadership must foster a mindset that embraces AI not as a threat but as a partner in driving growth and efficiency. However, integration challenges are inevitable—ranging from technical barriers and data limitations to employee resistance and regulatory concerns. Overcoming these hurdles requires strong change management, transparent communication, upskilling programs, and robust governance. By addressing these dimensions, businesses can align GenAI implementation with long-term goals, enabling scalable, responsible, and value-driven outcomes. Ultimately, successful GenAI adoption empowers organizations to remain competitive, agile, and forward-looking in an era where innovation is no longer optional but essential.

Exercise Questions

1. List and explain the key steps in adopting Generative AI tools.
2. What factors should be considered when selecting a GenAI tool?
3. Describe how GenAI can align with business strategy.
4. Identify three real-world business use cases of GenAI.
5. What does "building a culture of innovation" mean in the context of AI?
6. How can leaders encourage AI-driven experimentation?
7. Discuss the role of employee training in AI integration.
8. What are common barriers to GenAI adoption in businesses?
9. How can resistance to AI be effectively managed?
10. What ethical issues must be considered in implementing GenAI?
11. How does GenAI affect decision-making in organizations?
12. Describe the importance of data governance in GenAI systems.
13. Suggest strategies to evaluate GenAI ROI (Return on Investment).

14. How can small businesses start using GenAI effectively?
15. Propose a roadmap for implementing GenAI over 6–12 months.

CHAPTER 7
FUTURE TRENDS IN GENERATIVE AI

Generative Artificial Intelligence (GenAI) has emerged as one of the most transformative technological innovations of the 21st century. Initially recognized for its ability to generate human-like text, images, music, and code, GenAI is rapidly evolving into a foundational technology shaping industries across healthcare, education, finance, entertainment, and governance in Figure 7.1. As organizations move from experimentation to large-scale adoption, the future of GenAI lies not only in enhancing creativity and productivity but also in redefining how humans and machines collaborate. The coming years will see this technology mature into a powerful ecosystem that supports decision-making, automates complex tasks, and drives innovation at unprecedented speed. One of the most significant trends shaping the future of Generative AI is the movement toward multimodality. While current models specialize in individual domains such as text or images, future systems will seamlessly integrate multiple data formats text, audio, video, 3D models, and even sensor data into unified outputs. This will create richer, more contextually relevant AI interactions. For example, an educator could design immersive learning experiences where GenAI creates interactive textbooks that blend narrative, visuals, quizzes, and simulations in real time. Similarly, in medicine, multimodal AI could analyze medical records, diagnostic images, and patient speech to provide holistic assessments, significantly improving diagnostic accuracy. Another important direction is personalization at scale. Future GenAI systems will be deeply adaptive, tailoring outputs to individual preferences, cultural contexts, and professional needs. Unlike today's generalized outputs, next-generation AI will provide hyper-personalized services, from customized learning paths in education to adaptive therapeutic interventions in healthcare. Such personalization will be powered by advanced user profiling, federated learning, and secure data integration, allowing AI to deliver context-aware support without compromising privacy. This will transform customer experience strategies in industries, enabling businesses to differentiate themselves through unique, AI-driven engagements. The integration of GenAI with other frontier technologies will also define its future trajectory. Blockchain, Internet of Things (IoT), augmented reality (AR), and robotics are converging with AI to create ecosystems where generative models play a central role. For instance, blockchain can be leveraged to authenticate and secure AI-generated content, addressing issues of plagiarism and misinformation. Similarly, in smart cities, AI could generate predictive urban planning models by synthesizing data streams from IoT sensors, while AR applications will harness GenAI to create lifelike virtual experiences for training, design, or entertainment. Such convergence ensures that GenAI will no longer be a stand-alone tool but a backbone of interconnected digital ecosystems. As generative systems become more advanced, ethical and regulatory considerations will increasingly shape their development. Issues of misinformation, deepfakes, bias, and data privacy demand structured frameworks that balance innovation with accountability. Future trends point toward the rise of explainable AI, watermarking of generated content, and stronger international regulations to govern responsible use. This shift will encourage organizations to adopt ethical AI practices not only as a compliance requirement but as a competitive differentiator, ensuring trust among users and stakeholders. The challenge lies in aligning rapid technological innovation with equally robust governance mechanisms. Finally, the future of Generative AI will emphasize collaborative intelligence where AI augments human creativity rather than replacing it. We are moving toward a model where GenAI acts as a co-creator, offering suggestions, automating routine tasks, and expanding human imagination into unexplored territories. This will redefine roles in creative industries, research, and professional services, as humans focus on strategic, emotional, and value-driven aspects while AI handles data-intensive processes. By democratizing access to advanced tools, GenAI will empower individuals and organizations across diverse geographies and socioeconomic contexts, making innovation more inclusive. In essence, the future of Generative AI will be about synergy, trust, and human-machine collaboration driving global progress.

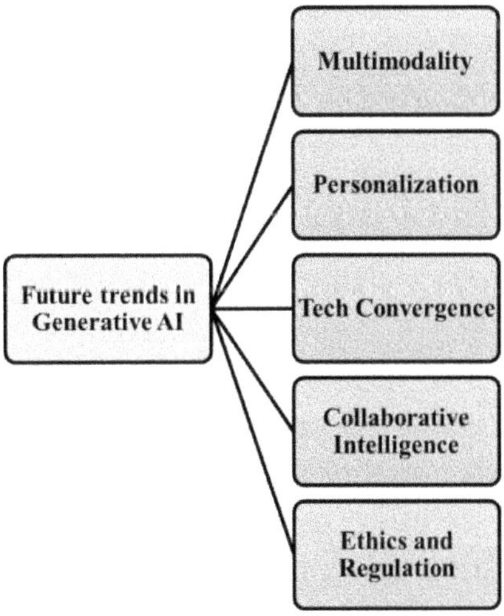

Figure 7.1: Future trends in Generative AI.

Emerging Technologies and Advancements

This Table 7.1 highlights key areas of innovation in generative AI, including autonomous agents, developer tools, media applications, computing infrastructure, strategic enterprise frameworks, and broader technology trends shaping the landscape in 2025.

Industry Developments & Strategic Shifts

The technology sector is undergoing rapid transformations driven by artificial intelligence, immersive experiences, and strategic collaborations. Companies are increasingly shifting focus toward integrating generative AI into mainstream products to enhance creativity, reduce costs, and improve user engagement. This shift reflects broader industry trends where content generation is no longer solely manual but supported by advanced algorithms capable of producing high-quality visuals, text, and interactive assets. Strategic alliances between major players allow faster scaling of innovations and ensure competitive advantage. By leveraging complementary strengths, these partnerships represent a pivotal movement shaping the future of digital content creation and engagement.

Meta & Midjourney Collaboration

Meta's recent collaboration with Midjourney highlights a strategic step in embedding advanced generative visual AI into its ecosystem. By licensing Midjourney's renowned image-generation technology, Meta seeks to elevate the quality of content produced across its platforms while reducing operational costs. This integration aims to provide users with powerful creative tools that enhance social interaction, storytelling, and digital expression. Beyond improving aesthetics, the move also targets higher engagement and retention by allowing creators, businesses, and casual users to effortlessly produce professional-grade visuals. The partnership reflects Meta's broader ambition to dominate the generative AI space, fostering both innovation and market leadership.

Media & Entertainment Transformation

AI orchestration is reshaping workflows by automating everything from highlight reel creation to synthetic anchors, multilingual translation, and predictive content caching. The NAB Show spotlighted generative tools being adopted for layered creative tasks, agentic systems for autonomous production work, and real-time content localization and monetization.

Autonomous, Agentic, and AI-Driven Systems

Autonomous, agentic, and AI-driven systems represent a new paradigm in which machines no longer act as passive tools but as proactive decision-makers. These systems combine autonomy, meaning the ability to act without constant human supervision, with agency, the capacity to pursue goals intelligently within dynamic environments. AI-driven layers add adaptability, enabling systems to learn, predict, and optimize tasks in real time. Together, they enable breakthroughs across industries such as robotics, finance, and healthcare, where speed, efficiency, and accuracy are critical. Such systems reduce human cognitive load while extending capabilities, creating new standards for intelligent automation and digital transformation.

Rise of AI Agents

The rise of AI agents has transformed industries by introducing autonomous systems capable of making complex, real-time decisions. In logistics, they optimize routes and manage supply chains with minimal human input. In cybersecurity, agents detect anomalies, respond to threats, and continuously adapt to evolving risks. Development processes now involve AI copilots accelerating code generation and bug detection. Content creation has also shifted as AI agents draft, edit, and personalize materials at scale. Their agentic nature ensures they don't simply execute commands but also anticipate needs, negotiate trade-offs, and operate in dynamic contexts, effectively acting as intelligent collaborators rather than tools.

Developer Productivity Gains

Generative AI has redefined productivity in software development, with studies showing gains of up to 30%. Instead of spending hours writing boilerplate code or debugging syntax errors, developers now rely on AI copilots for rapid generation, code reviews, and error detection. This shift allows human developers to focus on higher-order design, architecture, and creativity. Tasks that once required extensive repetition are now automated, making space for more innovative problem-solving. The productivity boost is not just quantitative but qualitative, as developers move beyond routine coding into orchestrating complex systems. This reshaping of workflows highlights how AI amplifies human ingenuity in development.

"Vibe Coding"

"Vibe coding," a term popularized in early 2025 by Andrej Karpathy, signals a cultural shift in programming philosophy. Instead of micromanaging every line of code, developers describe overall project goals or features to a large language model (LLM). The AI generates code iterations, which are then refined collaboratively in cycles of suggestion and feedback. Developers learn to trust the "vibe," relying on intuition and emergent results rather than rigid step-by-step control. This method reduces friction, speeds prototyping, and democratizes software creation by lowering barriers for non-technical users. Vibe coding reflects the growing trust between humans and AI as creative partners.

AI-Assisted Development Tools

AI-assisted development tools now permeate nearly every stage of software engineering. Large Language Models power intelligent autocompletion, enabling developers to finish complex functions with minimal typing. Automated bug detection identifies vulnerabilities early, while AI-driven test generation ensures broader code coverage and quality assurance. Static analysis tools highlight performance bottlenecks, security risks, and inefficiencies in real time. Beyond coding, AI copilots help with documentation, architecture suggestions, and workflow integration. Together, these tools streamline the development lifecycle, bridging the gap between ideation and deployment. They don't replace developers but enhance their capabilities, making modern software engineering faster, more accurate, and innovation-driven.

Multimodal, Video & Film Innovation

Multimodal generative AI is reshaping the creative industries, especially in video and film innovation. By combining text, images, audio, and motion data, AI systems now allow filmmakers to conceptualize scenes and generate visuals directly from textual prompts. This opens new avenues for pre-visualization, rapid prototyping, and cost-efficient production. Directors can experiment with styles, lighting, and framing without requiring expensive sets or crews. Moreover, the ability to blend modalities such as syncing generated visuals with natural language dialogue—makes storytelling more dynamic and inclusive. The democratization of these tools empowers independent creators while challenging traditional production pipelines.

Generative AI in Filmmaking

Recent surveys highlight groundbreaking advancements in text-to-image and text-to-video diffusion, neural radiance fields (NeRFs), avatar generation, and 3D synthesis. These technologies provide filmmakers with the ability to design characters, maintain stylistic consistency across scenes, and experiment with surreal or abstract effects impossible with conventional techniques. For instance, NeRFs allow realistic 3D environments from sparse image data, streamlining set creation and immersive backdrops. Avatar synthesis makes it possible to replicate actors or design entirely digital beings with expressive realism. Together, these innovations accelerate production timelines, reduce costs, and expand creative freedom, transforming filmmaking into a more technologically augmented art form.

Muse by Microsoft

Muse by Microsoft is an advanced generative model that demonstrates AI's role in gaming and interactive media. Using gameplay data from Bleeding Edge, Muse can generate visuals for gaming environments and even replicate controller input patterns. While its design focuses more on workflow acceleration and content preservation rather than full automation, its implications are far-reaching. For developers, it can streamline asset generation, automate repetitive tasks, and maintain stylistic cohesion in large projects. For researchers, it provides insights into how AI can model player behavior and simulate interaction dynamics. Muse represents a bridge between generative content creation and interactive experience design

Infrastructure, Compute, and Speed

Infrastructure, compute, and speed form the backbone of modern artificial intelligence systems, determining how efficiently and effectively models can be trained and deployed. The infrastructure involves highly specialized data centers equipped with optimized interconnects, cooling systems, and memory hierarchies to handle massive data flows required by large language models. Compute power, primarily driven by GPUs, TPUs, and emerging AI accelerators, dictates the scale of models that can be processed. Speed ensures real-time or near-real-time responses, which is critical for applications such as chatbots, autonomous vehicles, and generative AI tools. Together, these pillars define AI's capacity to scale globally.

Cerebras Breakthroughs

Cerebras Systems has redefined the landscape of AI computing with its wafer-scale engine, dramatically boosting inference capacity and throughput. By achieving a twentyfold increase in tokens-per-second generation, the company enables ultra-fast processing of large models. Its systems now outperform even high-end GPUs, offering nearly double the inference performance for advanced models like Llama 4. Such breakthroughs not only accelerate research but also power real-world services for companies like DeepSeek, Mistral, and

Perplexity, enabling them to deliver ultra-fast user experiences. Cerebras demonstrates how purpose-built architectures can challenge traditional GPU dominance in large-scale AI workloads.

Chips and Architectural Trends

The AI hardware landscape is undergoing a rapid transformation, shifting toward specialized architectures tailored for advanced workloads. McKinsey's 2025 outlook highlights "agentic AI"—systems with autonomous decision-making capabilities—as a rising priority, requiring chips optimized for context-aware reasoning. Alongside, specialized semiconductors are emerging to handle the unique demands of generative AI, including high parallelism, memory efficiency, and low-latency inference. These trends indicate a future where general-purpose GPUs may give way to custom accelerators for specific tasks. By aligning chip design with evolving AI paradigms, the industry is shaping a future of more efficient, scalable, and adaptive intelligent systems.

Ethical, Strategic & Organizational Frameworks

The integration of generative AI into modern systems requires a foundation built on ethical, strategic, and organizational frameworks. Ethical frameworks ensure that AI is deployed responsibly, reducing risks of bias, discrimination, and misuse. Strategic frameworks align AI adoption with business goals, ensuring investments create measurable value and innovation. Organizational frameworks focus on governance, clear roles, and accountability, enabling collaboration across leadership, IT, and compliance teams. Together, these three dimensions create a holistic approach where AI is not just a technological upgrade but a well-governed, strategically aligned, and ethically sound transformation. This balance builds trust and long-term sustainability.

Importance of Synthetic Data & AI Literacy

In high-stakes environments shaped by regulatory tightening, three pillars of resilience are vital: synthetic data, autonomous agents, and executive AI literacy. Synthetic data allows safe and privacy-preserving model training, enabling innovation without exposing sensitive information. Autonomous agents provide adaptive, real-time decision-making in dynamic contexts, such as healthcare, finance, or defense. Executive AI literacy ensures leaders understand AI's capabilities and risks, allowing them to govern responsibly, make informed investments, and ensure alignment with societal values. When combined, these elements protect organizations against regulatory risks, strengthen adaptability, and build confidence in AI systems while fostering responsible innovation at scale.

Data as the Competitive Edge

In the generative AI era, success hinges on the quality and availability of data. High-quality data ensures accurate, unbiased, and reliable AI outputs, while availability guarantees scalability across diverse applications. Organizations with exclusive or well-curated datasets gain a significant edge, as data fuels both innovation and differentiation in AI-driven products. Beyond volume, precision and contextual richness of data determine competitive advantage. Companies that invest in data governance, secure pipelines, and advanced curation techniques position themselves as leaders. In effect, data becomes the new "oil" for AI those who refine it well can dominate industries, shape markets, and sustain growth.

Key Trends from Broader Analyses

A snapshot of recurring themes across various expert reports and trend analyses:

AI-First Apps & Multimodal Interfaces

The evolution of AI-first applications marks a major shift from embedding AI features into existing tools toward designing entire platforms around artificial intelligence. Unlike earlier models that treated AI as an add-on, AI-first apps natively integrate reasoning, generative abilities, and contextual awareness. These platforms operate seamlessly across multiple modalities—text, image, video, audio, and even code—delivering fluid interactions. For instance, multimodal interfaces allow users to query in speech, receive visual outputs, or code suggestions in real time. This transformation is driving new ecosystems where AI acts not as a feature but as the very foundation of user experience.

Hyper-Personalization

Hyper-personalization leverages advanced analytics, real-time behavioral data, and AI-driven insights to deliver unique experiences tailored to individual users. It extends far beyond segmentation to provide one-to-one content recommendations, targeted marketing, and adaptive interfaces at scale. With machine learning models tracking preferences and contextual signals, businesses can dynamically adapt messaging, services, or product displays. For example, e-commerce sites present customized catalogs, while education platforms adjust lesson pacing for each learner. The ability to anticipate intent and predict needs makes hyper-personalization a defining trend, shaping customer loyalty and expectations in a world where generic interactions are no longer acceptable.

Human-In-The-Loop

Despite rapid automation, human-in-the-loop (HITL) remains essential in ensuring AI systems operate ethically, transparently, and effectively. HITL emphasizes a collaborative model where humans supervise, validate, or correct AI outputs, ensuring sensitive contexts—like healthcare diagnoses, recruitment, or cultural interpretation—retain human judgment. This approach mitigates risks of bias, misinformation, and over-reliance on machine outputs. By combining algorithmic efficiency with human oversight, organizations achieve balanced systems that are both scalable and trustworthy. HITL also provides valuable feedback for model refinement, ensuring continuous improvement. Ultimately, it safeguards accountability by embedding human values and domain expertise into AI-driven decision-making pipelines.

Generative Engine Optimization (GEO)

Generative Engine Optimization (GEO) is emerging as the next evolution of search visibility, adapting to how generative AI systems retrieve and present information. Unlike traditional SEO that targets keyword rankings in search engines, GEO focuses on structuring metadata, context, and semantic clarity so content is effectively surfaced by large language models. Businesses and creators must now optimize for conversational AI queries, ensuring their content is referenced in synthesized AI outputs. This includes clarity in factual information, embedding structured data, and aligning with AI training signals. GEO represents a paradigm shift, redefining how digital presence and discoverability will be maintained.

Causal AI

Causal AI represents a significant step forward in machine reasoning, moving beyond pattern recognition and correlations toward understanding cause-and-effect relationships. Unlike predictive models that only identify associations, causal AI can explain why outcomes occur, enabling robust decision-making even under shifting conditions. This capability is critical for applications like healthcare, finance, and climate modeling, where intervention strategies depend on causal understanding. By integrating structural causal models and counterfactual reasoning, these systems adapt to distributional changes, offering deeper insights and resilience. Causal AI thus provides not only accurate forecasts but also actionable explanations, empowering organizations to make reliable, evidence-based decisions.

AI in Electronic Design (EDA 4.0)

AI is revolutionizing the semiconductor industry through EDA 4.0, where design automation extends to previously human-intensive tasks. Traditional electronic design automation faced bottlenecks in high-level synthesis, verification, and analog design. With AI, these processes are accelerated and optimized, enabling faster iterations and reduced error rates. Machine learning models enhance chip layout, power efficiency, and performance tuning, while reinforcement learning aids in circuit optimization. Additionally, AI supports hardware-software co-design, bridging gaps between development stages. As semiconductor complexity grows, AI-driven EDA tools are crucial for sustaining Moore's Law, lowering costs, and empowering industries dependent on cutting-edge chips—from AI accelerators to IoT devices.

Table 7.1: Emerging Technologies and Advancements in Generative AI Across Domains.

Area	Emerging Advances
AI Agents	Autonomous decision-support across domains; boosting efficiency and resilience
Developer Tools	Productivity gains via code generation, testing, vibe coding, and orchestration
Media & Film	Multimodal content generation: video, visuals, stylization, 3D synthesis, avatars
Compute Infrastructure	Ultra-fast inference through Cerebras chips dramatically improving throughput
Enterprise Strategy	Synthetic data, governance, and AI literacy enabling safe adoption
Consumer Software	AI-first document interaction (e.g., Adobe Acrobat Studio)
Broader Trends	Hyper-personalization, GEO, multimodal AI, causal reasoning, AI in EDA

Generative AI's role in human-AI collaboration

Human–AI collaboration refers to systems where people and AI agents work together, combining human judgment, creativity, and contextual understanding with AI's computational power, speed, and ability to generate new possibilities. Generative AI plays a special role here because it not only processes data but also creates novel outputs—text, images, designs, code, and ideas—that humans can refine, guide, or deploy. This collaboration isn't about replacement but augmentation, where AI acts as a creative partner or co-worker.

Generative AI as a Creative Partner

Generative AI enables co-creation:

In writing, humans draft ideas while AI suggests expansions, rewrites, or stylistic adjustments. In art and design, AI generates multiple prototypes or variations, giving humans inspiration they can refine. In music and film, AI composes drafts or soundscapes, while artists provide direction and emotional nuance. This partnership democratizes creativity—people without advanced artistic or technical skills can bring their visions to life with AI support.

Enhancing Productivity and Efficiency

Generative AI enhances productivity by speeding up repetitive and cognitively heavy tasks. It can quickly produce first drafts of content, generate summaries of large documents, or even create initial versions of code snippets, saving significant time. Instead of spending hours drafting reports or parsing through research papers, professionals can leverage AI for the groundwork and then refine outputs with their expertise. This human-AI collaboration allows workers to focus on creativity, strategic thinking, and decision-making rather than mundane work. The overall efficiency comes from a blend of AI's speed and accuracy with human critical judgment and contextual understanding.

Workplace Documents

In the workplace, AI tools streamline the creation of essential documents such as reports, meeting minutes, and presentations. They can automatically capture key discussion points from transcripts or generate slide decks based on text inputs. Employees no longer need to manually structure every report or record conversation word-for-word, as AI can handle the bulk of the drafting. This leaves humans free to inject domain knowledge, critical insights, and context-specific details that AI alone cannot provide. The collaboration transforms documentation from a tedious task into a more value-driven process where human expertise polishes AI's groundwork into professional results.

Software Development

Generative AI has become an invaluable assistant for programmers by suggesting code snippets, identifying bugs, and generating unit tests. Instead of starting from scratch, developers can use AI to prototype faster, check syntax, or automate repetitive coding tasks. Debugging becomes less time-consuming as AI highlights potential errors and proposes fixes. Additionally, AI can create test cases that strengthen software reliability and accelerate quality assurance. This allows programmers to shift their attention to architectural design, scalability, and performance optimization. By handling lower-level coding work, AI ensures developers spend their energy on problem-solving and innovation, boosting overall software productivity.

Education

In education, AI empowers teachers by generating lesson plans, worksheets, quizzes, and summaries, significantly reducing preparation time. With AI drafting these resources, educators can devote more energy to engaging students, addressing individual learning needs, and fostering critical thinking. Rather than replacing teachers, AI acts as a supportive partner that enhances their capacity to personalize learning experiences. For example, it can create adaptive content suited for different student proficiency levels. This synergy ensures teaching remains human-centered, focusing on mentorship and interaction, while AI takes care of repetitive planning tasks. The result is a more dynamic and efficient classroom experience.

Human-AI Collaboration

Efficiency in using Generative AI does not come from AI operating in isolation but from a cooperative workflow where humans guide, validate, and refine its contributions. AI excels at handling volume and speed, but human oversight ensures accuracy, creativity, and ethical alignment. For instance, AI might produce a draft policy document or a research outline, but human experts ensure relevance, context, and correctness. This partnership prevents errors, reduces risks of misinformation, and ensures outputs align with organizational goals. By combining machine efficiency with human judgment, workplaces, classrooms, and development teams achieve higher productivity without sacrificing quality or integrity.

Human Oversight and Ethical Collaboration

A critical dimension of human-AI collaboration is responsibility. Generative AI may produce biased, misleading, or factually incorrect content.

Humans ensure:

1. Ethical boundaries (avoiding harmful outputs).
2. Cultural and contextual relevance (local adaptation of ideas).
3. Verification of accuracy (fact-checking AI content).

This oversight creates a "human-in-the-loop" model where AI amplifies capabilities but does not replace human judgment.

Adaptive Learning and Skill Development

Generative AI doesn't just output content—it helps humans learn:

Writers and students learn alternative phrasing

Generative AI acts as an adaptive learning partner for writers and students by presenting multiple ways to express the same idea. Instead of memorizing rigid structures, learners explore diverse sentence constructions, rhetorical devices, and stylistic approaches. This helps them expand vocabulary, refine tone, and strengthen analytical reasoning. For example, when a student drafts an essay, AI can suggest alternative thesis statements or counterarguments, encouraging deeper critical thinking. Writers benefit by seeing fresh narrative possibilities or ways to strengthen clarity. Over time, this process improves adaptability, creativity, and communication skills, transforming AI into an ever-evolving tutor.

Designers gain exposure to new artistic styles and layouts

Generative AI provides designers with inspiration that extends beyond their existing creative comfort zones. By generating visuals in various artistic styles, design patterns, and color palettes, AI enables designers to analyze and learn new forms of visual storytelling. For instance, a graphic designer can explore how minimalism contrasts with baroque-inspired styles or how typography shifts the overall impact of branding. Exposure to this diversity fosters innovation, adaptability, and skill refinement. Instead of replacing creativity, AI amplifies it, giving designers an expansive visual library to draw from. Ultimately, this leads to richer portfolios and more dynamic, future-ready design practices.

Professionals in law, medicine, or engineering

Generative AI supports professional skill development by creating realistic, domain-specific scenarios that enhance decision-making. In law, AI can simulate courtroom cases with varied arguments for practice. In medicine, it can model patient symptoms and treatment outcomes, helping doctors improve diagnostic accuracy. In engineering, AI may generate failure scenarios or design simulations, enabling proactive problem-solving. These interactive, risk-free environments allow professionals to rehearse responses, test strategies, and refine expertise without real-world consequences. By engaging in continuous simulated practice, learners develop confidence, resilience, and adaptive problem-solving skills that are vital for high-stakes, knowledge-intensive professions.

Transforms AI into a collaborative tutor rather than a static tool

The essence of generative AI lies in its ability to shift from being a passive tool to becoming an active collaborator in human learning. Unlike static systems that merely provide outputs, AI interacts, adapts, and evolves based on user needs. This dynamic relationship makes AI function like a personalized tutor offering guidance, alternative perspectives, constructive feedback, and adaptive challenges. Learners no longer just consume information; they co-create knowledge with AI. This collaborative approach fosters continuous growth, where both creativity and critical thinking are sharpened. In this role, AI not only accelerates learning but also makes education more interactive and future-oriented.

Decision-Making Support

In domains like healthcare, law, and business strategy, generative AI helps by simulating possible outcomes: Doctors increasingly use AI to explore possible treatment pathways, but the ultimate decisions remain grounded in clinical expertise. AI can process large datasets, analyze similar case histories, and propose evidence-based options, helping doctors to see alternatives they may not have initially considered. However, physicians rely on their professional judgment, patient history, and contextual nuances to decide whether an AI-suggested treatment is appropriate. Similarly, lawyers employ AI to draft arguments and structure legal documents, but they refine the drafts with precedent, reasoning, and professional interpretation of the law. This ensures that legal outputs are not only technically correct but also strategically aligned with the client's case. Managers also benefit from AI in modeling strategic scenarios and testing potential consequences before committing to a plan. By simulating different business environments, market conditions, and organizational changes, AI provides managers with insights into risks and opportunities. Yet, final decisions rest on human judgment, shaped by experience, ethical considerations, and organizational culture. In all these fields, AI serves not as a replacement but as a collaborative advisor a partner in thought that supports professionals without supplanting their authority or accountability.

Future Directions

Human–AI collaboration with generative AI is moving toward:

Multimodal collaboration

The future of human–AI collaboration will be characterized by seamless multimodal interaction, where text, image, video, and audio are integrated to create richer experiences. Instead of relying on a single mode of communication, individuals will be able to express ideas through multiple channels at once, and AI systems will understand and respond accordingly. For instance, a designer might explain an idea verbally, sketch it on a digital canvas, and receive real-time AI-generated visuals or prototypes. This convergence allows knowledge workers, educators, and creatives to engage with AI in more natural, human-like ways, breaking barriers between mediums and enhancing productivity.

Personalized collaboration

Generative AI is increasingly moving toward highly personalized interactions, where assistants adapt to individual preferences, contexts, and working styles. Over time, AI will learn not just the content of user queries but also tone, priorities, and long-term goals. For example, a researcher may prefer structured summaries with citations, while a manager may want concise visual dashboards. Personalized AI can adjust outputs accordingly, acting almost like a professional partner who anticipates needs. Such personalization fosters trust, reduces cognitive load, and empowers individuals by aligning technology with unique workflows, making collaboration with AI both efficient and tailored to personal aspirations.

Collective intelligence systems

The next frontier involves collective intelligence systems in which humans and multiple AI agents collaborate as distributed teams. These systems will assign specialized roles to different AI models some focusing on data analysis, others on creativity, problem-solving, or communication. Working alongside human expertise, they will tackle complex challenges such as climate modeling, medical research, or strategic business planning. Humans provide contextual judgment and ethical reasoning, while AI accelerates computation, exploration, and ideation. Together, this synergy creates a hybrid intelligence where the collective outcome surpasses what either could achieve alone, fostering innovation, resilience, and groundbreaking solutions to global challenges.

Co-evolution of humans and AI

These directions signal a broader trajectory of co-evolution, where humans and AI systems continuously learn from each other. Rather than replacing human roles, AI will augment capabilities, enabling individuals to operate at new levels of creativity, insight, and efficiency. Humans, in turn, will guide AI development with feedback, values, and domain expertise, shaping systems that are more aligned with human goals. This reciprocal learning relationship establishes a dynamic ecosystem of shared growth. Over time, the distinction between human and machine collaboration will blur, leading to environments where human ingenuity and artificial intelligence evolve together to redefine problem-solving and innovation.

Predictions for the next decade

Between 2025 and 2035, generative AI is expected to evolve from powerful content creation tools into deeply integrated collaborators across industries. Models will move beyond producing text, images, or audio separately to seamlessly handling multimodal inputs and outputs, enabling richer, context-aware interactions that resemble human creativity. Healthcare, education, design, and research will see generative systems becoming embedded partners, providing not just outputs but co-developing ideas, solutions, and simulations. Advances in personalization will allow AI assistants to learn individual work patterns, emotional cues, and domain-specific knowledge, making them indispensable as adaptive collaborators. At the same time, generative AI will mature in reliability, transparency, and governance. Over the next decade, the field will focus on reducing hallucinations, ensuring factual grounding, and embedding ethical constraints through regulation and technical safeguards. Decentralized and edge-based generative systems may emerge, giving users more control over data privacy and ownership. Collective intelligence platforms, where humans and AI agents jointly tackle global challenges like climate change, healthcare, and economic planning, will likely expand. By 2035, generative AI may shift from being seen as a "tool" to being recognized as a partner in human progress—reshaping industries, education, and creativity while raising new questions of accountability and trust.

Executive summary 12 big shifts

1. Agentic AI becomes standard

AI systems evolve from reactive assistants into autonomous agents capable of planning, calling external tools and APIs, and managing multi-step workflows. By default, these models include auditing, logging, and verification to ensure safety and accountability. Such agentic AI reduces human micromanagement, as machines not only answer but act, coordinate, and self-monitor. This shift unlocks productivity in enterprises where repetitive or orchestrated tasks dominate, from IT operations to customer service. Businesses will increasingly view AI agents as digital colleagues with governance mechanisms, transforming workflows across industries and blurring the line between automation and intelligent collaboration.

2. Multimodality everywhere

Future AI models seamlessly integrate text, image, audio, video, 3D data, and time-series into a unified learning framework. This convergence allows cross-modal reasoning: describing a video in text, editing a 3D design by voice, or generating time-series predictions from multimodal cues. Video and 3D synthesis will reach cinematic "post-production" quality, enabling film, gaming, and digital twins to be produced on demand. Multimodal intelligence extends accessibility, allowing inclusive interfaces for education, healthcare, and design. By embedding all sensory and symbolic forms into one pipeline, multimodality reshapes creativity, communication, and simulation, creating an "all-in-one" foundation for next-generation AI ecosystems.

3. Reasoning improves via tooling

Instead of scaling model size endlessly, future reasoning strength will derive from structured tooling. AI integrates program-aided reasoning, retrieval-augmented generation, and verifiable pipelines such as proofs, tests, and sandboxes. This ensures outputs are traceable, testable, and logically consistent rather than opaque guesses. For example, medical or legal AIs will provide both conclusions and reproducible chains of evidence. In scientific discovery, verified computational reasoning prevents spurious correlations. Tool-grounded reasoning elevates AI from prediction engines into reliable partners in logic and problem-solving. Enterprises and regulators alike will prefer verifiable systems, creating a new standard of accountability and trust in intelligent automation.

4. On-device small models

Lightweight AI models in the 1–10B parameter range will run efficiently on laptops, smartphones, and edge devices, giving users private "edge copilots." These local models handle contextual, personalized tasks offline while orchestrated by more powerful cloud LLMs for complex reasoning. The dual system balances privacy, latency, and performance. For instance, a phone-resident model can summarize notes instantly while the cloud counterpart manages research or enterprise knowledge queries. On-device intelligence reduces dependence on persistent internet connectivity and enables highly customized, secure use cases. This shift democratizes AI access globally, bridging the digital divide while decentralizing computational power.

5. Synthetic data flywheels

Synthetic data generation becomes central to AI progress, with curated datasets, automated curricula, and advanced simulation environments powering training pipelines. By creating diverse, scalable data, AI systems overcome real-world scarcity, bias, or privacy barriers. Flywheels emerge: models generate synthetic data, refine on it, and iterate toward stronger capabilities. Data provenance, verification, and watermarking become mandatory to prevent misuse and ensure integrity. Industries such as healthcare, finance, and robotics rely on simulated datasets to model rare events or future conditions. Synthetic data thus accelerates innovation while shifting the competitive edge from mere compute to intelligent data pipeline design.

6. World-modeling & simulation

AI shifts toward long-horizon prediction, enabling sophisticated world-models for science, economics, climate, policy, and robotics. These models anticipate cause-effect dynamics and support simulations for decision-making. Before deploying robots in factories or cars on roads, agents are trained extensively in synthetic environments. Policymakers model pandemic responses or carbon reduction strategies in virtual scenarios. Financial institutions stress-test portfolios against diverse futures using AI simulations. This development moves AI beyond reactive systems into foresight engines, were planning spans months, years, or decades. By merging predictive analytics with causal inference, world-modeling fosters safer real-world applications through rigorous, low-risk pre-deployment training.

7. Software 2.0 shops

Software development undergoes radical transformation in “AI-first” repositories. Autonomous coding agents not only write but also test, benchmark, and ship software modules. Human engineers act less as coders and more as product managers, safety reviewers, and visionaries. Development cycles shorten dramatically as AI automates bug fixing, documentation, and integration. These shops blur traditional distinctions between programming and product design, with AI copilots handling both routine and advanced coding tasks. Organizations adopting Software 2.0 pipelines gain exponential productivity, accelerating innovation. Safety, however, becomes crucial, requiring rigorous oversight of generated code to prevent vulnerabilities or malicious dependencies from propagating.

8. Domain copilots > general chat

General-purpose AI chatbots give way to domain-specific copilots that embed deeply into verticals such as healthcare, law, engineering, or education. These specialized systems come with licensing, compliance guardrails, and liability frameworks tailored to regulated environments. For example, medical copilots provide decision support under clinical guidelines, while legal copilots analyze cases with jurisdiction-specific reasoning. Educators deploy copilots as adaptive tutors that align with curriculum standards. Unlike broad assistants, domain copilots prioritize safety, explainability, and expert-level accuracy. This specialization reflects market demand for trustworthy, sector-aligned AI that augments professionals rather than serving as casual conversational partners.

9. Energy/efficiency becomes a moat

As AI adoption scales, energy and compute efficiency become strategic differentiators. Training and inference costs push innovation in sparsity, quantization, model distillation, and specialized hardware such as optical processors, analog chips, or 3D stacked architectures. Organizations that achieve breakthroughs in energy efficiency gain a competitive moat, delivering faster, cheaper, and greener AI services. Governments and enterprises will prioritize sustainable AI deployment, linking efficiency to regulatory compliance and environmental targets. Edge devices and low-latency systems particularly benefit from these optimizations. Thus, energy management evolves from a backend concern into a central pillar of AI competitiveness and responsibility.

10. Security & policy harden

With AI embedded across industries, robust security and governance frameworks become non-negotiable. Model supply chains face scrutiny, requiring provenance tracking, integrity checks, and red-teaming protocols. Watermarking, usage logs, and incident reporting evolve into compliance checklists enforced by regulators. Enterprises integrate AI audits into risk management strategies. As adversarial attacks and data poisoning threats grow, AI security converges with cybersecurity, demanding layered defenses. Policy frameworks also mature, aligning liability, certification, and ethical boundaries. Together, hardened security and policy infrastructure establish resilience and public trust, ensuring that AI innovation unfolds responsibly in sensitive domains such as defense, healthcare, and finance.

11. Human-AI UX matures

User experience evolves from simple chat interfaces to "ambient copilots" seamlessly integrated into workflows. AI becomes embedded in IDEs, documents, AR glasses, and dashboards, supporting context-aware assistance without constant prompts. Transparency and control improve, with explainable outputs, editable reasoning chains, and traceable suggestions. This creates a sense of partnership rather than black-box mystery. Workers experience AI not as an external tool but as an ambient, adaptive collaborator woven into their environment. The shift democratizes access to advanced AI, enhancing productivity, creativity, and decision-making while reducing cognitive friction. Mature UX thus defines the mainstream adoption curve of AI.

12. Open + closed hybrid

AI ecosystems stabilize into a dual structure: open models thrive at the edge, in research, and for experimentation, while closed models dominate regulated, high-stakes verticals such as healthcare, finance, or national security. Standards emerge for interoperability, allowing hybrid deployments where open and closed systems cooperate. For instance, an open edge copilot may preprocess data before handing tasks to a proprietary cloud model under compliance frameworks. This balance ensures both innovation and accountability, preventing monopolistic lock-in while maintaining quality in sensitive applications. The hybrid paradigm becomes the pragmatic compromise driving sustainable, inclusive, and resilient AI growth globally.

Capabilities & Modalities

AI systems are rapidly moving toward unified multimodality, where a single backbone can seamlessly ingest and emit text, images, audio, video, sensor streams, and even 3D environments. This means future models will not just generate isolated media but entire multi-sensory experiences, blending narrative, visuals, sound, and interactivity. For example, video generation will achieve coherence across several minutes, controlled by high-level scripts or storyboards. Similarly, 3D asset generation will embed physics and material realism, allowing direct use in simulations, games, or design. Speech systems will offer fine-grained voice identity controls, enabling dynamic, authentic personalization while preserving safety and ethical boundaries.

Structure-Aware Generation

The next generation of AI will excel at structure-aware generation, where outputs conform to precise formats such as JSON, SQL queries, CAD files, LaTeX manuscripts, or Building Information Models (BIM). This will be achieved by integrating constrained decoding with formal validators, ensuring correctness and compliance before output is finalized. The result will be a leap in reliability, as enterprises can plug AI directly into pipelines without risk of malformed outputs breaking downstream systems. This structured reliability transforms AI from a creative tool into a trusted automation partner across sectors like engineering, finance, legal, and academia, where precision and integrity are non-negotiable.

Memory & Long Context

A defining frontier is memory and long-context reasoning. While context windows already scale to millions of tokens, sheer size alone does not solve continuity and recall challenges. What matters more is grounded, durable memory linked with retrieval over personal and organizational knowledge bases. Such systems will remember projects, preferences, and historical interactions, enabling continuity across weeks or months. Combined with intelligent search and summarization, this allows users to revisit past decisions, refine ongoing projects, and collaborate with AI as a persistent knowledge partner. Instead of starting fresh each session, AI will evolve into an adaptive assistant that learns, recalls, and reasons contextually.

Agentic AI & tool use

Planning & decomposition: Multi-agent architectures where specialists (reasoner, searcher, coder, checker) collaborate, with verifiable artifacts (tests, proofs, citations).

APIs & robotic process automation: Agents operate CRMs, ERPs, code repos, and lab instruments; human-in-the-loop dashboards approve actions and set policy.

Evaluation & trust: Agents ship with scorecards (task success, latency, cost, safety incidents) and sandboxed "dry-run" modes.

Reasoning, retrieval & verification

RAG 2.0: Retrieval pipelines evolve

RAG 2.0 represents the next generation of retrieval-augmented generation where retrieval pipelines move beyond simple keyword or vector search. Learned indexers adapt to context and domain, ensuring better alignment of retrieved information with user queries. Multi-hop queries allow models to connect information across multiple sources instead of relying on isolated facts. Table and diagram parsers extend retrieval beyond plain text, enabling structured knowledge extraction from complex data formats. Citation faithfulness checks further ensure that the evidence provided truly supports the generated claims, reducing hallucinations. Together, these advancements enhance precision, reliability, and trustworthiness in AI-driven knowledge systems.

Program-Aided Reasoning

Program-aided reasoning empowers AI models to go beyond static outputs by dynamically calling external solvers, such as mathematical engines, logical proof systems, or simulation frameworks. Instead of producing approximate answers, models can query precise tools and integrate the results into their reasoning chains. This approach mirrors how humans use calculators, spreadsheets, or software to verify complex tasks. Additionally, models perform unit testing of their own outputs, identifying inconsistencies or errors before presenting results. By iteratively revising until constraints are satisfied, program-aided reasoning improves accuracy, reduces error propagation, and makes AI more dependable for critical applications like science, law, or engineering.

Self-consistency with evidence

Traditional large language models often relied on majority voting across multiple sampled outputs, known as self-consistency, to stabilize responses. However, future systems emphasize evidence-weighted reasoning where claims are not just popular but supported by verifiable proof. Outputs are expected to include references, supporting documents, test logs, or even step-by-step proofs to justify conclusions. This paradigm is especially important in high-stakes domains such as medicine, law, or finance, where unverifiable answers are unacceptable. By shifting from "what the model thinks is most likely" to "what the evidence confirms," self-consistency evolves into a more rigorous, transparent, and accountable reasoning framework.

Data, provenance & IP

Licensed + Synthetic Blends

In the future, datasets will be treated much like software, with explicit licenses defining how they may be used, shared, or commercialized. This shift provides clarity to researchers, developers, and enterprises about ownership and permissible usage. At the same time, synthetic data plays an increasingly important role, serving as a controlled supplement to real-world datasets. By adjusting parameters such as bias and variance, organizations can generate training material that fills representational gaps, improves fairness, and reduces overfitting. Most importantly, synthetic data lowers intellectual property risks by minimizing reliance on potentially restricted or copyrighted content while still preserving model performance.

Provenance

Provenance in the data and AI ecosystem ensures transparency and accountability. As generative models grow more powerful, enterprises and regulators demand ways to verify the origin of both training inputs and model outputs. Emerging tools include cryptographic signatures, watermarking, and content credential frameworks that allow any file—text, image, video, or dataset—to carry verifiable proof of authenticity. Such credentials become the norm in enterprise settings, where uploads and outputs without provenance are considered non-compliant or insecure. This shift not only supports regulatory requirements but also strengthens user trust, as consumers can confirm that AI-generated content comes from trusted, auditable sources.

Data Markets

Data markets are evolving into structured ecosystems where creators, organizations, and even individuals can license their archives and contributions for AI training. Unlike ad-hoc data scraping, these markets emphasize transparency, fair compensation, and compliance. Revenue-sharing models enable equitable distribution, rewarding data owners while granting enterprises reliable access to diverse datasets. Enforcing these agreements requires mechanisms like training attestations statements or proofs confirming licensed data was indeed used—and independent audits that validate compliance. Over time, this fosters a sustainable data economy, reducing legal risk for AI developers and incentivizing high-quality data curation, thus ensuring innovation thrives without undermining ownership rights.

Efficiency, Cost & Hardware

Training

Modern AI training strategies are increasingly focused on maximizing efficiency while reducing costs. Mixture-of-experts (MoE) architectures distribute workloads across specialized subnetworks, activating only relevant experts per token, thereby lowering compute requirements. Sparsity techniques further cut costs by ensuring only necessary parameters are updated during training. Low-rank adapters enable model fine-tuning without retraining entire networks, saving both memory and compute power. Curriculum learning introduces data in progressive difficulty, stabilizing convergence and reducing wasted training cycles. Combined, these approaches slash the cost per token and make large-scale AI training financially sustainable without sacrificing performance or model generalization.

Inference

Inference efficiency has become as critical as training. Quantization using 4-, 3-, or even 2-bit precision reduces memory and compute loads while maintaining accuracy, making it the industry standard. Speculative decoding accelerates generation by predicting multiple tokens at once and verifying them, dramatically improving throughput. Caching mechanisms allow models to reuse previously computed representations, cutting redundancy in repeated queries. Additionally, serverless "burst" inference dynamically scales compute resources to meet spikes in demand without maintaining idle servers, reducing infrastructure costs. These innovations enable faster, cheaper, and more accessible AI inference, critical for real-world deployment at scale in consumer and enterprise applications.

Hardware

Hardware advances underpin the next leap in AI cost and efficiency. Domain-specific accelerators optimize workloads beyond general-purpose GPUs, tailoring compute units for AI primitives like matrix multiplications. Optical interconnects vastly improve bandwidth and reduce latency between chips, a bottleneck in large model deployment. Near-memory compute minimizes energy-hungry data movement by performing operations close to where data is stored. Parallel to performance improvements, greener datacenter designs emphasize renewable integration, efficient cooling, and reduced energy leakage. Carbon reporting per inference is emerging as a standard, allowing companies to track environmental costs alongside financial ones, pushing AI innovation toward a more sustainable trajectory.

Personalization, Privacy & Edge

Personalization in AI enables systems to adapt responses, recommendations, and interactions to individual user preferences and behaviors. However, achieving this requires careful attention to privacy and edge computing. Edge-based personalization ensures that sensitive user data is processed locally on the device rather than being transmitted to external servers, reducing exposure to potential breaches. This not only safeguards private information but also enhances latency and user experience. By maintaining data within the device ecosystem, organizations can respect privacy regulations while still delivering highly customized outputs. This approach balances convenience with ethical responsibility in AI-driven personalization.

Private Fine-Tuning

Private fine-tuning emphasizes tailoring models without compromising user data security. Instead of sharing raw inputs with central servers, small on-device adapters can learn a user's style, preferences, or domain-specific patterns safely. The cloud infrastructure may only receive encrypted gradients, minimal metadata, or sometimes nothing at all, ensuring sensitive information never leaves the device. This design is particularly useful in industries where compliance and confidentiality are critical, such as healthcare or finance. It empowers users with safe, personalized AI while giving organizations control over privacy-preserving methods. Ultimately, it makes fine-tuning both secure and adaptive to individual needs.

Policy-Aware Outputs

Policy-aware outputs allow organizations to embed compliance rules directly into AI responses. These runtime guards ensure that generated content respects sensitive information boundaries, such as personally identifiable information (PII), regulatory compliance frameworks, or company-specific brand guidelines. If an output violates a rule, it is either blocked or automatically redacted before being delivered. This mechanism prevents accidental data leaks, regulatory breaches, or brand inconsistencies while still enabling flexible AI use. It effectively combines governance with productivity, allowing AI systems to align with organizational policies dynamically. By integrating safeguards at the generation stage, organizations minimize risks without stifling innovation.

Federated + Split Learning

Federated and split learning enable AI training across multiple entities without exchanging raw data, ensuring data sovereignty and privacy preservation. In federated learning, models are trained locally at each node, and only aggregated updates are shared with a central server. Split learning takes this further by dividing the training process itself between client and server, so neither has complete visibility of the dataset. These methods are highly beneficial for sensitive sectors like healthcare, finance, and defense, where raw data cannot leave institutional silos. By fostering collaborative learning without data exposure, these approaches unlock innovation while maintaining strict confidentiality.

Safety, Security & Governance

Safety, security, and governance form the foundation of responsible AI deployment. Safety ensures that models behave predictably, avoiding harmful or biased outputs. Security focuses on protecting systems, data, and models from theft, tampering, or adversarial attacks. Governance involves transparent oversight, regulatory compliance, and the establishment of ethical frameworks that guide development and usage. Together, these pillars build trust and accountability, ensuring that AI systems serve society without undermining human rights or safety. Proper governance also includes auditability, explainability, and the involvement of multidisciplinary stakeholders to ensure long-term alignment with public values and societal well-being.

Standardized Red-Teaming: Continuous Adversarial Testing

Standardized red-teaming embeds continuous adversarial testing within the CI/CD pipeline to strengthen AI systems against evolving threats. This practice systematically probes models for vulnerabilities such as prompt injections, jailbreaks, data exfiltration attempts, and model theft. By simulating real-world adversarial behavior, red-teaming reveals weaknesses before malicious actors can exploit them. Integrating it into CI/CD ensures every update undergoes rigorous checks, reducing the risk of unsafe outputs slipping into production. Standardized frameworks also enable consistent benchmarking across organizations, fostering industry-wide resilience. Ultimately, this proactive approach transforms security from a one-time audit into a continuous defense mechanism for AI systems.

Abuse-Resistant Generation: Safer Defaults

Abuse-resistant generation emphasizes designing AI systems with safer defaults that prevent harmful or unethical use. These safeguards focus on reducing risks in sensitive areas such as chemical or biological dual-use research, extremist propaganda, and synthetic media like deepfakes. Context-aware refusals play a key role, ensuring models recognize misuse attempts and decline outputs appropriately without disrupting legitimate use cases. Beyond refusals, layered safety techniques—like content filters, alignment with ethical standards, and adaptive guardrails—make systems more resilient to exploitation. By embedding these controls at the design level, developers ensure that AI benefits users responsibly while limiting potential avenues for abuse.

Incident Response: AI-CERT Style Reporting

An effective incident response framework for AI mirrors cybersecurity's CERT (Computer Emergency Response Team) model, often termed "AI-CERT." This involves structured reporting mechanisms to identify, share, and resolve vulnerabilities in real-time. Complementing this, Model Bills of Materials (MBOM) document datasets, checkpoints, and guardrails used in development, ensuring traceability across the supply chain. Supply-chain attestations verify integrity at each stage, minimizing risks of tampered data or compromised models. Together, these practices create a transparent ecosystem where issues can be quickly addressed, accountability is maintained, and trust in AI systems is reinforced. Incident response thus becomes central to resilient, ethical AI deployment

Robotics & Embodied AI

Robotics and embodied AI represent the convergence of artificial intelligence with physical systems capable of interacting in the real world. Unlike purely digital AI models, embodied AI learns through experience in environments, combining perception, reasoning, and motor control. Modern research explores how robots acquire generalized intelligence by grounding knowledge in sensorimotor actions rather than static data. This approach allows machines to develop human-like adaptability—navigating dynamic spaces, manipulating objects, and responding to unexpected events. As robots evolve beyond factory lines into healthcare, homes, and logistics, embodied AI becomes crucial for enabling autonomy, contextual decision-making, and safe collaboration with humans.

Sim-to-Real: Foundation Policies + Diffusion Policies

A major challenge in robotics is bridging the gap between simulation and reality, known as the sim-to-real problem. Recent advances leverage foundation models trained in highly realistic simulated environments and then transferred into the real world. Photorealistic simulations allow robots to practice endlessly without risk, while diffusion-based policies help in fine-tuning control for complex and stochastic actions. By combining these approaches, robots gain the ability to perform household chores, warehouse logistics, and even assistive care tasks with greater reliability. This reduces costs of training, accelerates deployment, and brings robots closer to viable solutions for everyday applications.

Multisensor Fusion: Language + Vision + Force + Audio

Robotic intelligence is strengthened when multiple sensory modalities are integrated. Multisensor fusion enables robots to interpret language instructions, recognize visual cues, perceive force feedback, and process auditory signals simultaneously. For instance, a robot could follow narrated demonstrations while sensing the resistance of objects it manipulates and confirming placement through visual inspection. This approach enhances contextual learning, allowing robots to better understand complex environments and adapt to human interactions. By combining linguistic reasoning with embodied perception, machines can execute nuanced tasks such as cooking, caregiving, or assembly, making them more versatile and responsive to human intent.

Safety: Constraints, Monitors & Teleoperation

Safety is a fundamental requirement in robotics, especially as robots operate alongside humans. Formal safety constraints, such as geofencing and force limits, ensure robots remain within acceptable boundaries of motion and power. Runtime monitors track real-time performance, detecting anomalies and preventing dangerous failures. Furthermore, human-in-the-loop teleoperation serves as a critical fallback, allowing operators to intervene during unexpected conditions. These layered safeguards create trust in robotic systems, especially in sensitive environments like healthcare, logistics, and domestic assistance. By combining autonomous control with rigorous safety frameworks, robots can be deployed widely while maintaining reliability and human-centered oversight.

Risks & counter-trends

Data scarcity & copyright drag

A major risk for the continued progress of generative AI is data scarcity combined with copyright restrictions. Current large models thrive on vast amounts of diverse and high-quality data, but as public internet sources become exhausted or legally restricted, future training may hit plateaus. Copyright disputes and lawsuits are already highlighting tensions between creators, publishers, and AI companies, potentially slowing the availability of licensed datasets. Without either large-scale licensing agreements or reliable synthetic data generation, model improvements may stagnate. Counter-trends include advances in data augmentation, self-play, federated learning, and synthetic data generation that reduce dependence on copyrighted material.

Energy/compute constraints

Another significant barrier is the immense energy and computational cost of training and deploying frontier models. Training state-of-the-art systems requires thousands of GPUs running for weeks, consuming massive amounts of power, which raises costs and environmental concerns. Regulatory scrutiny may also intensify around sustainability, carbon emissions, and energy usage, restricting unconstrained scaling. If unchecked, rising costs could limit access to only a few major players. On the other hand, counter-trends include efficiency breakthroughs in model compression, hardware acceleration (e.g., TPUs, custom AI chips), and algorithmic optimization that enable leaner yet powerful models. Governments may also incentivize greener AI innovations.

Safety/regulatory shocks

Generative AI faces the risk of abrupt safety or regulatory shocks. A single high-profile incident such as misinformation causing public harm, bias leading to discrimination, or catastrophic misuse in sensitive domains could trigger strict caps on deployment. Regulators might respond with heavy compliance burdens or restrictive licensing schemes, slowing down research and innovation. However, counter-trends exist: proactive adoption of safety standards, explainable AI, transparent governance, and international frameworks could ease tensions. Industry collaboration on ethical guidelines and self-regulation could preempt extreme policies. Ultimately, embedding safety-by-design principles may help maintain public trust and reduce the likelihood of disruptive regulatory shocks.

Over-Automation

The risk of over-automation arises when organizations rely too heavily on AI systems, prematurely removing human oversight. This can create brittleness in decision-making processes, as models may fail in unanticipated contexts without human judgment to intervene. Critical sectors like healthcare, law, and finance could face severe consequences if errors go unchecked. Counter-trends point to a renewed appreciation for human-in-the-loop frameworks, where AI assists but does not replace experts. Hybrid systems that integrate human review, contextual reasoning, and accountability may gain more trust. This balance underscores the lasting value of domain expertise, creativity, and ethical judgment alongside AI efficiency.

Conclusion

The future of Generative AI holds immense promise, marked by rapid advancements in technology and expanding applications across diverse domains. Emerging trends indicate a shift toward more efficient, multimodal, and adaptive models capable of integrating text, images, audio, and video, thereby creating richer and more dynamic outputs. These developments will enhance creativity, problem-solving, and decision-making in sectors ranging from healthcare and education to design and entertainment. A central theme in this evolution is the role of human–AI collaboration. Rather than replacing human intelligence, Generative AI is increasingly seen as a partner that augments human creativity, productivity, and innovation. By streamlining repetitive tasks and offering new perspectives, AI empowers humans to focus on higher-order thinking and strategic decision-making. Looking ahead to the next decade, we can expect Generative AI to become more aligned with ethical, transparent, and responsible frameworks. Issues such as bias mitigation, intellectual property, and sustainability will remain key considerations. With responsible governance, Generative AI has the potential to transform industries and reshape societal norms, making human–AI synergy a defining characteristic of future progress.

Exercise Questions

1. Define Generative AI in your own words and explain why it is considered transformative.
2. What are the key emerging technologies shaping the future of Generative AI?
3. Discuss how multimodal AI models differ from traditional models.
4. Explain the importance of efficiency and scalability in next-generation AI systems.
5. How can Generative AI enhance creativity in fields like design and art?
6. What role does Generative AI play in advancing healthcare innovation?
7. Describe how AI can support educators and students in the future.
8. Why is human–AI collaboration considered essential rather than optional?
9. Provide two examples of how Generative AI reduces human workload.

10. What ethical challenges must be addressed as AI systems evolve?
11. How can bias in Generative AI models be identified and minimized?
12. Predict two possible transformations in society due to Generative AI in the next decade.
13. What governance and policy measures are necessary for responsible AI adoption?
14. Explain the concept of "human–AI synergy" with an example.
15. Do you think Generative AI will replace or complement human intelligence? Justify your answer.

CHAPTER 8
CONCLUSION

Key Takeaways and Lessons Learned

This final chapter reinforces the central theme of the book: Generative AI is not just a technological trend, but a strategic enabler for future-focused organizations. The key takeaways include:

Generative AI transforms business models by shifting focus from traditional automation to creativity and adaptability: Generative AI represents a paradigm shift in how businesses view technology. Unlike earlier waves of automation that primarily focused on efficiency, cost savings, and repetitive task reduction, Generative AI emphasizes creativity and adaptability. It allows organizations to reimagine their models, enabling the design of entirely new products, services, and customer experiences. By producing novel solutions, businesses can move beyond rigid processes and develop adaptive frameworks that respond to evolving market dynamics. This adaptability ensures resilience in fast-changing environments, giving companies the agility to experiment, innovate, and sustain long-term growth while staying ahead of competitors.

It empowers organizations to generate content, automate design, and personalize customer experiences at scale, across industries: Generative AI equips organizations with powerful tools to amplify creativity and efficiency. It can generate diverse types of content—ranging from marketing campaigns to technical documentation—while automating design processes that once demanded extensive human effort. Beyond creation, its strength lies in personalization. By analyzing customer data, preferences, and behaviors, Generative AI can tailor experiences that feel individually crafted, thereby deepening customer engagement. This scalability ensures that personalization, once reserved for luxury or niche markets, is now achievable across industries such as healthcare, retail, finance, and entertainment. The result is not just efficiency but a richer, more meaningful connection with customers.

Enterprises that adopt generative AI see measurable gains in productivity, cost-efficiency, innovation speed, and customer engagement: Organizations that successfully implement Generative AI quickly witness tangible benefits across multiple dimensions. Productivity increases because tasks that would require extensive time, such as drafting documents, designing prototypes, or generating code, can now be achieved within minutes. Cost-efficiency follows as AI reduces the need for excessive resources while maintaining quality outputs. Innovation speed accelerates, enabling rapid experimentation and faster product cycles. At the same time, customer engagement improves, as businesses can deliver highly personalized services that resonate with individual needs. These measurable gains demonstrate that Generative AI is not just a futuristic concept but an immediate driver of operational excellence.

The difference between surviving disruption and driving it lies in how effectively companies integrate AI into their core operations—not just as tools, but as strategic assets: The key differentiator between companies that thrive and those that merely survive disruption is their approach to Generative AI. Treating AI as a peripheral tool provides incremental benefits, but embedding it into the core operations transforms it into a strategic asset. This integration allows AI to influence decision-making, business strategy, and long-term planning rather than just task execution. Companies that weave AI into their culture and workflows can anticipate market changes, innovate continuously, and disrupt industries rather than being disrupted. In this sense, AI becomes a force multiplier, ensuring businesses lead transformation rather than struggle to keep pace.

The chapter reminds readers that early adopters are already witnessing a competitive edge, and the pace of transformation will only accelerate: The conclusion underscores a crucial insight: the benefits of Generative AI are already visible among early adopters. Organizations that embraced AI sooner are gaining competitive advantages through faster innovation, stronger customer relationships, and more efficient operations. Their lead is expanding as the pace of AI transformation accelerates globally, creating a widening gap between pioneers and latecomers. This chapter serves as both inspiration and warning—those who act now can shape industries, while those who delay risk obsolescence. The message is clear: readiness and adaptability to integrate AI are no longer optional, but essential for securing a sustainable, profitable future.

Encouraging Experimentation and Adaptability

A central lesson from the Generative AI revolution is the need for a mindset shift within organizations:

1. Companies must foster a culture of experimentation encouraging teams to test generative tools for idea generation, design, marketing, and strategy.

2. Leaders are urged to stay adaptable, iterating quickly based on feedback and evolving technology.
3. Generative AI isn't a one-size-fits-all solution. Its real strength lies in co-creation with humans, where creativity, critical thinking, and contextual judgment play crucial roles alongside machine intelligence.

This section emphasizes that risk-taking and adaptability are core competencies in the AI-driven future.

Harnessing Generative AI to shape a sustainable and profitable future

The chapter ends on a visionary note: organizations that strategically integrate generative AI can not only stay competitive but also redefine industry standards. The future is one where:

AI augments human potential across creative, operational, and strategic domains: Generative AI stands as a transformative force that enhances human capacity rather than replacing it. By automating repetitive tasks, AI allows professionals to focus on higher-order creativity, innovation, and problem-solving. In creative fields, AI tools can draft designs, compose content, or generate prototypes, enabling humans to refine and lead the vision. Operationally, it streamlines workflows, predicts bottlenecks, and reduces human error. Strategically, AI analyzes complex datasets, providing insights that sharpen decision-making and long-term planning. This augmentation ensures that human ingenuity is amplified, allowing organizations to achieve breakthroughs that would be difficult or slow without such intelligent support.

Businesses can scale hyper-personalization, agile development, and predictive intelligence while

reducing waste and inefficiencies: Generative AI empowers businesses to deliver hyper-personalized experiences to customers by analyzing individual behaviors, preferences, and feedback in real time. Marketing campaigns can be dynamically tailored, products can be customized, and services can adapt instantly to user needs. Agile development also benefits as AI automates testing, code generation, and iterative improvements, accelerating time-to-market. Predictive intelligence helps companies anticipate customer demands, supply chain issues, and market shifts with greater precision. At the same time, AI reduces waste by optimizing resource use, energy consumption, and material allocation, ensuring processes are lean and efficient. This dual impact drives both profitability and sustainability.

Generative AI becomes a foundation for sustainability optimizing resource use, reducing manual effort, and enabling smarter decision-making: Sustainability is no longer optional but central to modern business strategy, and generative AI provides the tools to achieve it. Through advanced simulations and optimization models, AI enables organizations to use resources such as energy, water, and raw materials more efficiently. Automated processes reduce manual labor in repetitive or hazardous tasks, lowering human fatigue and errors while cutting operational costs. Furthermore, AI-driven decision-making ensures that sustainability goals align with profitability, identifying greener alternatives without sacrificing efficiency. Whether in manufacturing, logistics, or services, AI allows companies to implement eco-conscious strategies at scale, shaping industries that are both environmentally responsible and future-ready.

Profitable and sustainable enterprise of tomorrow will be built today by those who embrace and shape AI responsibly: The organizations that act now to integrate generative AI responsibly will define tomorrow's success stories. Responsible adoption involves ensuring fairness, transparency, and accountability in AI systems, as well as addressing ethical concerns such as bias, data privacy, and workforce impact. Leaders who embrace AI not merely as a cost-cutting tool but as a driver of long-term value will build enterprises that thrive financially while contributing to global sustainability. The businesses that invest today in experimentation, responsible governance, and cross-disciplinary integration of AI will shape industries, set benchmarks, and secure a future that balances profitability with social and environmental good.

Bibliography

Ali, H., & Aysan, A. F. (2023a). What will ChatGPT Revolutionize in Financial Industry? SSRN Electronic Journal. https://doi.org/10.2139/ssrn.4403372

Ali, H., & Aysan, A. F. (2023b). What will ChatGPT revolutionize in the financial industry? Modern Finance. https://doi.org/10.61351/mf.v1i1.67

B N, M. K., A, R., Shaik, A., Shaik, M. B., & Abrar, M. (2024). Empowering Customer Support: Using Generative AI and Pre-trained LLM's in a Chatbot Revolution. International Journal of Innovative Research in Computer and Communication Engineering. https://doi.org/10.15680/ijircce.2024.1201020

Brem, A. (2023). Artificial Intelligence in Engineering Management - An Editor's Perspective (2023). IEEE

Engineering Management Review. https://doi.org/10.1109/EMR.2023.3284708

de Souza, B. C., Serrano de Andrade Neto, A., & Roazzi, A. (2024). The generative AI revolution, cognitive mediation networks theory and the emergence of a new mode of mental functioning: Introducing the Sophotechnic Mediation scale. Computers in Human Behavior: Artificial Humans. https://doi.org/10.1016/j.chbah.2024.100042

Ferrara, E. (2023). GenAI Against Humanity: Nefarious Applications of Generative Artificial Intelligence and Large Language Models. SSRN Electronic Journal. https://doi.org/10.2139/ssrn.4614223

Ferrara, E. (2024). GenAI against humanity: nefarious applications of generative artificial intelligence and large language models. Journal of Computational Social Science. https://doi.org/10.1007/s42001-024-00250-1

Fintech's Generative AI Revolution How AI is shaping the Future of Banking and Financial Services. (2023). International Research Journal of Modernization in Engineering Technology and Science. https://doi.org/10.56726/irjmets47516

Frank, S. (2023). The fall of creativity A librarian's role in the world of AI. College and Research Libraries News. https://doi.org/10.5860/crln.84.11.439

Ha, D. J. (2023). Generative-based AI and the possibility of Chinese language education revolution. The Society for Chinese Humanities in Korea. https://doi.org/10.35955/jch.2023.04.83.411

Howell, M. D., Corrado, G. S., & Desalvo, K. B. (2024). Three Epochs of Artificial Intelligence in Health Care. In JAMA. https://doi.org/10.1001/jama.2023.25057

Hwang, Y. S., Um, J. S., Pradhan, B., Choudhury, T., & Schlueter, S. (2024). How does ChatGPT evaluate the value of spatial information in the 4th industrial revolution? In Spatial Information Research. https://doi.org/10.1007/s41324-023-00567-5

Hyunjin, C. (2020). A Study on Application of Generative Design System in Manufacturing Process. IOP Conference Series: Materials Science and Engineering. https://doi.org/10.1088/1757-899X/727/1/012011

Ibanez, A. (2023). Intellectual cyborgs and the future of science. In Trends in Cognitive Sciences. https://doi.org/10.1016/j.tics.2023.06.004

Ikeda, K. (2023). Quantum extensive-form games. Quantum Information Processing. https://doi.org/10.1007/s11128-022-03806-0

Juncker, S. (2023). Dreaming with AI. Poligrafi. https://doi.org/10.35469/poligrafi.2023.418

Lazic, S. E. (2022). Artificial Intelligence and Causal Inference. Journal of the Royal Statistical Society Series A: Statistics in Society. https://doi.org/10.1111/rssa.12986

Lee, S.-W. (2023). A Study on China's Generative AI Regulations. LAW RESEARCH INSTITUTE CHUNGBUK NATIONAL UNIVERSITY. https://doi.org/10.34267/cbstl.2023.14.1.115

Levine, S., & Hausman, K. (2024). Using Big Data to Make Robots More Capable. IEEE Spectrum. https://doi.org/10.1109/MSPEC.2024.10418906

Li, Y., Pan, Q., Wang, S., Yang, T., & Cambria, E. (2018). A Generative Model for category text generation. Information Sciences. https://doi.org/10.1016/j.ins.2018.03.050

Liu, T. Y. A., & Wu, J. H. (2022). The Ethical and Societal Considerations for the Rise of Artificial Intelligence and Big Data in Ophthalmology. Frontiers in Medicine. https://doi.org/10.3389/fmed.2022.845522

Mannuru, N. R., Shahriar, S., Teel, Z. A., Wang, T., Lund, B. D., Tijani, S., Pohboon, C. O., Agbaji, D., Alhassan, J., Galley, J. Kl., Kousari, R., Ogbadu-Oladapo, L., Saurav, S. K., Srivastava, A., Tummuru, S. P., Uppala, S., & Vaidya, P. (2023). Artificial intelligence in developing countries: The impact of generative artificial intelligence (AI) technologies for development. Information Development. https://doi.org/10.1177/02666669231200628

Mesko, B. (2023). The ChatGPT (Generative Artificial Intelligence) Revolution Has Made Artificial Intelligence Approachable for Medical Professionals. In Journal of Medical Internet Research. https://doi.org/10.2196/48392

Onuh Matthew Ijiga, Idoko Peter Idoko, Lawrence Anebi Enyejo, Omachile Akoh, Solomon Ileanaju Ugbane, & Akan Ime Ibokette. (2024). Harmonizing the voices of AI: Exploring generative music models, voice cloning, and voice transfer for creative expression. World Journal of Advanced Engineering Technology and Sciences. https://doi.org/10.30574/wjacts.2024.11.1.0072

Orduño-Osuna, J. H., Cota-Rivera, E. I., Raygoza-L., M. E., Jimenez-Sanchez, R., Limón-Molina, G. M., Bravo-Zanoguera, M., Mercado-Herrera, A., & Rico, F. N. M. (2023). Exploring the challenges and applications of generative AI on engineering education in Mexico. In Facilitating Global Collaboration and Knowledge Sharing in Higher Education with Generative AI. https://doi.org/10.4018/9798369304877.ch011

Popenici, S., Rudolph, J., Tan, S., & Tan, S. (2023). A critical perspective on generative AI and learning futures. An interview with Stefan Popenici. Journal of Applied Learning and Teaching. https://doi.org/10.37074/jalt.2023.6.2.5

Prather, J., Denny, P., Leinonen, J., Becker, B. A., Albluwi, I., Craig, M., Keuning, H., Kiesler, N., Kohn, T., Luxton-Reilly, A., MacNeil, S., Petersen, A., Pettit, R., Reeves, B. N., & Savelka, J. (2023). The Robots are Here: Navigating the Generative AI Revolution in Computing Education. ITiCSE-WGR 2023 - Proceedings of the 2023 Working Group Reports on Innovation and Technology in Computer Science Education. https://doi.org/10.1145/3623762.3633499

Prieto, I., & Blakely, B. (2024). Proposed Uses of Generative AI in a Cybersecurity-Focused Soar Agent. Proceedings of the AAAI Symposium Series. https://doi.org/10.1609/aaaiss.v2i1.27704

Qian, Y., Siau, K. L., & Nah, F. F. (2024). Societal impacts of artificial intelligence: Ethical, legal, and governance issues. Societal Impacts. https://doi.org/10.1016/j.socimp.2024.100040

Qu, X., Yang, J., Chen, T., & Zhang, W. (2023). Reflections on the Implications of the Developments in ChatGPT for Changes in Medical Education Models. Journal of Sichuan University (Medical Science). https://doi.org/10.12182/20231360302

Sarker, I. H. (2021). Deep Learning: A Comprehensive Overview on Techniques, Taxonomy, Applications and Research Directions. In SN Computer Science. https://doi.org/10.1007/s42979-021-00815-1

Sobhanmanesh, F., Beheshti, A., Nouri, N., Chapparo, N. M., Raj, S., & George, R. A. (2023). A Cognitive Model for

Technology Adoption. Algorithms. https://doi.org/10.3390/a16030155

Sobo, E. (2023). Could ChatGPT Prompt a New Golden Age in Higher Education? Teaching and Learning Anthropology. https://doi.org/10.5070/t36160114

Sturm, N., Mayr, A., Le Van, T., Chupakhin, V., Ceulemans, H., Wegner, J., Golib-Dzib, J. F., Jeliazkova, N., Vandriessche, Y., Böhm, S., Cima, V., Martinovic, J., Greene, N., Vander Aa, T., Ashby, T. J., Hochreiter, S., Engkvist, O., Klambauer, G., & Chen, H. (2020). Industry-scale application and evaluation of deep learning for drug target prediction. Journal of Cheminformatics. https://doi.org/10.1186/s13321-020-00428-5

Ubal Camacho, M., Tambasco, P., Martínez, S., & García Correa, M. (2023). El impacto de la Inteligencia Artificial en la educación. Riesgos y potencialidades de la IA en el aula. Revista Interuniversitaria de Investigación En Tecnología Educativa. https://doi.org/10.6018/riite.584501

Vafadar, M., & Moradi Amani, A. (2024). Academic Education in the Era of Generative Artificial Intelligence. Journal of Electronics and Electrical Engineering. https://doi.org/10.37256/jeee.3120244010

Vidal-Alaball, J., Panadés Zafra, R., Escalé-Besa, A., & Martinez-Millana, A. (2024). The artificial intelligence revolution in primary care: Challenges, dilemmas and opportunities. Atencion Primaria. https://doi.org/10.1016/j.aprim.2023.102820

Waisberg, E., Ong, J., Kamran, S. A., Masalkhi, M., Zaman, N., Sarker, P., Lee, A. G., & Tavakkoli, A. (2023). Bridging artificial intelligence in medicine with generative pre-trained transformer (GPT) technology.

Journal of Medical Artificial Intelligence. https://doi.org/10.21037/jmai-23-36

Wang'ang'a, A. W. (2024). Consequences of Artificial Intelligence on Teaching and Learning in Higher Education in Kenya: Literature Review. East African Journal of Education Studies. https://doi.org/10.37284/eajes.7.1.1718

Wang, J. J., & Ye, F. Y. (2023). A Probe into the Generative AI and GPT-type Technical Applications with Transform for Information Management and Communication. Journal of Library Science in China. https://doi.org/10.13530/j.cnki.jlis.2023047

Wang, S., Huang, X., Liu, P., Zhang, M., Biljecki, F., Hu, T., Fu, X., Liu, L., Liu, X., Wang, R., Huang, Y., Yan, J., Jiang, J., Chukwu, M., Reza Naghedi, S., Hemmati, M., Shao, Y., Jia, N., Xiao, Z., ... Bao, S. (2024). Mapping the landscape and roadmap of geospatial artificial intelligence (GeoAI) in quantitative human geography: An extensive systematic review. In International Journal of Applied Earth Observation and Geoinformation. https://doi.org/10.1016/j.jag.2024.103734

Xu, X. (2024). Navigating the AI Revolution: Implications for Business Education and Pedagogy. Journal of Curriculum and Teaching. https://doi.org/10.5430/jct.v13n1p371

Yafei, X., Wu, Y., Song, J., Gong, Y., & Lianga, P. (2024). Generative AI in Industrial Revolution: A Comprehensive Research on Transformations, Challenges, and Future Directions. Journal of Knowledge Learning and Science Technology ISSN: 2959-6386 (Online). https://doi.org/10.60087/jklst.vol.3n2.p20

Zimina, L. V. (2023). Neural Networks in the Book Publishing Industry. Bibliography and Bibliology. https://doi.org/10.25281/2411-2305-2023-2-48-66

He Jiayi. (2023). Analysis of ChatGPT and AI Painting Collaborative Design System under the Generative Artificial Intelligence Revolution. Design. https://doi.org/10.12677/design.2023.84304

References Books

1. Supremacy: AI, ChatGPT and the Race That Will Change the World by Parmy Olson (2024)
2. AI Snake Oil: What Artificial Intelligence Can Do, What It Can't, and How to Tell the Difference by Arvind Narayanan & Sayash Kapoor (2024)
3. Life 3.0: Being Human in the Age of Artificial Intelligence by Max Tegmark (2017)
4. The Singularity Is Nearer: When We Merge with AI by Ray Kurzweil (2024)
5. All In on AI: How Smart Companies Win Big with Artificial Intelligence by Thomas H. Davenport & Nitin Mittal (2023)
6. Agentic Artificial Intelligence: Harnessing AI Agents to Reinvent Business, Work, and Life by Thomas H. Davenport (2025)
7. Working with AI: Real Stories of Human-Machine Collaboration by Thomas H. Davenport (2022)
8. The AI Advantage: How to Put the Revolution in Artificial Intelligence to Work by Thomas H. Davenport (2018)
9. Competing on Analytics: The New Science of Winning by Thomas H. Davenport & Jeanne Harris (2007, revised 2017)
10. Generative AI Revolution: Transforming Industries Through Innovation (hypothetical or descriptive title found on Amazon)